MW00526737

# MORE DIRTY LITTLE SECRETS
## VOLUME II

# MORE DIRTY LITTLE SECRETS ABOUT BLACK HISTORY, ITS HEROES AND OTHER TROUBLEMAKERS

## VOLUME II

Claud Anderson, Ed. D.,
and
Brant Anderson

**Power**Nomics
CORPORATION *of* AMERICA

MARYLAND

Copyright © 2006 by Dr. Claud Anderson and Brant Claud Anderson

Published by the PowerNomics ® Corporation of America
P.O. Box 30536
Bethesda, Maryland 20814
(301) 564-6075
www.powernomics.com


Printed in the United States of America
ISBN 0-9661702-3-7 (9780966170238 beginning in 2007)


We gratefully acknowledge the Dwight D. Eisenhower Presidential Library and Museum for permission to reprint the photo of Ida Stover Eisenhower, The Harvest Institute for the photo of Emmett Simmons and *The Michigan Citizen* newspaper for the Detroit Sambo Awards.


Editors: Joann Anderson, Ph.D. and Edward Sargent
Cover design and layout: Gary Scott, A3arts
Copy editor: Alanna Boutin
Interior Layout Design: Caldonia Joyce


All rights reserved. No part of this book may be reproduced or transmitted in any form or by any means, electronic or mechanical, including photocopying, recording or by any information storage and retrieval system, without the written consent of the publisher.

# OTHER BOOKS AND EDUCATIONAL MATERIALS BY THE AUTHOR

## Books

*PowerNomics: The National Plan to Empower Black America*

*Dirty Little Secrets About Black History, Its Heroes and Other Troublemakers*

*Black Labor, White Wealth: The Search for Power and Economic Justice*

## Videos & DVDs (available in both formats)

*A Vision Beyond the Dream*

*PowerNomics:Inappropriate Behavior*

*On the Firing Line: Questions and Answers with Dr. Claud Anderson*

*Reparations: Now or Never*

## Audio CDs

*How Blacks Lost Their Economic Rights*

*On the Firing Line: Questions and Answers with Dr. Claud Anderson*

*Inappropriate Behavior*

*Preview of More Dirty Little Secrets*

Contact your local bookstore or PowerNomics Corporation for any of the above products. PowerNomics is the exclusive publisher of Dr. Claud Anderson's books and producer of his multimedia materials.

At the conclusion of the famous decade-long trial that ended in 1938 involving the Scottsboro boys (a trial that was a hot racial issue), Clarence Darrow, the popular attorney of the 1930s and 40s, looked at the crowd of Blacks who were whooping and shouting outside of the courthouse celebrating the acquittal and said: "If the people of your race would spend less time singing, dancing and praying, and more time standing up for yourselves, White people would not spend so much of their time beating up on you."

# ACKNOWLEDGMENTS

This book marks some very special points in my life. I was inspired by and wrote this book with my son, Brant. We have always been a team. I have been blessed by his love and very existence, and I appreciate his assistance as co-author. This book symbolizes my passing the mantel to him.

My career as a writer has been fulfilling and very unusual because each of my books has been a number one best seller. I want to acknowledge those who have played a role in my success. First, I thank my family, my children, Paige and Brant, and my wife, Dr. Joann Anderson, for giving me inspiration, strength and the reason to do the often grueling intellectual work that has gone into each of my books. I am especially indebted to my wife, who has always encouraged me and offered guidance.

Second, I want to thank Dr. Rosie Milligan and the staff of Milligan Books in particular Linda Tidwell for their excellent service and support. I also want to acknowledge my readers who are loyal, supportive and intellectually curious and the Library of Congress for permission to reprint some of the photos from their collection. This book is my appreciative THANK YOU to all.

# TABLE OF CONTENTS

# INTRODUCTION

The first *Dirty Little Secrets About Black History, Its Heroes and Other Troublemakers* has been a best-selling book in Black America for over eight years. This phenomenal feat suggests that the book satisfied a real thirst in its readers for the truth about our nation's history, institutions and sacred leaders. For centuries, scholars, historians and most authors have assumed a White perspective of human history. The truth about Black people, slavery and Jim Crow segregation was intentionally omitted from volumes of religious history, military history, cultural history, economic history and all other kinds of history. Very little history existed that accurately presented the significant presence and contributions of Black people in the development of this nation and the Western world. For instance, there has been no positive recognition or appreciation of Black people as the world's original people, this nation's super-patriotic soldiers and athletes and the world's music and performance arts geniuses, who made phenomenal contributions to mankind while suffering an African holocaust.

The burden of correcting historical omissions and creating accurate racial images of Black people now rests upon their own shoulders. Even at the risk of appearing biased, they have no choice but to research, then reconstruct history to include the true story of Black people. All people should know that Black history is an integral part of the history of the United States and is more than slavery and Jim Crow segregation. It is more than Booker T.

Washington, Frederick Douglass, Rev. Martin L. King and the other few personalities who appear on school bulletin boards during Black History Month. It is the intention of *More Dirty Little Secrets* to contribute clarity to the historical record.

By no means is the material contained herein definitive history. It is anecdotal history, written to educate and entertain, and most importantly, to trigger and direct much needed scholarly research of the issues raised. Each factoid debunks racial myths, lies and omissions or provides fascinating historical information surrounding events and personalities. Just like the first *Dirty Little Secrets*, this book is filled with enlightening, refreshingly interesting, heart-rending and humorous factoids about the historical journey of an enslaved people.

# CHAPTER 1

# NOTABLE FIRSTS AND LASTS

*In the final days, the last shall be made first!*

## Mini Facts

◆ *In 1519, after accompanying Cortez in his exploration of Mexico, Juan Garrido, a Black African, became the first person to sow and reap wheat in the New World.*

◆ *In 1758, Frances William, a Black Jamaican, graduated from Cambridge University, becoming the first Black college graduate in the Western Hemisphere.*

◆ *In 1844, Macon B. Allen passed the Maine bar examination and became the first licensed Black lawyer in the United States.*

◆ *In the 1940s, Benjamin O. Davis, a brigadier general in the U.S. Army, became the first Black American officer to command White officers and enlisted men.*

## ❦ SAMBO AWARDS: NEW GROUP ❦ ACCOUNTABILITY

As conservatism and anti-Black public policies have escalated, Black Americans have begun to take a more protective group posture. One change in behavior is that Blacks are beginning to hold other Blacks accountable when their actions harm the race. It is a constructive change in behavior for Blacks to "Call Out Sambos." A Sambo is a Black person who knowingly degrades and betrays the race. Calling Out Sambos is a phenomenon that is sweeping the country. Communities call out "Sambos" in a number of different ways. The most frequent form is an awards ceremony that usually takes place during the last week in February, Black History Month. Sometimes Sambo Awards are announced on radio talk shows. Other times the lists are made up into flyers and distributed throughout the community. The commonality between the Sambo Awards is that they identify, acknowledge and present to the public Sambos in that city or region. They say in effect: "If you sell us out, you will not be able to do it undercover and you will suffer public consequences."

Despite the variety of formats, Sambo awards combine the Black tradition of Calling People Out with the customary Black History Month ritual of recognizing Black Americans whose personal achievements and accomplishments have lifted the race. How do these groups determine who to call out? The lead community organization begins the process. It solicits from the community nominations of individuals considered guilty of Samboing, compiles a list and makes up a ballot. Once the ballot is complete, the community votes. The organization then presents the awards, always with fanfare and publicity, sometimes in formal ceremonies, sometimes in other ways. Awards have included Sambo plaques, Toby trophies, Hayward Shepard certificates, shoeshine boxes, head rags and watermelons. In 2004, Sambo Awards were presented in cities such as Dallas, Columbus, Ohio, Los Angeles and New York. But the one that attracted the most attention was in Detroit, Michigan.

## ❦ FIRST SAMBO AWARDS ❦

In Detroit in February 2004, Call 'Em Out, a community organization "dedicated to stamping out Samboing," hosted a 'Beans and Cornbread Festival,' the first regional Sambo Awards ceremony. Former Detroit Mayor Dennis Archer received the "Sambo Lifetime Achievement Award." Kay Everett, a Detroit city councilwoman, was runner-up. Call 'Em Out recognized Archer and Everett for their consistent anti-Black behavior. They hid behind the concepts of color-blind, race-neutral myths, then used them as excuses to structure public policies that benefited Whites and others while underserving the city's Black majority.

At the Sambo Awards ceremony, Call 'Em Out recounted how Mayor Dennis Archer justified awarding nearly 100 percent of the city's contracts, control of the city's school system, entertainment centers, prime land and casino licenses to Whites, then proclaimed he "would not make a Black man rich." Councilwoman Everett, a loyal supporter of Archer, received the runner-up Sambo Award for numerous anti-Black actions. She ranted publicly that she was "sick of hearing of Blackness, and that Blacks could kiss her rooty-toot-tooty." Call 'Em Out cited just a few of Everett's offensive votes, which included:

- ◆ *seizing the land and homes of longtime Detroiters and turning them over to private developers;*

- ◆ *severely curtailing bus services;*

- ◆ *tearing down low-income housing for Blacks and replacing it with townhouses and condominiums devel-*

*oped by Whites from outside the city for occupancy of
Whites from outside the city.*

Call 'Em Out presented Councilwoman Everett with specially
selected items for her Sambo Award — an Aunt Jemima head rag
and a shoeshine box.

*The Michigan Citizen announces Detroit
Sambo Awards, March 6, 2005.*

In 2005, nearly 500 people attended the Call 'Em Out awards
ceremony, which featured speakers, entertainment and food. The
winners were current Detroit Mayor Kwame Kilpatrick and, once
again, Councilwoman Kay Everett. Local Black newspapers
hailed the event, while mainstream newspapers denounced the

local Black community, in effect saying, "How dare you call our Negroes, Sambos!"

Everett continued her award-winning behavior and on October 11, 2004, received yet another recognition for her activities, this time from the government. After years of proclaiming she was race-neutral and refusing to do anything to help the city's majority Black population, the news media splashed across the front pages the story of FBI indictments that alleged Everett had, in fact, been using her elective office to support and give city resources to one race ... the White race. The FBI indicted Everett on 28 separate accounts of corruption and misuse of public office. The charges included taking bribes and other payoffs from White casino owners and land developers. The indictments even included a charge that Everett had demanded eighteen pounds of sausage from one White developer as penalty for giving her a check that bounced. Where did the FBI get its information? A developer, stressed with Everett's constant demand for payoffs, recorded telephone conversations and meetings with her. The media reported that the 28 counts could result in more than 400 years of imprisonment and that additional counts would soon be announced. Local Black radio stations and the Black-owned Michigan Citizen newspaper labeled her "the Sausage Queen." On the 24th of November, 2004, two months after her federal indictments, Councilwoman Everett suddenly passed away. The harm she did to Blacks in Detroit, unfortunately, did not.[1]

## ❦ THE FIRST AFRICAN EXPLORER ❦

Africans discovered the Americas long before the Europeans did. Since civilization developed first in Africa, it is logical that Africans would be the first people to migrate and explore the world. Unfortunately, over the course of time, most archeological artifacts of the earliest African Blacks were stolen, accidentally destroyed or misidentified with later population groups. However, a few written records survived.

According to Arab historical and geographical documents, a Black Islamic king named Abubakari II instructed his people to build a large reed boat for crossing the Atlantic Ocean. With his crew, Abubakari sailed due west from the West African coast in 1311, following the prevailing ocean currents. Historians believed that he and his crew landed on the north coast of South America and proceeded overland to Panama and Mexico. In the late 1900s, a well-publicized transatlantic expedition using reed boats tried to replicate the path of Abubakari and his crew. They, too, followed the prevailing currents in the Atlantic Ocean. The currents carried them across the Atlantic to nearly the same spot where Abubakari is reputed to have landed. The success of this modern day, Africa-to-Western World expedition would lead one to conclude that Black Africans rather than White Europeans were most likely the first transatlantic explorers.[2]

## 🐛 DUEL OVER SLAVERY 🐛

Which United States senator was killed by a Supreme Court justice in a duel over the enslavement of Africans? If you guessed David C. Broderick, you were right. David S. Terry, chief justice of the California Supreme Court, shot David C. Broderick at ten paces in a gun duel at 5:30 a.m., Monday, September 12, 1859, on a ranch near San Francisco, California. Hit by a bullet and lying on the ground dying, Senator Broderick looked up at the crowd around him and said: "They killed me because I was opposed to their corruption and the extension of slavery." Broderick died a few days later.

The duel was over whether Southern property rights, which included owning slaves, would become legal in California. David C. Broderick was a liberal opposed to slavery. David Terry was a pro-slavery conservative. Terry challenged Broderick to the duel because he was offended by remarks Broderick had made about slaveholders. In death, Senator Broderick became a martyr and accomplished more than he could have imagined. Many Californians considered his death a political assassination. In the 1860 presidential election, Abraham Lincoln carried California by 614 votes and on the same ballot, California citizens voted to keep California a slave-free state. Terry lived until 1889, when he was shot to death at a train stop by a bodyguard of another U.S. Supreme Court justice. What goes around comes around.[3]

## ❧ QUOTABLE QUOTE ❧

"In order to get beyond racism, we must first take an account of race. There is no other way. In order to treat persons equally, we must first treat them differently."U.S. Supreme Court Justice Harry Blackmun made this statement in 1978 in the opinion he wrote for the minority in the Regents of the University of California vs. Bakke case.

## ❧ FIRST ALL-BLACK MILITIA ❧

The image of the nation's Minute Men has always been White; however, Blacks have been called to militia movements several times in history. In the mid-1800s, the Reverend John Mars, a pastor in Springfield, Massachusetts, called upon the Black men in his congregation to organize themselves into a militia, secure arms and prepare to fight in response to the federal Fugitive Slave Law. The militia swore blood revenge upon any White slave catcher caught kidnapping free or bonded Blacks. Scattered Black towns as far away as Kansas and Missouri established similar militant organizations to protect themselves.

Following the Civil War, Adelbert Ames, a White Republican governor of Mississippi, called on Blacks to arm themselves to counter violence by White Democrats. The call to arms, however, was short-lived. Governor Ames lost his nerve, disarmed Blacks then betrayed them for a worthless "We'll be nice" pledge from an all-White Democratic Party.

Across the nation, the Black militia movement demonstrated two truisms and failed primarily because of Blacks themselves. The truisms are: 1) it is unrealistic for Blacks to expect protection from Whites; and 2) Black people have proved unwilling to protect themselves. Black politicians in the Republican Party were 100 percent opposed to Blacks arming themselves because White party leaders were opposed to Blacks fighting in defense of their own special interests. Black leadership proved timid and compromising. They only wanted to "get along." They were socially conditioned to see any action independent of Whites as impractical and unwise. That attitude and behavior evolved and was infused into a nonviolent civil rights movement that focused on social integration in the 1900s.[4]

## ❦ FIRST OFFICER TO LEAD BLACK ❦ CIVIL WAR SOLDIERS

In the Union Army during the Civil War, only White officers commanded Black soldiers. James H. Lane was the first White officer assigned to lead Black Union troops into battle against Southern Confederate troops. Before the Civil War started, Lane could best be called a "total segregationist." Lane didn't just oppose racially integrated communities or schools, he opposed both free and enslaved Blacks even entering the state of Kansas. When Lane was drafted and commissioned as an officer in the Union Army, his life took an unexpected and ironic twist. Lane was assigned to military duty in the Midwest, which compelled him to alter his negative racial attitude and do what he could never have dreamed of doing when he was a civilian. He had to value the lives of Blacks over Whites by leading Black troops into combat against slaveholders and Southern Confederate soldiers. Military records indicate Lane carried out his orders successfully.[5]

## ❦ FIRST BACK-TO-AFRICA MOVEMENT ❦

Paul Cuffee (1759–1817), a Black man, was the first person to actually carry out a "Back-to-Africa Movement." The Constitution of the United States was written following the Revolutionary War and it mandated an end to international slave trading by the year 1807. This Constitutional mandate and the fact that slavery hit a low in the ten-year period between 1789 and 1799 led many Whites to believe slavery would be nonexistent by 1807. Paul Cuffee, a free Black ship captain and merchant, appealed to both the federal government and free Blacks to support his Back-to-Africa relocation plan for all freed slaves. Over the course of twenty years, Cuffee personally transported 38 African Americans to Freetown, Sierra Leone. The White-sponsored American Colonization Society was more successful. During the same period, in its Back-to-Africa Movement, the society transported nearly 10,000 Blacks, at a cost of $1,800,000. Rather than spending approximately $180 in transportation costs per ex-slave, some slaveholders felt it was cheaper to simply set them free to be on their own in America. A few thousand Blacks received meritorious manumission in the late 1790s.

Neither the 1807 date established in the Constitution for the end of international slave trading nor the nation's first Back-to-Africa Movements noticeably impeded the growth of the institution of slavery. Growth actually exploded in the early 1800s. Paul Cuffee, the American Colonization Society and all subsequent "Back-to-Africa Movements" failed for a number of reasons, but primarily because of the costs associated with relocation, reparations to slave owners and the fact that too many Blacks identified with America as their home and refused to be relocated. But there were other more subtle reasons why the Back-to-Africa Movement failed. In the early 1800s, the federal government initiated immigration polices that encouraged European Whites to migrate to America. The government knew mainstream White society and the economy would need Black people as an unpaid, noncompetitive labor class, captured consumers and as an official out-group to elevate newly arriving immigrants. Twenty generations of immigrants have used native Black Americans as a political and economic platform for Americanization.[6]

## 🐾 FIRST IN THE ELECTRIC CHAIR 🐾

Henry Bookman, a 28-year-old Black man who lived in the state of Oklahoma, was the first person in the nation publicly executed in an electric chair. Throughout history, humans have executed other humans, especially across racial lines. In the late 1800s, Thomas Edison and the Westinghouse Corporation demonstrated how electricity could be used to kill. They invented the electric chair. Requiring only 2400 volts of electricity for thirty seconds, they hailed their electric chair as economical, more effective and less gruesome than the old-fashioned public firing squads and hangings. One of the first customers for the electric chair was the Oklahoma state prison system, but it went unused for nearly thirty years.

In the early 1900s, the state of Oklahoma got its first chance to test the electric chair on a living human. Henry Bookman was tried and convicted of killing his White employer, Richard Horseman, for some unknown reason. Prior to a brief trial, local Whites made two unsuccessful attempts to break Bookman out of jail and lynch him. In 1915, on the day he was scheduled to die in the Westinghouse-built electric chair, Bookman exercised his right to make a last request. He asked to be buried in a black suit. The prison did not have a black suit so it gave Bookman a brown suit instead. When the switch was pulled on the never-before-used electric chair, Bookman received two jolts of 2400 volts. The doctor who examined Bookman and pronounced him dead noticed that Bookman had received his last request. The electric currents were so hot that they not only killed Bookman, but turned his brown suit black. In the death of Henry Bookman, there are lessons for the living: be careful what you ask for and be even more careful where you sit.[7]

##  FIRST REVOLT OF INDIAN HELD SLAVES

In 1842, one of the nation's first and biggest slave revolts occurred in the newly established Oklahoma territory between Indians slaveholders and their enslaved Blacks. Black slaves revolted, killed a large number of Indians and took off for freedom in Mexico. Just like White slave owners, Indians pursued the runaway Blacks nearly to the Mexican border. En route, the Blacks armed themselves and had running battles with the Indians. A final battle took place just a short distance from the Mexican border. Many Blacks and Indians died in the battle, but Indians captured a large number of the runaway Blacks and returned them to slavery in the Oklahoma territory. They remained slaves throughout the Civil War. While this nation was at war, the five civilized Indian tribes held no less than 10,000 African Blacks in captivity. Although in 1865, the United States government signed freedom agreements and paid all the tribes to free their Black slaves, the Choctaws and the Chickasaws did not free their Black slaves for another two to three years. The freedom agreements required Indians not only to free Blacks they were holding in captivity, but to also give the slaves money and free land. The

Indians did not release their Black captives in the agreed upon time frame and never gave them land or money.[8]

## ❦ FIRST BLACKS TO HOLD ❦ INDIANS ACCOUNTABLE

Immediately following the Civil War, former Black Union soldiers were converted into Buffalo Soldiers and assigned to police duty in the developing Western frontier. This was the first time the Black Buffalo soldiers got a chance to reverse roles with American Indians who had sided with European Whites in slavery and the Civil War. Black Buffalo soldiers fought successful battles with various Indian tribes from the Mississippi River to California. One Black Buffalo soldier wrote a poem that reflected their racial pride and the confidence that the Blacks had in their military skills and commanding White officer:

The Ninth marched out with splendid cheer,
The Bad Lands to explore,
With Colonel Henry at their head,
They never fear the foe.
So, on they rode from, Christmas eve,
'Till dawn of Christmas day;
The Red Skins heard the Ninth was near,
And they fled in great dismay.

Conflict between Indians and Black Americans continues to this very day. Before 1970, American Indians were accepted as a subcategory of Whites. They receive reparation benefits by claiming even an infinitesimal amount of so-called "Indian Blood." Blacks and Indians matched and mixed occasionally during the 400 years this country was developing. But today, Indian tribes, especially the Cherokee and Seminoles, have petitioned the federal government to exclude Blacks who claim to have Indian blood from land grants, inherited rights or financial settlements between the federal government and Indians. Since there are no benefits associated with being Black, Indians like others, distance themselves from Blacks.[9]

## ❧ FIRST NATIONAL SYMPATHY FOR SLAVES ❧

The novel *Uncle Tom's Cabin* was a first in many respects. It was first published in 1852 as a serial, in the *National Era*, an abolitionist newspaper. It became an instant hit when later published as a novel. *Uncle Tom's Cabin* carried a subtitle often forgotten today: *Or, Life Among the Lowly*. It sold more than 300,000 copies in its first year alone and became the first national best seller. Harriet Beecher Stowe achieved her most significant first as the first writer to bring dignity to millions of enslaved Black people. She presented Black people to the world as just as human as White people with the same range of human feelings, needs and morals. Most White Americans were exposed to Harriet Beecher Stowe's *Uncle Tom's Cabin* for the first time as a musical play in the late 1800s.

In 1903, a twelve-minute motion picture of Harriet Stowe's novel gave this nation its first American Black movie character: Uncle Tom. However, the first Uncle Tom film character was portrayed by a White person, who smeared his face and hands with black shoe polish. Two decades later, Black minstrels imitated White minstrels by covering their hands and faces with black shoe polish. They mocked themselves for laughs.[10]

## ❦ FIRST BLACK AUTOMOBILE MAKER ❦

In the early 1900s, Henry Ford put America on wheels. Ford's Tin Lizzies and Model T Fords moved an eager nation into the automobile future. However, instead of having a Ford in their future, a few Black Americans dreamed of driving a Patterson-Greenfield automobile. This "dream machine," or automobile, was built by Black Americans. In 1873, The C.R. Patterson & Son Carriage Company of Greenfield, Ohio, became the nation's and the world's first Black-owned automobile manufacturing company. Charles Patterson was born a slave on a West Virginia plantation. After the Civil War, he earned a living as a blacksmith using skills that he had mastered as a slave and quickly established a reputation as a fine blacksmith. Patterson got a job at the Dines and Simpson Carriage and Coach Makers Company. He was promoted to management and went into partnership with a White man named J.P. Lowe. The company manufactured high quality buggies and popular wagons. When J.P. Lowe died, Charles Patterson and other members of his family took full control and ownership of the business.

While continuing to produce fine wagons, the Patterson Company entered the world of automobile manufacturing. The Patterson automobile was reportedly a better quality than Henry Ford's Tin Lizzie, but could not compete with Ford's mass production assembly lines. Less than 150 Patterson automobiles were produced. By 1930s, the company began shifting its production into buses, hearses, moving vans and trucks. A few years later, the company closed it doors. Reportedly, some wagons and buggies manufactured by the Patterson & Son Carriage Company are displayed at the Greenfield, Ohio, Historical Society Building, but there are no known Patterson automobiles still in existence.[11]

## ❦ FIRST MILITARY DRAFT ❦

The first Conscription Act that drafted American males into military service was passed by Congress in 1862 during the American Civil War. The Conscription Act pulled the sheet off of self-proclaimed patriots who, in truth, had no stomach for fighting. Wealthy Whites avoided the draft by paying poor Whites to sign up in their place. White Irish males ignited "draft riots" across the country to show their disapproval of the conscription law, even though they were just arriving as guests in America. They went on racial rioting rampages in Troy, New York; Boston, Massachusetts; Portsmouth, New Hampshire; Rutland, Vermont; and Wooster, Ohio. Other ethnic groups joined the Irish Whites and directed their anger to defenseless Blacks in urban cities, murdering nearly 1,200 within a week's time. White rioters did not riot against and lynch Black people for something that they had done. The rioters raped, robbed and killed Blacks simply because Whites did not want to fight what they called a "Nigger War" and Black communities were unarmed and could not defend themselves.

The attitudes of the White rioters reflected the words expressed by Ulysses S. Grant, a slave-holding Northern general in the Union Army, who became president of the United States. General Grant said if he thought the Civil War was being fought over slavery, he certainly "would not be fighting it." Most Whites knew the Civil War had little to do with freeing enslaved Blacks. The war was an economic and power struggle between the North and South for control of slavery-generated wealth, industry and political representation in Congress; moreover, the North wanted to industrialize and develop the West. Once the Civil War was over, the North was totally indifferent to what happened to five million newly freed Blacks.[12]

## ❧ FIRST PRESIDENT WAS BLACK ❧

Millions of tourists and students visit the District of Columbia annually just to see the Washington Monument and hear tour guide tales of George Washington, reportedly the first president of these United States. George Washington may have been many things, including a slave owner, but he certainly was not this nation's first president. It is not well-known that the first president of the United States was John Hanson, a Black man. The Articles of Confederation were adopted in 1777. In 1781, when the Maryland colony officially signed the Articles of Confederation, uniting the thirteen colonies into thirteen united states, those united states became an actuality. John Hanson, the man who signed for the Maryland colony, was immediately elected president of the assembled and united states. John Hanson's formal title was "President of the United States in Congress Assembled." John Hanson then became the first functional president of the United States of America.

The Founding Fathers and officials of the assembled states recognized John Hanson as the president the United States. Even George Washington, the ranking general of the American Army, addressed Hanson with the highest title and honor in the land. When George Washington won a great military victory in York-town, John Hanson sent General George Washington a letter of congratulations. When George Washington responded with his own letter, he addressed it to "John Hanson, President of the United States." George Washington was the second president. If you look very closely at the back of a two dollar bill, John Hanson, the Black man sitting in the fifth seat on the left, was the first president of the United States.[13]

*Two dollar bill with John Hanson in the first seated row, fifth from the left.*

## 🐛 FIRST POST-SLAVERY BLACK GOVERNOR 🐛

In the ten years of Reconstruction following the Civil War between 1865 and 1875, a few Black ex-slaves participated in this nation's highest corridors of political power. Pinckney Benton Stewart Pinchback was one of those few. Besides being a governor, Pinchback distinguished himself in many ways. Pinchback was born on May 10, 1837, as one of 10 siblings who belonged to a White Mississippi planter who allowed Pinchback to learn a few skills. In his youth, Pinchback worked as a steward on steamboats and learned how to steer boats up and down the Mississippi River, Missouri River and Red River. During the Civil War, Pinchback became the only Black officer in the Union-controlled Louisiana Native Guard. He distinguished himself by leading his troops through Confederate blockades of the Mississippi River around the city of New Orleans, Louisiana, which the Confederate Army controlled.

After the war, Pinckney Pinchback became very active in the Republican Party. In 1868, Pinchback became the first Black delegate to a Republican presidential convention. In that same year, he was elected to the state senate and named pro tempore. He became lieutenant governor of Louisiana upon the death of Governor Oscar Dunn, and was the acting governor until another was elected. A few years later, in 1872, he was elected to the United States Congress.[14]

## 🐝 FIRST HUMANS WERE BLACK 🐝

The mother and father of all humankind were Black people in Africa. Genetic markers found in chromosome studies indicate that all humans around the world have a single common Black ancestry. In 1997, paleontologists announced a startling discovery of skull and body remains in the African country of Ethiopia. According to scientific tests, these artifacts are the oldest and best preserved evolutionary record of modern man and date back more than 160,000 years. Scientists from the University of California said: "This discovery filled in a big gap in the African human fossil record and supports the genetic evidence that modern humans arose from Africa and not from multiple locations in Europe, Asia and Africa as some researchers suggest." DNA genetic coding, carbon testing and archeological artifacts allow scientists not only to track the origin of mankind back to Africa, but to also proclaim "the first humans on earth were Black people."

In 2002, the Discovery Channel aired a two-hour research docudrama entitled, *The Real Eve*, that used DNA studies to reconstruct how the first human life, which was Black and free, first existed in Africa. The offspring of Black Africans migrated to other parts of the world in search of cooler and more favorable climates. Over time, genes mutated to adapt to the new, cooler environments. The discovery that modern humans definitely originated in Africa puts to rest nonscientific speculations that Europeans or Asians are the oldest Homo sapiens.[15]

## ❦ FIRST BLACK KING IN THE AMERICAS ❦

It is common knowledge that Africa had Black kings, but how many people are aware that there was at least one Black king in the Western Hemisphere? Henri Christophe, who became a Black king, was born in 1767, on the island of Grenada in the Caribbean. His parents, who were originally slaves, were brought to the islands to work in the sugar cane industry. While still a child, Christophe's father sold him to a White ship captain, who subsequently sold him to a French sugar planter in Haiti. Raising and cutting sugar cane was brutal labor and caused much discontent among the slaves in Haiti. Having witnessed the suffering of his people, Christophe joined in the great Haitian slave revolt that overthrew the French colonists.

Christophe performed so well during the Haitian revolt that he was recognized by General Toussaint L'Overture and promoted to the rank of sergeant. After the Haitian revolt, the island was divided into two independent republics and Christophe was elected president of the Northern State in February 1807. He successfully introduced many social, educational and economic reforms. However, to continue to improve the quality of life for his people, he decided to create the first Black kingdom in the Western world. On March 28, 1811, Christophe declared Haiti a kingdom and himself King Henri. Years later a stroke left him partially paralyzed. To keep his enemies from capturing and mutilating him, he eventually committed suicide. Henri Christophe had arisen from a poor little Black boy to the only king in the Western hemisphere.[16]

## ❦ FIRST FREEDOM RIDERS ❦

History will always repeat itself, especially when its lessons are ignored. When the Congress of Racial Equality (CORE) launched the Freedom Rides in the early 1960s, most people thought they were a totally new concept. However, they weren't! Freedom Rides occurred much earlier in the mid-1940s. Those rides, called Journey of Reconciliation, lasted two weeks. Riding on Greyhound buses, the first freedom riders traveled to fifteen different eastern cities in the states of Virginia, North Carolina, Tennessee and Kentucky. As it has been throughout history, the 1940s freedom riders were threatened with arrest, which, fortunately, did not actually happen.

What triggered these Freedom Rides, or the Journey of Reconciliation? It was Irene Morgan, a Black woman. In 1944, while riding from Virginia to Maryland, a Greyhound bus driver asked Irene Morgan to surrender her seat to a White person and move to the rear of the bus. When Irene Morgan refused, she was arrested, charged and tried for disorderly conduct in the circuit court in Middlesex County, Virginia. She was found guilty and fined $10. With the assistance of the NAACP, she sued both the bus company and the city in the U.S. Supreme Court. The court trial lasted for years, but she finally prevailed with a positive courtroom decision. On June 3, 1946, the Supreme Court reversed a lower court decision and struck down segregated interstate bus travel. Actually, when Irene Morgan and Rosa Parks refused to give up their seats, their protests were a continuation of strong Black womanhood that modeled Sojourner Truth's transportation protest in the District of Columbia in the mid-1800s.[17]

## ❦ FIRST BLACK BICYCLING CHAMPION ❦

For nearly a century, Black athletes dominated professional and amateur sports, such as jockeying, boxing, track and field, basketball and baseball. In recent times, Black athletes began dominating such sports as fencing, soccer, tennis and golf. In the 21st century, cycling has been dominated by Whites. Lance Armstrong established international bicycling records. But did you know that nearly a century ago, a Black man named Marshall W. Taylor was an undisputed national and international bicycling champion? Since bicycle racing started back in 1878, and cycling today is not a high-profile professional sport, it might be somewhat difficult to envision a Black bicyclist as a sports hero. However, Marshall Taylor was the first Black American professional bicyclist to earn worldwide fame and set cycling records around the world. At the end of the 1800s, bicycling was a popular mode of transportation and a competitive sport in America and across Europe.

Marshall Taylor was born on a farm near Indianapolis, Indiana, in 1878. As an early victim of racism and social exclusion, he directed his energy and anger into sports. Taylor acquired a bicycle and became an expert trick rider. To gain acceptance and recognition, Taylor moved to Massachusetts, where he could compete in local bicycle races in a less racially hostile environment. At the age of 16, Taylor was a world-class sprinter, a professional cyclist at 18 and a world champion at 20. By the end of the 1901 season, Taylor was only 22, but he had competed against and defeated the cycling champions of every major European country. In Europe, Taylor won forty-two of fifty-seven bicycling races. He was a conquering hero. Taylor was the first Black athlete to have a commercial sponsor, establish a world record and compete regularly in open, integrated competitions for an annual championship. He became a wealthy man while he was in Europe. When Taylor returned to America, he returned to being a victim of racism and was denied access to restaurants, hotels, bicycle tracks and a source of income. In 1932, while still the victim of racism in his own country, Marshall Taylor died in poverty.[18]

## 🐞 WHITES' FIRST BLACK HERO 🐞

It is a rare event in American society for a Black man to be anointed a hero by White society. It is not only rare but a shocking surprise, especially when such recognition occurs during slavery. In 1861, the schooner *S.J. Waring* was en route from New York to South America with a three-man crew. One of the crew was a Black man named William Tillman, a steward and cook. A few hours away from its New York port, the schooner was boarded and taken over by a group of eight pirates, or bandits. The notorious criminal named Jeff Davis led the bandits. After they seized control of the boat, Jeff Davis proclaimed himself the new captain and diverted the boat to a port in Charleston, South Carolina. Jeff Davis told William Tillman that he should consider himself acquired property, a slave, who would be sold as soon as the boat reached Charleston.

Davis locked up the two Whites of the original crew. Believing that most Blacks were docile and could never be more than servants, Davis allowed William Tillman to remain unbound to attend to the personal needs of the new captain and his seven-man bandit crew. Tillman waited for the right moment to make his move. The rebel bandits fell off to sleep one by one. Finally only one was left to guard the boat, and he was drinking himself into a stupor. William Tillman was a free Black man who was not going to allow anyone to take away his freedom. Fearing slavery, especially in the Deep South, Tillman decided that the moment was at hand for him to fight and win his freedom or die trying. He found a hatchet and went below deck to the captain's quarters, where the ringleader, Jeff

Davis, was sleeping. He entered the captain's quarters and struck a fatal blow to Davis' head. Tillman next proceeded to the adjoining cabins and killed three more sleeping bandits. Tillman then went back onto the main deck and attacked another bandit, who was on guard duty. Unfortunately, the blow to the guard's head did not kill him. The bandit drew a pistol and screamed for help. But before the few remaining bandits could arrive on deck, Tillman delivered a death blow and took the guard's pistol. Tillman then forced the remaining three bandits below deck at gunpoint and locked them in chains. He released the members of his original crew, but proclaimed himself captain of the boat. Tillman turned the boat around and informed his old crew that he was taking it back to New York.

Five days later, the *S.J. Waring* arrived in the New York harbor under the command of Captain William Tillman, a Black patriot. The *New York Tribune* said this about Tillman and the incident with the Southern bandits: "To this colored man was the nation indebted for the first vindication of its honor on the sea." Others said that Tillman's victory offset the North's military loss at Bull Run. To show the nation's appreciation and indebtedness to Tillman for the capture and return of the schooner, the federal government gave William Tillman $6,000. It is not known what Tillman did with the money or whether he ever took any more ocean cruises to South America.[19]

## 🥭 LAST BIG SLAVE AUCTION 🥭

In March of 1857, just four years before the start of the Civil War, one of the nation's largest sale of Black slaves took place at a race track in Savannah, Georgia. Pierce Butler, a White slave owner of a large Georgia plantation, sold 436 of his 900 slaves to satisfy his personal debts. Butler loaded the 436 Black men, women and children that he owned onto railway cars and steamboats, then transported them to the racetrack to be auctioned off to the highest bidders. The slaves feared the breakup of their families and the separation of parents from children and sisters from brothers.

While a few slaves put on a show to impress their new masters, most begged and cried not to be sold away from their loved ones. When the auction was over, the slaves sat brooding, filled with sorrow and rocking back and forth. Pierce Butler, on the other hand, popped champagne corks because he had just netted more than $300,000 from his auction sale. One observer of the human suffering wrote in his diary that even though the sale appeared cruel, it was not. The author noted that Whites must not only make money off of Blacks at every opportunity, but: "The Negroes of the South must always be slaves because the South will not free them and become Africanized." The Southerner acknowledged no sympathy or concern for the pain and suffering of Black people.[20]

## ❦ THE LAST BUFFALO SOLDIER ❦

John Collins, reportedly the last living Buffalo Soldier, died in California in 2002. At the time of his death, he was the minister of the Westside Seventh Day Adventist Church of Fresno, California. The Buffalo Soldiers were a Black segregated unit of the United States Army that received its name from Native Americans during the Indian wars of the late 19th century. John Collins served in World War II as a trooper in the segregated 2nd Cavalry. In various forms, the Buffalo Soldiers existed from 1866 to 1943.

Before his death, John Collins expressed his disappointment that military and United States history both ignored the contributions and achievements of Black soldiers in winning the West, the Spanish-American War, World War I and World War II. Collins was proud of the fact that during the Indian Wars and the Spanish-American War, 23 Black soldiers received the Congressional Medal of Honor for extraordinary heroism. A Western historian,

William L. Katz, writes: "It is ironic that these brave Black soldiers served so well in the final and successful effort to crush American Indians, the first victims of White racism on this continent."[21]

## 🐝 BLACKS BECOME THIRD-CLASS CITIZENS 🐝

On May 30, 2005, the cover of *Newsweek* agazine heralded the first Hispanic-elected mayor of the city of Los Angeles, California, and how Hispanics, as the new majority-minority, would change American politics. Forty million Hispanics made 36 million Black Americans economically and politically obsolete. For more than 400 years, Black Americans were second-class citizens as the nation's majority-minority. Now they are third-class citizens. A Mexican immigrant told a radio talk show host that while Black Americans were marching and singing that they would overcome some day, legal and illegal Hispanics poured into the country and overwhelmed. According to the 1900 census, there were eleven and half million Blacks and only 100,000 Latinos in America. Both groups had an identical birth rate. By 2000, Latinos caught and passed Black Americans in population. Why? Because during the 20th century, natural births and legal and illegal immigration allowed the nation's Hispanic population to increase by 4,000 percent. Race-based immigration laws and natural birth rates restricted Black population increases to only 300 percent over a 100-year time period.

Between 1970 and 1990, the Hispanic population in the United States tripled. Today, 92 percent of this nation's Hispanic population has been in this country less than 25 years. Black Americans were further disadvantaged by the fact that Hispanics receive unearned benefits by being classified as a minority, when in fact, until 1970, they were classified in the U.S. Census as White. Hispanics are an ethnic group with immigration papers and drivers' licenses that list them as White. They have not been customarily or legally denied access to this nation's educational, economic or political systems because they were not living in this country. It is an injustice to equate the poverty and low educational skills that Hispanics and other immigrants bring with them into this country with the poverty and low educational achievement of Blacks that are the direct legacies of centuries of slavery and Jim Crow imposed on them.

Hispanics constitute a language group. Why should they be treated any differently from Whites who speak French, Greek or Russian? What historical damages have Hispanics suffered at the hands of the U.S. government that qualifies them for affirmative action, reparations or any other special governmental considerations? The legacies of slavery and structural racism have been placed on the backburner. What will happen to Black Americans who cannot compete in their hamstrung condition? Hispanics have displaced Blacks, and some projections are that by the year 2015, the combined populations of Asians and Arabs will push Blacks out of third-class citizenship into fourth-class citizenship. Blacks received practically nothing after centuries of second-class citizenship. How do they expect to be treated now that they are third-class citizens or when they become fourth-class citizens?[22]

## ❦ HOLLYWOOD'S FIRST BLACK STAR ❦

Lincoln Theodore Monroe Andrew Perry, better known as Stepin Fetchit, was White Hollywood's first Black movie star. Stepin Fetchit was born in Key West, Florida, in 1902. He developed an interest in show business at a very early age. For a number of years, he performed in vaudeville with a dancing partner. His first big break in movies occurred in 1929, when White movie studios chose him to play in an all-Black talkie entitled, *Hearts in Dixie*. Through the 1930s and 1940s, Stepin Fetchit appeared in a number of movies with some of Hollywood's White superstars.

However, in all of his films, Stepin Fetchit played the same gawky, mumbling, shuffling, lazy Black man. He was so good at presenting the White image of a Black man that he became one of the nation's highest paid movie stars. By the late 1950s, with the emergence of "positive Blackness," Black actors who played the role of an Uncle Tom or Sambo had become an embarrassment to Black people. Movie roles for Stepin Fetchit and similar Black character actors dried up. Fetchit died in California in 1985 as a penniless, has-been Negro actor.[23]

## ❦ FIRST SCALPINGS ❦

South Carolina was the first colony to authorize scalp hunting in America. In the beginning, neither Indians nor colonial Whites were the victims of scalping. Instead, they were the scalpers of runaway slaves or troublesome free Blacks. In the late 1600s and early 1700s, so many enslaved Blacks accepted Spain's offer to runaway and live free in Florida that it drove the American colonists crazy. To stop the runaways, who were attracted to places like St. Augustine, Florida, the South Carolina assembly devised a plan to instill fear in the minds and hearts of slaves. In 1739, the South Carolina Assembly approved paying bounties to man hunters who chased and returned slaves to their owners or the scalps of slaves who could not be returned alive.

White and Indian man hunters cooperated in chasing and scalping runaway Black slaves for the bounty. The South Carolina Assembly posted a proportional fee schedule based upon the sex of the returned slave and for the scalps. Typically, a bounty of $40 was paid in South Carolina for the return of a Black man; $25 for a Black woman; and $10 for children under twelve. However, for the scalp of any Black man, women or child with both ears attached, the public treasury was willing to pay $20. It was not unusual to see White and Indian slave chasers return from the wilderness of Georgia and Florida with sacks of Black scalps. It was ironic that when the Indian Wars started between Whites and Indians, both groups used their scalping skills on each other.[24]

## ❧ FIRST BLACKS TO BACK IMMIGRANT RIGHTS ❧

For centuries, Black Americans served as an economic stepping stone for a torrent of immigrants who impeded Black economic and political progress, and more importantly, displaced Blacks from the nation's conscience. The negative impact of immigrants on Black Americans did not go unnoticed. National Roper surveys conducted in the post-Civil Rights era of the 1970s and 1980s indicated that approximately 92 percent of Black Americans opposed the country's open-door immigration policy. During and after slavery, national Black leaders, such as Frederick Douglass, Sojourner Truth, Harriet Tubman, Booker T. Washington, W.E.B. DuBois, Marcus Garvey, Carter G. Woodson and A. Philip Randolph, worked actively to close the nation's doors until Black Americans had received long overdue justice. But during the 1960s Black Civil Rights Movement, a disconnection occurred between Black America and its visible, institutional civil rights leaders. Dr. Martin Luther King, Rev. Jesse Jackson, Rev. Benjamin Hooks, Vernon Jordan and their respective civil rights organizations signed onto full-page advertisements supporting an increase of immigrants into the United States from Indo-China. These ads ran in major urban newspapers across the country and erroneously linked the historical dilemma of Black Americans with immigration policies and immigrant rights.

This public endorsement encouraged immigration advocates and fueled an unprecedented surge of immigrants into the United States. Though the group self-interest of the arriving immigrants was adverse to and competitive with native Black Americans, civil rights leaders embraced the immigrants into a vague minority category and promoted their inclusion in affirmative action programs. Black Americans qualified for affirmative action and preferences because all levels of government had used their powers to exclude, subordinate and exploit Blacks. Civil rights leaders pushed to have Hispanics, Asians, Arabs and women included into affirmative action based solely on their ethnicity, language, culture, gender, religious and country of origin. The inclusion of immigrants in affirmative action and compensatory programs made the programs unjustifiable and made Black Americans appear foolish. In September 2004, civil rights leaders underscored their shift away from Black interests by calling for and participating in a national march in Washington, D.C., for immigrant rights. The civil rights movement has achieved its goal of forging a "color-blind" society. In the midst of women's rights, gay rights, minority rights, veteran's rights, Indian rights, Asian rights, Hispanic rights and immigrant rights, Black rights remain invisible. In their naiveté, civil rights leaders have become irrelevant, buried the unique history of Black Americans and denied an enslaved people justice.[25]

## 🌺 FIRST SLAVE REVOLT IN AMERICA 🌺

In his book, *Before the Mayflower*, Lerone Bennett documented that the first and most successful slave revolt in North America occurred in1526 on the San Miguel settlement, near the Pee Dee River, in South Carolina. Spanish colonizer Lucas Vasquez de Ayllon founded the settlement. He had followed the ocean route of Amerigo Vespucci and landed at the mouth of the Pee Dee River in the winter of 1526. Ayllon was accompanied by 500 Spaniards and 100 enslaved Africans from Haiti. The settlement was short-lived because malaria took the lives of half the Spaniards, including Allyon himself. The enslaved Africans revolted, set fire to the settlement and fled to live among native

Indians. The remaining Spaniards fled America's East Coast back to Haiti, allowing the 100 Black Africans to remain and establish the first permanent settlements within the confines of the present day Eastern United States. After the revolt, some Blacks remained along the Pee Dee River; however, most moved to Florida, which was Spanish territory, and built Maroon colonies to avoid European Whites, who began arriving in North America in the 1600s. A few Blacks migrated North along the Eastern Seaboard. In part, this explains the presence of 32 Blacks in Jamestown, Virginia, population records though only 20 Black slaves had supposedly arrived in 1619 onboard a Dutch slave ship.

*Drawing of a runaway Maroon. (Library of Congress)*

The little known Pee Dee River played an important role in the life and times of Black Americans. Over two centuries after the Pee Dee River revolt, Stephen Foster wrote a song about the Pee Dee River and enslaved Blacks. His brother thought Foster should pick another river for the name of his song. After looking through an atlas, the brother came upon the Suwannee River in Florida and convinced Foster to change the song's title to "Suwannee River." Thus, few Blacks have longed for their home on the "Old Pee Dee River."[26]

## ❦ FIRST TERRORIST FLAG IN AMERICA ❦

President George W. Bush launched his reelection campaign in 2004 against an emotional backdrop of airplanes being flown into the World Trade Center towers in New York on September 11, 2001. The burning towers symbolize terrorism, fear, death and destruction on American soil. George Bush used the public's fear of terrorism to help his reelection. But there is another, much older symbol of terrorism in this country. The Confederate flag is the nation's oldest symbol of terrorism. For nearly a century and a half, the Confederate flag has been highly visible over battlefields, state capitals, Ku Klux Klan rallies and in neo-Nazi literature. It is even on clothing and automobile bumper stickers. The Confederate flag has aided an endless number of conservatives and racists get elected to public office.

The rebel or Confederate flag symbolized Southern culture and history, but more importantly, it symbolized historical tyranny of Black Americans and terrorist/traitorous behavior against the United States of America. The Civil War lasted four years at a cost of a nearly a half million lives. After the war, Jefferson Davis, the president of the Southern Confederate States of America, and supporters of the Confederate South were indicted for treason. It is ironic that Southerners value patriotism and love for America, while defending the rebel or Confederate flag that symbolizes anti-Americanism.

There is little doubt that red-blooded Americans would be upset if Al Queada supporters in this country displayed images of the burning World Trade Center towers on articles of clothing, automobile license plates or atop public buildings. Terrorist organizations, like the Ku Klux Klan, Black Horse Brigade, American Nazi Party, Skin Heads and other White Aryan organizations, hold the Confederate flag in the highest esteem and use it to symbolize anti-Black, anti-Jewish and anti-American feelings. So, rather than taking down the Confederate flag, it ought to be waved high and acknowledged as the original symbol for terrorism on American soil.[27]

## 🍒 FIRST RACE WAR 🍒

History books refer to the Seminole Wars as wars between the United States Army and Seminole Indians. In truth, the Seminole Wars were Black-White race wars. Mainstream history books misdirect their readers by failing to indicate that most of the Indians were Black Seminoles. Three centuries of runaway Black slaves had inter-bred with various Indian tribes and produced a mixed bred of Indians and Blacks called Seminoles. The U.S. Army was fighting Black Seminoles and runaways. This little known fact was noted by General Sidney T. Jesup, the military's most knowledgeable U.S. Army officer in Florida, who wrote letters to his superiors in Washington, D.C., saying: "This, you may be assured, is a nigger and not an Indian war." General Jesup continued: "Throughout my operations I have found Negroes the most active and determined warriors; and during the conferences with the Indian chiefs I ascertained they exercised an almost controlling influence over them." The three (Black) Seminole Wars lasted for nearly four decades and at times tied up half of the Army's troops. The United States Congress spent nearly $40 million and the lives of 1,500 soldiers on the wars. The three Seminole Wars represented the single largest and longest Black slave resistance and race war in the nation's history. General Jesup summed the situation up when he further stated: "I would rather fight 500 White men than do battle with 50 Black Seminoles." When the 50 years of Seminole Wars ended, Black Seminoles, as well as incorrigible Black runaways, were marched on the Trail of Tears into Oklahoma Territory and into oblivion.[28]

## ❦ FIRST PONY EXPRESS RIDERS ❦

History has shortchanged Black frontiersmen. How many people know that the first Pony Express riders in the West were Black? Two of these riders were George Monroe and William Robinson. Since Blacks attended the nation's field animals and were the first cowboys and race horse jockeys, it was a natural progression for Blacks to become the first Pony Express riders. Why? Because Pony Express riders tended to be expendable people who had short life expectancies and few other options for earning a living. Riding a horse at breakneck speed through harsh terrain and Indian territory was dangerously hard work. Blacks transferred their long history of raising, training and riding horses to success in the Pony Express. Of the people passing through their territory on a regular basis, American Indians found Black riders less intimidating than White riders.

Though Hollywood movies have yet to feature a Black Pony Express rider, when you see the modern day mailman and his mail truck, close your eyes and picture a Black man riding at full gallop with Indian arrows sailing passed. Then appreciate the role that the Black Pony Express rider played in establishing the United States postal system.[29]

## ❦ FIRST BLACK BANK ❦

Today, Black Americans are often criticized for not being thrifty and not saving a greater portion of their income. In the late 1860s, nearly 5 million newly freed slaves made a Herculean effort to save money by banking their limited resources with the Freedmen Savings and Trust Company banks that were chartered by the United States Congress. In these banks, Blacks were the only depositors "with two-thirds of the deposits to be invested in securities of the United States." The sources of these ex-slaves' deposits were life savings, military wages, bounties, freedom dues, church tithes and donations from philanthropic organizations and benevolent societies. Over the course of nine years, these ex-slaves deposited $57 million in 37 different branches of the Freedmen Banks located in major American cities, such as New York, Washington, D.C., Philadelphia, Atlanta, Nashville, Memphis, Charleston and Savannah. Although the federal government created those banks specifically to provide financial support for former slaves, the government destined the banks to fail when they appointed racist White bank managers and gave them total and unsupervised control over the ex-slaves' monies. Without any protection for depositors and all of the Freedmen Banks controlled by White boards of trustees, should anyone be shocked that all 37 branches in different cities went insolvent at exactly the same time? Within ten years, the White bank managers invested Freedmen Bank funds in speculative ventures for their own self-enrichment and fleeced the newly freed slaves of their limited properties and life savings.

Five years after the Civil War ended, newly enacted Black Codes were effectively turning the mood of the nation against the recently freed Black slaves. Northern congressmen opposed and killed a bill to grant each ex-slave forty acres, a mule and $100. Calls for states' rights were locking Blacks into semi-slavery called a peonage, or sharecropping system. And, following the U.S. Supreme Court Slaughter House decision, which stipulated that the 13th, 14th and 15th Amendments to the Constitution were solely for Blacks, the executive, judiciary and legislative branches entered into a conspiracy to end Civil War Reconstruction and its Freedmen programs. Consistent with historical policies, the government's public explanation for this inhumane fleecing of ex-slaves' total resources was simply, bank mismanagement and an economic downturn. Just as White society has never paid a penalty for the pain and suffering it has inflicted on Black people for over 500 years, the White managers of the Freedmen Banks were never held accountable for conflict-of-interest borrowing, fraudulent investment ventures and outright theft.

When the Freedmen Banks collapsed, Black Americans lost more than their life savings. Many Blacks lost their faith in banks, business development and elected officials. To this present time, Black Americans have not pressed Congress to investigate, hold public hearings or to reimburse the nearly half million Black depositors for the losses imposed on them. Maybe there is still time for justice to prevail on behalf of Black Americans.[30]

## ❦ THE FIRST TO BAN EDUCATING BLACKS ❦

It is no big secret that during slavery in most states, it cost a person $100 and 39 lashes with a whip if they were caught teaching a Black person to read and write. Black slaves caught writing and reading, especially a newspaper, were often beaten or even killed. Blacks who could read or write had to dumb down in the presence of Whites. Whites harbored little fear of illiterate Blacks. Whites did fear educated Blacks and used the law to impose ignorance on them. South Carolina has the dubious honor of being the first state to forbid teaching a Black to read and write. In the early 1700s, when the British first established the colonies, there was strong opposition to educating slaves. The ruling Whites resisted the efforts of missionaries to teach Blacks to read the Bible and write because they knew it was easier to control an ignorant slave than an educated one. The Stono slave uprising in the early 1700s made matters worse. Out of fear, the ruling White overclass argued that they "would exercise all measures to insure that no light would enter the Black slaves' brain." For more than three centuries, they succeeded.[31]

## ❦ FIRST MERITORIOUS MANUMISSION AWARDS ❦

Meritorious manumission was a slavery control that rewarded and set free any Black slave who saved a White person's life, protected White property, created an invention from which the White slave owner could profit or informed on anyone planning a slave revolt or escape. Meritorious manumission was first established by the Virginia and South Carolina colonies in 1710. South Carolina's first meritorious manumission award was to a slave named Nigger Willis, who betrayed slaves who were planning a revolt. Between 1710 and 1865, meritorious manumission was such a strong enticement that out of 260 recorded slave revolts, a Black person informed in every one. By the early 1800s, so many slaves were being meritoriously manumitted that some states passed anti-manumission laws.

How many slaves actually received their freedom in meritorious manumission is not known. However, in the instance of informers, they placed their personal gain and need for White approval above the lives and well-being of other members of their race. Even in the four most noted slave uprisings in America's history — the Stono revolt, Gabriel Prosser's revolt, Denmark Vesey's revolt and Nat Turner's revolt — Black informants ended the revolts and sentenced thousands of Blacks seeking freedom to their deaths. The Civil War may have ended the "peculiar institution" of slavery, but there have been no private- or government-sponsored program to deprogram the descendants of slaves and end America's meritorious manumission policy.[32]

## ❦ FIRST BLACK BABIES IN THE WHITE HOUSE ❦

Black slaves and laborers not only built the White House in Washington, D.C., but they also lived in it and birthed Black babies in it. In December 1806, a Black baby was born to Fanny and Eddie, a slave couple who belonged to Thomas Jefferson and worked for him in the White House. Unfortunately, the young slave child died in the White House of unknown causes just prior to its second birthday.

There is a little doubt that other Black children were born in the White House. During the hundred years before the Civil War, nearly every president owned slaves, so the White House was home for hundreds of them. Before the White House was built, George Washington, who is recognized as the first president, resided in a red brick mansion on Chestnut Street in Philadelphia, Pennsylvania. Washington's household was composed of 32 people, including approximately 20 of his Black slaves. Thomas Jefferson, the third U.S. president, had a Black mistress and Black babies on his Monticello plantation in Virginia. As president, he took several slaves from his Monticello plantation to work in and around the White House executive mansion. By the end of his term, Jefferson told his daughter that he might switch to White servants, because: "When they misbehave, they can be fired." Slaves could not be fired.

All the presidents from Washington's era to the decade after the Civil War were or had been slave owners at one time. They either brought their own slaves to the mansion or used slave laborers assigned to the White House during their term of office. In the White House, the slave living quarters were either the cellar or attic. Andrew Jackson, the seventh president, brought slaves from his Tennessee plantation. His personal body slave slept on the floor in Jackson's bedroom. James Polk, the eleventh president, went so far as to replace all White staff with Black slaves from his Tennessee plantation and Louisiana sugar mills. His slaves also lived in the basement and attic. When Zachary Taylor became president, anti-slavery sentiments were high in the District of Columbia. Fearful of political repercussions, Taylor hid his slaves from the public by restricting them to the eight attic rooms, the presidential private rooms and the executive kitchen. With all those slaves living and sleeping all over the White House for nearly a century, a calculator would be needed to compute the number of Black babies that were born there. After the Civil War, President Ulysses S. Grant reversed President Polk's action of using only Black slaves in the White House. Grant hired White servants to work inside the White House and ordered most of the newly freed slaves to work outside.[33]

## ❦ FIRST BLACK NOVELIST ❦

In 1859, *Our Nig: Or Sketches from the Life of a Free Black*, by Harriet E. Wilson, a Black woman, was the first novel published by a Black person in the United States. Harriet E. Wilson was born in Fredericksburg, Virginia, in 1808, and died in 1870 in Boston, Massachusetts.

Unlike most books of that time, *Our Nig* was neither poetry nor about the life of a runaway slave. Its topic was the oppressive experiences of a young Black woman in a White home in the heart of American abolitionism. Sadly, few Blacks could read at that time. It was well after the Civil War before mainstream American society chose to commit itself to building a literate society by funding a national system of public schools to teach every citizen how to read and write. Ironically, one of the first novels published carried the racial epitaph "Nig" in the title, and 150 years later, the NAACP successfully pressured the Miriam Webster Company to remove the word "nigger" from its dictionary.[34]

## ❦ FIRST BLACK TO JOIN UNION ARMY ❦

History has heretofore recognized the first Black entry and participation in the Civil War based upon when the Union Army was authorized to recruit free Blacks in 1862. The racial barrier to the Civil War, however, had been broken earlier. On August 23, 1861, James Stone of Ohio enlisted and became the first Black to fight for the Union during the Civil War. He was a very light-skinned man married to a White woman. Since the military officials didn't know he was Black, Stone received military rank, pay and privileges comparable to any White soldier. His racial identity as a Black person was not publicly revealed until after his death in 1862.

James Stone's ability to pass as a White man was not unique. His case simply points out that Black people are not always easily categorized. Some are clearly identifiably Blacks, while others are Black because they declare themselves to be. Millions of Black people pass for something other than Black and that started way before James Stone joined the military. Throughout this nation's history, White society has had a poor record of determining who was Black.[35]

## ❦ FIRST BLACK GUEST IN THE WHITE HOUSE ❦

George Washington was the first president of the United States to invite a Black person into the White House. George Washington met with Phillis Wheatley and thanked her for a poem that she had written in tribute to him. Phillis Wheatley's poem about George Washington fit her pattern of writing about mainstream issues and people. Her poems were often of a religious nature and rarely, if ever, about slavery or Black people. Phillis Wheatley became the first popular and published Black poet in America. Also, in 1773, she became the first Black American to publish a book. In great measure, Phyllis Wheatley was allowed to succeed because she avoided race matters and garnered many White supporters.[36]

## ❦ FIRST BLACK PAINTER ❦

In the late 1700s, a Black slave painted himself out of slavery. The particulars of just how Joshua Johnston was able to gain his freedom from his master is unknown, but by 1796, he was advertising his painting services in a Baltimore, Maryland, newspaper. What is clear is that Joshua Johnston was America's first notable Black artist and painter. In the late 1700s and early 1800s, Joshua Johnston earned his living in Baltimore, Maryland, and Washington, D.C., by painting portraits of wealthy White people. Apparently, not all of his work was attributed to him. Modern art historians began to raise questions about Joshua Johnston when J. Hall Peasants, an art historian in Baltimore, realized that there were similarities in painting styles in a number of unsigned colonial portraits. He began a search of the city's directories, newspaper advertisements, libraries, county records and other sources to find more information about Johnston. Finally, in 1971, the National Gallery of Art in Washington, D.C., located a portrait with Johnston's signature on it.

Now more than 50 oil portraits are attributed to Joshua Johnston. A number of his paintings are held by the Maryland Historical Society, the Corcoran Gallery of Art and private collectors. Joshua Johnston painted the world as he saw it, through the eyes and faces of wealthy Whites.[37]

## ❦ First Black College Graduate ❦

The first African-American to graduate from an American college was Alexander Lucius Twilight. He was also the nation's first elected Black representative. Born free in Bradford, Vermont, in 1795, Twilight received a bachelor's degree from Middlebury College in 1823. He taught school in Peru, New York. He later studied theology and was licensed to preach by the Presbyterian church. In 1829, he became principal of the Orleans County Grammar School in Brownington, Vermont, and served as minister of a local congregation as well. Twilight led a fund-raising campaign for a new, larger intermediate school named the Brownington Academy. He shepherded the building of the three-story granite structure with little funding from public or private sources. Twilight served in the Vermont state legislature from 1836 to 1837, then returned to his educational and ministerial career.[38]

## ❦ First Black Woman Doctor ❦

For centuries, the best medical services available to Blacks were faith healers, witch doctors, midwives and herbalists. Public policies and laws prohibited Black people from attending medical schools and legally practicing medicine. However, a few Black men and women broke the barriers and became medically trained doctors. The first African-American woman to earn a medical degree was a native of Richmond, Virginia, Rebecca Lee. She graduated from the New England Women's Medical College in Boston, Massachusetts, in 1864. After practicing medicine for several years, Dr. Lee published the *Book of Medical Discourses*, which advised women how to care for themselves and their children. Dr. Lee was a credit to her gender, the Black race and to the human race.[39]

## ❦ FIRST BLACK BASEBALL PLAYER ❦

Although Jackie Robinson received credit for integrating professional baseball, Moses Fleetwood Walker was an earlier pathmaker. He entered professional baseball less than 20 years after the Civil War. Walker's place in history is more ambiguous and less prominent than Jackie Robinson's because he integrated professional baseball nearly a hundred years before Jackie Robinson. Moses Fleetwood Walker was born in Steubenville, Ohio, on October 7, 1857. He was the son of Moses W. Walker, a physician, and his wife, Caroline, a midwife. In Steubenville where Walker grew up, and later at Oberlin College, a Quaker institution famous for its anti-slavery roots and its liberal outlook on race, he enjoyed significantly more freedom and social equality than most Black Americans of his time. Nevertheless, he did have to confront the harsh realities of 19th century America.

While attending Oberlin College, he played on the varsity baseball team. After leaving college in 1883, Walker signed up to play with the Toledo Mud Hens, a White baseball team. The Mud Hens won the National League baseball pennant and the next year were invited to join the American Association, a major baseball league that rivaled the National League in popularity. When Walker accepted the team's offer, he became history's first African-American major league ballplayer. Within a year, Walker was injured. Both he and his team fell out of the big leagues. For another half century until Jackie Robinson integrated the Brooklyn Dodgers in 1947, no African-Americans played professional baseball except in the Negro League.[40]

## ❦ FIRST BLACK PROFESSIONAL JOCKEYS ❦

Black men were the most popular horse racing jockeys from the earliest colonial period through the early 1900s, when they were replaced by Hispanic and Italian jockeys. When Black jockeys dominated horse racing, they established records that have yet to be broken. There were outstanding Black Kentucky Derby-winning jockeys like Oliver Lewis (1875), Billy Walker (1877), Isaac Murphy (1884/1890), Babe Hurd (1882), George Lewis (1880), Willie Simms (1896/1898), Jimmie Winkfield (1901/1902), Erskine Henderson (1885), Alonzo Clayton (1892), James Perkin (1895) and Jess Conley. George "Spider" Anderson rode his mount to victory in the 1889 Preakness. Riding Aristides, a thoroughbred named after an ancient Greek general, Oliver Lewis won the first Kentucky Derby at Churchill Downs in Louisville, Kentucky, on May 17, 1875. Black jockeys continued to dominate horse racing and had no peers until jockeys began to draw large salaries. Then Black jockeys began to disappear. By the early 1920s, Black jockeys had been replaced.[41]

## ❦ FIRST BLACKS IN CONGRESS ❦

In 1868, John W. Menard of Louisiana grabbed the honor of being the first Black elected to the U.S. Congress. Menard was the son of French Creole parents. He moved to Louisiana after the Civil War to specifically work for the Republican Party. Taking advantage of his political contacts and Black Americans' newly acquired voting rights, he ran for and was elected to the U.S. House of Representatives. When he rose to argue that he should be accepted into the "hallowed halls of Congress," Menard became the first officially recognized Black person to speak on the floor of Congress. Racism, however, prevailed. White congressmen would not let him be officially seated. Menard was awarded full salary as a congressman, but the committee on elections responded to pressures from White congressmen and ruled that it was too soon to admit a Black person to Congress. After speaking on the floor of Congress, but refused his seat, Menard accepted a position as the inspector of customs for the port of New Orleans, Louisiana.

Blacks did a little better in the United States Senate. Two years later, in January 1870, the Mississippi state legislature chose Hiram Rhoades Revels, a Black man, to fill the unexpired term of Confederate President Jefferson Davis in the United States Senate. Thus, Revels was the second Black person to become a member of the U.S. Congress. Though Whites opposed a Black man becoming a United States senator, Revels' heavy Black support put him into office. While holding the position, Revels was a strong champion of Black rights and justice. However, after only one year in the U.S. Senate, he left the position to become the president of Alcorn University, a Black school in Mississippi.[42]

## ❦ First Black Killed in the ❦ Revolutionary War?

On March 5, 1770, Crispus Attucks and several of his colonial compatriots confronted a contingency of British Redcoats in a Boston square. In the ensuing pushing and jeering, Crispus Attucks, a Black man, was shot twice in the chest and died. Despite White opposition, "Crispus Attucks Day" was inaugurated by Black abolitionists in 1858. Three decades later in 1888, a bronze and granite statue was erected to Crispus Attucks on the Boston Commons that recognized him as the first person to die in the Boston Massacre that ignited the American Revolutionary War. More recent research, however, shows that five people were killed in the so-called massacre, and it raises questions about Crispus Attucks' patriotism and behavior.

It now appears that Crispus Attucks was not the first person killed in the Revolutionary War. Apparently, a Black youngster named Christopher Snyder had been killed by British soldiers a few days earlier. Further, rather than seeing Crispus Attucks as a patriot and hero, it seems that White colonists viewed Attucks as a troublemaker. John Adams, a future president of the United States, went so far in a public hearing as to defend the British soldiers who killed Crispus Attucks. A jury of White colonial Americans blamed Crispus Attucks for inciting a riot and found the British soldiers not guilty of killing Attucks, a Black man. Black Americans honored Crispus Attucks as a national hero and patriot, while Whites labeled him a criminal outsider. Some people just wondered what Crispus Attucks, a runaway slave, had hoped to gain by his behavior in the first place.[43]

## 🦋 THE END OF THE BUFFALO SOLDIERS 🦋

The first opportunity that Black men had to formally enter the nation's military forces occurred during the Civil War. After the war, the United States government maintained a segregated U.S. Cavalry: one White and one Black. The Black cavalry, called "Buffalo Soldiers," fought Indians and outlaws in the frontier West. By the end of the 1800s, they were pulled out of the West and assigned to fight as a cavalry with Teddy Roosevelt's Rough Riders in the Spanish-American War in the Caribbean and Pacific Islands. In all major battles, the Buffalo Soldiers distinguished themselves but received little recognition.

With the start of World War II, the last remnant of the Black cavalry, or the old Buffalo soldiers, was converted into military support units of drivers, cooks, waiters, construction workers, maintenance crews, butlers and body servants. For most of World War II, Black soldiers were only issued weapons in emergency situations. In the closing years, they were issued weapons and allowed to fight as infantrymen alongside White soldiers. Being able to fight and defend themselves with a gun in their hands rather than a broom or skillet gave Black soldiers some dignity and restored their masculine image.[44]

*Black Rough Riders. (Library of Congress)*

## ❦ FIRST BLACK TO WIN NATION'S ❦ HIGHEST RECOGNITION

The Civil War movie, *Glory*, depicted a suicidal attack by an all-Black Union military unit attacking Fort Wagoner, which protected the Charleston Harbor in South Carolina. Nearly all the Black troops were killed in the attack. While the 54th Massachusetts Infantry had the distinct honor of being the first all-Black regiment recruited to fight in the Civil War, Sergeant William H. Carney added to the unit's glory by being the first Black American to be awarded the Congressional Medal of Honor, the nation's highest military recognition. In Fort Wagner, on July 18, 1863, William H. Carney led the charge carrying the American flag. Although critically wounded, Carney held the flag high and proclaimed that he never allowed it to touch the ground during the battle. For his heroism, he won the nation's highest award for bravery and gallantry in combat.[45]

## ❦ FIRST PRESIDENTIAL VETO ❦

President Andrew Johnson has the dubious honor of being the first president to use the presidential veto to kill off civil rights benefits for Black Americans. In national politics, the president of the United States is always the big man with the biggest stick. But apparently, when Lincoln emancipated the slaves following the Civil War, his actions gave the U.S. Congress some backbone. The first time the United States Congress ever overrode a presidential veto was for the 1866 Civil Rights Act, passed by the Radical Republicans over the wishes of conservative Southern President Andrew Johnson. Johnson had angered Congress earlier when he vetoed the Civil Rights Acts of 1865 and 1866. When President Johnson vetoed the Civil Rights Act of 1866, Radical Republican members of Congress fought back and overrode his veto. The original intent of the 1865 civil rights law was to place Black ex-slaves in a protected class similar to the Doctrine of Trust that protects American Indians. By consistently vetoing these Civil Rights laws, President Johnson weakened Congressional support for the measures. Instead of getting forty acres, a mule and $100, the best that the radical members of Congress could get for Blacks was the establishment of the Freedmen Bureau, which lasted only a couple of years.[46]

## ❦ THE FIRST ARRESTED FUGITIVE SLAVE ❦

The Compromise of 1850 ended slave trading within the District of Columbia, but it imposed the more stringent Fugitive Slave Act of 1850 on the rest of the nation. The Fugitive Slave Act provided for the appointment of federal commissioners who could use federal marshals and private citizens in any state to capture and return runaway slaves to their White masters. James Hamlet was the first Black person arrested under the new Fugitive Slave

Act. Hamlet was captured in New York and returned to the South by slave catchers.

In a few instances, free Blacks as well as White abolitionists tried to stop the slave catchers from seizing and returning runaway slaves to their masters. However, the abolitionists were rarely successful. The federal government's fugitive slave law itself scared anti-slavery groups, because they knew they could be arrested and fined for aiding a fleeing slave. Abolitionists' commitment to runaways was too weak to justify fighting the power of federal and local governments, as well as White slave catchers.[47]

## 🐛 FIRST INTERRACIAL SEX WHIPPINGS 🐛

One of the first acts of the early colonies was to regulate sex between Blacks and Whites. As early as 1638, the Maryland colony enacted the Doctrine of Exclusion that mandated social separation between Blacks and Whites. This doctrine, soon adopted by other states, stipulated that: "Negroes should never be permitted to enjoy the fruits of White society." Apparently, sex was one of their sacred fruits because in 1639, the Court of Chancery in Virginia tried and convicted Hugh Davis, a White man, for having engaged in sexual relations with a Black female. For his sentence, Davis was whipped before an assembly of Negroes and others for having abused and defiled his body by sharing the "fruit."

A year later in 1640, a Black woman was tried and ordered whipped at a whipping post for having engaged in interracial sex with a White man in colonial Virginia. Twenty-five years later, when Black enslavement laws were enacted, it became legal and customary for a White male to indulge in sex with a Black woman anytime he so wished. The probability was high that any Black female would become a victim of rape or become a concubine of a White male. It took another three hundred years for anti-miscegenation laws to be repealed in most states so that Blacks and Whites could date and even marry.[48]

## ❦ FIRST BLACK DOCTOR IN ❦ THE WESTERN WORLD

The first Black to be trained to practice medicine in the Western world was James Africanus Beale Horton. Horton attended several European schools, but completed his medical training in London in 1858. When he returned to his home in Nigeria, he not only practiced medicine, but began to do medical research in tropical medicine. Horton's contributions to modern medical knowledge evolved from his work on mosquitoes and malaria. In his research, he confirmed that many indigenous African plants had therapeutic value in the treatment of tropical ailments such as cholera, dysentery and fevers. He became widely known and respected by other medical practitioners for his knowledge of Africa's natural coastal vegetation and food plants that could be used for medicinal purposes. Although he only lived to be 48, Horton served as a major link between Africa and Europe, synthesizing the information and values of both cultures.[49]

## ❦ THE FIRST BLACK HOSPITAL ❦

In May 1891, the Provident Hospital and Training School was founded in Chicago, Illinois, by Dr. Daniel Hale Williams. It was the first hospital in the nation that was built, owned and operated by Blacks. Provident Hospital offered the first training program for Black nurses. Dr. Williams performed the first open heart surgery at Provident two years after the facility was opened. When James Cornish, a Black man, was stabbed in the chest in a barroom fight in 1893, and rushed to Provident Hospital, Dr.

Williams opened his chest and successfully operated on him without the benefit of X-rays, blood transfusions and high-tech medical equipment. When James Cornish completely recovered from his wounds and this never-before-attempted operation, Dr. Williams became famous across the country.

The hospital filled many needs of the Black community. It was nearly impossible for Black patients to enter other hospitals, for Black doctors to do internships and for Black nurses to receive training. Though Provident was the nation's first and only Black hospital, it was, ironically, criticized for being racially segregated. An even greater irony is that staff-wise, Provident was the only hospital in the nation with an interracial staff. Fifty years later, when social integration came, Black patients deserted Provident Hospital, causing it to fall on hard financial times. Provident Hospital and Dr. Daniel Hale Williams remain magnificent monuments to a struggling race. [50]

## ❦ THE NATION'S FIRST BLACK BOYCOTT ❦

James Forten, a wealthy, free Black man who lived in Philadelphia, Pennsylvania, in 1760, was a strong and wealthy abolitionist. Forten can be credited with organizing the first Black boycott. He started the Free Produce Movement, which rallied people to boycott and refuse to consume food or any other commodities produced by Black slave labor. If most White abolitionists, Blacks and others who opposed slavery had followed Forten's lead and had boycotted slave-produced products and commodities, it is highly unlikely that slavery would have lasted a year.

As a free Black, James Forten worked hard to earn money to aid his people. When the Founding Fathers declared their war of independence against the English crown, Forten enlisted in the Revolutionary Navy as a "powder monkey." Young men like

Forten were paid to scramble between the decks on warships, bringing powder for the ship's cannons. After the Revolutionary War, Forten used his savings to start a sail-making shop. He prospered in the shipping business, amassing over $100,000, making him the equivalent of a modern day millionaire. Unlike most Blacks who achieved their financial dreams, Forten knew money was not the end, but a means to an end. So, for most of his life, he used his energy and wealth to support economic boycotts, other abolition causes and a back-to-Africa movement.[51]

## ❦ UNDERGROUND RAILROAD FIRSTS ❦

It is generally believed that the Underground Railroad came into existence during the 1820s and stretched from the Southern states into Canada. One legend has it that a runaway slave in Kentucky swam the Ohio River and disappeared so fast that the pursuing White slave master said that he "must have gone on an underground road." In 1839, a Washington newspaper reported that a tortured young boy revealed to slave chasers that he was "supposed to go North on a railroad and the railroad went underground all the way to Boston." This was one of the earliest print references to a runaway slave network being both a railroad and underground. However, the Underground Railroad was not a physical rail line. Instead, it was a loose network of individuals who opposed slavery and performed the dangerous and noble service of aiding slaves who attempted to escape the inhumane institution of slavery.

The first Underground Railroad did not run north. Instead, it ran south. Ferandina Beach, Florida, was the terminus of the earliest southbound Underground Railroad. In the early 1500s, enslaved Africans revolted against Whites exploring the Southeastern coast of North America. After seizing their freedom, they migrated along the coastlines of present day North Carolina,

South Carolina and Georgia, then crossed the St. Mary's River into Spanish Florida. The southern border of Georgia was an international line that divided colonial English territory from Spanish Florida. The various runaway routes that led to and across the St. Mary River were the first Underground Railroad lines.

The Spanish government promoted this Underground Railroad by making public proclamations that any enslaved Black runaway who migrated into Florida, helped build and defend settlements like St Augustine and converted to Catholicism would be granted full rights and privileges of Spanish citizenship. Over 12,000 runaway slaves migrated to Florida and built Maroon communities. Since slaves were not American citizens, they officially became this nation's first and largest body of Spanish citizens.[52]

## ❦ First Underground Railroad ❦ Conductor

A replica of William Still, who many called the father of the Underground Railroad, was unveiled at the National Underground Railroad Family Reunion which took place on July 27, 2003, at the Loew's Hotel, in Philadelphia, Pennsylvania. It is amazing that with the exception of Harriet Tubman, Blacks get practically no credit for their part in establishing and operating the Underground Railroad that rescued and transported runaway slaves to freedom. Historians, teachers and history books give the lion's share of the credit and recognition for the Underground Railroad to White abolitionists. This omission of fact denies Black people an important lesson in extending themselves to help their own people. [53]

## ❦ First Black Insurance Company ❦

The first Black insurance company was established in Philadelphia, Pennsylvania, in 1810, by three Black businessmen.

James Porter, William Coleman and Joseph Randolph knew Whites were not inclined to insure or bury Black people. Black bodies, especially those that remained from public executions by legal or extra-legal agents, were often allowed to conspicuously rot. The African-American Insurance Company came into existence for the specific purpose of providing funds for a proper burial of Black Americans. The insurance company stayed in business for more than thirty years.[54]

## ❦ THE FIRST LEGAL BLACK TOWN ❦

As early as 1526, Black runaways were building Maroon towns throughout the Southeastern states. Fugitive slave laws said Maroon towns were illegal. However, according to Dana Mackenzie, in an article entitled, "Ahead of Its Time," the first legal Black town was built in rural Pike County, Illinois, in 1831. The town, called New Philadelphia, was started by Frank McWorter, a newly-freed slave. McWorter had been a slave in Kentucky before he bought his freedom. He purchased his own freedom at the age of 42 by using profits from a saltpeter manufacturing business that he started. After farming for a number of years, he earned enough money to purchase land from the federal government, which he used as the site for New Philadelphia. He also purchased 16 family members out of slavery. William Butler, John Walker and many other freed slaves joined McWorter in building his dream town.

New Philadelphia, with its 85-foot wide main streets, became an active urban center for Blacks and a minor commercial district. Over 100 Whites took up residence in the city. During the city's heyday, Black and White children went to school together and even intermarried. Today, New Philadelphia is not even a ghost town. All of its commercial and residential buildings have been torn down and bulldozed. Main Street and Broadway, once the town's major streets, are now gravel driveways leading to a farm-house. With only a highway marker and small flag, New Philadelphia is but a memory of biracial cooperation in a Black town before the Civil War.[55]

## ❦ THE FIRST MASS TRANSIT PROTESTS ❦

In 1865, Congressman Charles Sumner obtained passage of a bill that prohibited segregation on horse-drawn streetcars in the District of Columbia. Long before Irene Morgan and Rosa Parks, it was Sojourner Truth, the tireless Black female activist, who decided to test the effectiveness of the new transportation law. She boarded a horse-drawn streetcar that regularly ran on a main street in Washington, D.C. Upon boarding, a White conductor tried to make her ride on the outside platform, which had been designated as the Colored section. She refused and threatened to sue the conductor if he persisted in trying to remove her from the main section. Sensing Sojourner's determination, the White conductor finally gave in and allowed her to ride in the White section.

Several days later, she chose another streetcar to test. After boarding, Sojourner again refused to move to the designated colored section. This time, the White conductor attempted to physically remove her. He slammed her against the door in his effort to throw her from the horse-drawn car into the street. The conductor slammed her so hard against the side of the coach that she was injured. Sojourner Truth then summoned a police officer and had the conductor arrested. The conductor was fired from his job. Within a short time after these two incidents, some White conductors would stop their streetcars and wait for Black women to reach the corner and board. Nearly a hundred years before the Black Civil Rights Movement, Sojourner Truth stood up and demanded that as a Black woman she be allowed to sit any place she chose on a District of Columbia street car.[56]

## ❧ FIRST SUPREME COURT ACTIVIST ❧

Though all Whites benefited from slavery and structural racism, there were some Whites who placed the welfare of lowly Black slaves above their own personal gain. John Jay, the first chief justice of the United States Supreme Court, was such a person. John Jay gave meaning to the flowery words of the Declaration of Independence, "all men are created equal and are endowed with certain inalienable rights of liberty, justice and the pursuit of happiness." In the late 1700s, while most slaveholders dreamed of enriching themselves through the ownership of slaves, John Jay began purchasing Black slaves from slaveholders. Jay invested his money in the purchase of slaves, not for personal profit, but to have the legal right to set them free. The United States Supreme Court has never had that kind of human compassion and out-of-court judicial activism for Black people before or since Jurist John Jay.[57]

## ❧ FIRST BLACK FEMALE AVIATOR ❧

Bessie Coleman was the first Black female aviator. Born in Texas in 1892, Coleman spent her youth working hard in cotton fields and taking in laundry. After graduating from high school, she moved to Chicago in hopes of finding a better way of earning a living. While attending a beauty school and working as a manicurist, she became interested in aviation. Her interest in flying motivated her to read everything she could about flying. She applied for admission to a local flying school, but was refused because of her race and gender. Rather than giving up, she instead saved her money, learned French, then in 1920 applied for admission to the Ecole d'Aviation des Freres Caudron at Le Crotoy in the Somme, in France. On June 15, 1921, Bessie Colman was awarded a pilot's license by the Federation of Aeronautique International in France. Coleman became not only the first African-American woman to be a licensed pilot, but also the first woman to earn an international aviation license.

Bessie Coleman returned to the United States, determined to earn a living in aviation and use some of her money to start a school for Black Americans. No White corporation would hire her, so she embarked on independent tours of air shows across the country to raise enough money to start her own flying school. Tragedy struck while she was flight testing an airplane that she had just purchased for an air show in Jacksonville, Florida. The plane went into a tailspin while Bessie Coleman, with an unfastened seat belt, was leaning out of the window to check the field runway. Bessie Coleman plunged to her death, ending her dream of teaching Black Americans to fly. Officials and representatives of the Bessie Coleman Foundation (BCF) plan to visit the small French village where Bessie Coleman first learned to fly and to publicly thank the Caudron brothers, who were her instructors.[58]

## ❦ FIRST MEXICANS WERE BLACK ❦

The first Mexican was Black. Until the 16th century, there was no Mexico nor Mexicans. Mexicans are a by-product of the racial and cultural mixing of Asian-African Indians, White Spaniards and African Blacks. Following Columbus' discovery of the Americas, Mexico, as a country, was originally called New Spain. In 1519, Hernando Cortes and more than 300 African Blacks set out to explore New Spain and Central America. Upon his arrival, he was greeted by Zambos, people of African-Indian mixtures, who treated Cortes like a god. As Cortes entered Tabasco, the Indian Aztec capital, he was given a Black female slave named Doria Marina. She was the stepchild of an aristocratic Spanish family, a princess who had been secretly sold into slavery. Doria Marina initially acted as Cortes' aide, interpreter and chief negotiator.

Though her negotiating skills probably saved Indian lives, many Indians eventually began to view her as a traitor. Cortes was sexually attracted to her and made her his mistress. Doria Marina became pregnant and bore Cortes a son. Cortes and his Spanish explorers, as well as the local Aztec Indians in the 1500s, recognized the son as the first official Mexican.

Within the very same time period, Spanish slave traders were further blackening Mexico and Central America. Between 1500 and 1650, Spanish slave traders and explorers imported millions of African slaves into New Spain, or Mexico, to dig in the mines for silver and gold. The intermingling of millions of Black slaves with White Spanish conquistadors and African-Aztec Indians created a hybrid ethnicity. By the 19th century, people of African descent had been completely absorbed into Mexico's Mestizo population. Today's mestizos are a biological and cultural mixing of White Europeans, Indians and people of African descent, people who try to erase their Black heritage by labeling themselves Mexicans, Hispanics, Latinos and Chicanos.[59]

## 🍒 THE FIRST SLAVERY APOLOGY 🍒

In 2004, the J.P. Morgan Corporation gave Black America the first public slavery apology and pledge of Black reparation funds. Why did they do it? Because the National Reparation Convention (NRC) members succeeded in persuading the Chicago city council to approve a resolution that required all corporations seeking to do business in Chicago to disclose whether or not their corporation had ever directly or indirectly participated in and profited from Black enslavement. A signed and sworn disclosure document subjected corporations to a financial penalty for false information. Two years after the resolution passed, the J.P. Morgan Company approached the city seeking to open an additional bank in Chicago. Officers of J.P. Morgan Company indicated in their disclosure statement that the company had never engaged in or profited from slavery. Alderwoman Dorothy Tillman, the president of the NRC, requested Dr. Claud Anderson, the president of The Harvest Institute, and other members of the Reparation group, to research historical documents to ascertain whether or not J.P. Morgan enterprises had engaged in slave trading.

Research of museums and Library of Congress files in Washington, D.C., bore fruit. The slave bills of sales and other documents provided evidence that J.P. Morgan, now called J.P. Morgan Chase & Company, had, in fact, been heavily involved in the slave trade. On January 21, 2005, J.P. Morgan Chase & Company publicly announced and filed a disclosure statement with the city of Chicago acknowledging that two of its predecessor banks had received thousands of slaves as collateral before the Civil War. J.P. Morgan officials issued a public apology for their corporation's involvement and promised to set up a $5 million dollar education fund for Black students. While J.P. Morgan's offer of funds for education acknowledged past wrongs, the offer was rejected. The National Reparations Committee, instead, supports reparation funds that are earmarked for economic development and industrialization of Black America.[60]

# CHAPTER 2

# HEROES AND HEROINES

*Heroes not only know what to do,
they do it!*

## Mini Facts

◆ *In 1739, near Stono River, South Carolina, a Black slave named Cato led a major slave revolt. Cato tried to escape to Spanish Florida through the southern Underground Railroad.*

◆ *In 1822, Denmark Vesey, a slave in Charleston, South Carolina, won $1,500 in a lottery. He used the money to buy his freedom, then planned the nation's best organized slave revolt.*

◆ *Between 1831 and the 1840s, Black Seminoles and Black Maroons fought the Second Seminole War, the longest war this nation has experienced in its history.*

◆ *In 1841, a Washington, D.C., court ruled that Joseph Cinque, an African slave, and his fellow mutineers aboard the Spanish slave ship, Amidstad, were not guilty and ordered them released.*

## ❧ A BLACK OFFICER IN THE ❧ REVOLUTIONARY WAR

A few Blacks who fought in the Revolutionary War did not fight for the American cause and yet are entitled to be called Black heroes. A Black slave named Titus, later known as Colonel Tye, was such a hero. Titus was the property of John Corlies, one of the few Quakers in Monmouth County, New Jersey, who refused to educate or set his Black slaves free, defying an edict from his church when it began to oppose slavery. Titus's future was a future of slavery until General Dunmore of the British Army issued a proclamation that promised to free any Black slaves who joined the Brits. In November 1775, a few days after General Dunmore's Emancipation Proclamation was issued, 22-year-old Titus escaped his master and joined the British Army. Titus quickly learned the art of military warfare and rose through the ranks. While not formally commissioning Black officers, the British bestowed the title of Colonel on Titus out of military respect. Titus then changed his name to Tye and became Colonel Tye, the most feared and respected guerrilla commander in the British Ethiopian Regiment.

Colonel Tye and his Black Brigade used their knowledge of swamps, rivers and woods to raid and destroy military units and supplies. Colonel Tye's feats inspired Blacks to run away to the British while debilitating and demoralizing the patriot forces. The patriots rejoiced when in 1780, Colonel Tye was shot in the wrist and later died from a fatal case of lockjaw. Tye's fighting reputation lived on among the American patriots, who confessed that the Revolutionary War would have ended sooner had Colonel Tye been on their side.[1]

## ❧ THE LEGEND OF GEORGE MONROE ❧

George Monroe was born the son of an early Black gold miner and grew up to become one of California's most famous

Pony Express riders and stage drivers. In the early years of his life, George Monroe established a reputation as the most knowledgeable and dependable stagecoach driver on the run between Merced and Mariposa, California. His reputation finally brought him public recognition and personal satisfaction. In 1879, Monroe was chosen by the federal government to drive the stagecoach that took President Ulysses S. Grant along the treacherous Rocky Mountain "S-curve" trails into Yosemite Valley. Apparently Monroe lived up to his reputation. To immortalize George Monroe's fame as a driver, the Monroe Meadows in the Yosemite National park was named after him.[2]

## ❦ JAMES BECKWOURTH: ❦ HERO OR SCOUNDREL?

The best known Black pioneer frontiersman of the West was an ex-slave named James Beckwourth, whose frontier exploits placed him on a level with Kit Carson, Buffalo Bill Cody and Davy Crockett. Beckwourth was born in Fredericksburg, Virginia, in 1798, but moved to St. Louis, Missouri, when he was a teenager. After a short apprenticeship as a blacksmith and a horse trader, he moved further West into Crow Indian country. There he married an Indian woman and became a leader of her tribe and a skilled frontiersman. But like most frontiersmen, Beckwourth had a dark side. In the 1830s, Beckwourth traveled over 2,000 miles back East, from Colorado to Florida, to join and scout for the U.S. Army in its fight with runaway slaves, Black Maroons and Black Seminole Indians. When the Seminole War ended in the 1840s, President Zachary Taylor ordered that Cherokee, Choctaw, Creek, Black Seminole Indians as well as incorrigible runaway slaves would be relocated into Indian territory in the West. Beckwourth played a major role in the Trail of Tears march into the Oklahoma Territory. Blacks made up over one-third of the Trail of Tears marchers.

When the war ended, Beckwourth went back to his old frontiersman profession of guiding wagon trains through the Rocky Mountains. In 1850, Beckwourth discovered a pass through the Sierra Nevada Mountains near what is now Reno, Nevada. For over a decade, he operated a trading post for wagon trains. After the Civil War, he returned to his Indian wife and his old Crow tribe as a friendly gesture. When he refused to stay with them, they poisoned him so that at least his spirit would remain with them forever.[3]

## ❦ ALAMO DEFENDERS WERE ❦ POOR ROLE MODELS

The Battle of the Texas Alamo produced many myths that obscure the truth about the nature of the battle and the Alamo's defenders. The defenders were not fighting for their freedom. Instead, they were fighting to expand and maintain Black slavery. Worse, the most famous Alamo defenders had questionable characters. They appear not to have been good role models. Do slaveholders who openly invade another country and thumb their noses at its anti-slavery laws qualify to be called heroes? Or was their defeat at the Alamo a just reward? Of the 182 Alamo defenders, only six survived the two-week battle. Antonio Santa Anna, the victorious Mexican general, immediately ordered three of them shot and their bodies doused with oil and burned. The remaining three — a White woman named Susanna Dickinson, her 15-year-old son, and Joe, the Black slave of Colonel Travis — were spared. They were set free and told to go forth and warn all White Americans that what happened at the Alamo would happen to them if they came on Mexican territory to set up slave plantations.

Not much is known about the three survivors, but there are some little-known facts about the defenders. All of the better-known personalities perished, including Colonel Travis, Davy Crockett,

Stephen Austin and the Bowie brothers. Colonel Travis, who commanded the Alamo mission, was a killer and liar who abandoned his wife and family. Most White folk heroes were slave owners or slave traders. Rezin Bowie, a White Texan, and father of the celebrated Colonel James Bowie, hero of the Alamo and inventor of the Bowie knife, was a major slave trader who worked directly with an African chief named John Ormond or Mungo John.

Though Jim Bowie was most noted for his fights with his namesake knife and the Battle of the Alamo, Jim and his brother were equally noted for owning and smuggling slaves. Colonel William B. Travis was a slaveholder and had one of his favorite slaves, Joe, with him in the Alamo. Stephen F. Austin was a slaveholder who lied to the Mexican authorities about owning slaves. Thousands of Blacks were being brought into Texas to work the cotton fields. A year before the Alamo, Austin had been arrested and jailed for holding slaves in Texas. Austin claimed his Blacks were not slaves because they had signed a contract to work for him for the rest of their lives without pay. Mexico did not buy Austin's explanation.

Dave Crockett was a juvenile delinquent, wife-deserter and local braggart long before he became a professional woodsman. Crockett did not live up to the reputation as a crack shot and woodsman. In a shooting match, he missed a large buffalo and got himself lost in the woods. After winning two terms to the United States Congress as a representative from Tennessee, he lost his third term, then in social-political disgrace, he immediately left the state. Would these Alamo defenders still be heroes if it were widely known that they were not fighting for their personal freedom and independence but to enslave Blacks and use them to raise cotton on Mexican-owned land? Moreover, according to comments made by the survivors, the White Alamo defenders would have fled had they known help would not arrive in time to save them. The Alamo heroes were fighting to take away from

Black people their freedom, independence and the fruits of their labor. There is little likelihood they will ever be heroes in the eyes of most Black people.[4]

## 🍎 UNCLE TOM'S ELIZA WAS A REAL PERSON 🍎

Eliza, a major female character in Harriet Beecher Stowe's novel, *Uncle Tom's Cabin*, was modeled after a real female slave who became known as Eliza Harris. And, like in Stowe's novel, Harris was a slave who fled with her two-year-old baby in her arms across the ice floes in the Ohio River that divides the states of Kentucky and Ohio. Harris had lost two children previously due to natural causes. She decided to cross the icy river after over-hearing her owners' plan to sell her and her child. Though there was no bridge over the river, her fear of losing her only child pushed her to try crossing the icy river or perish in the attempt.

By a miracle of God, she made it to the other side while being chased and was pulled up the snow-covered embankment by a man who had watched the entire event. Levi and Catherine Coffin, a Quaker family that ran a station on the Underground Railroad, gave her the name Eliza Harris once she reached their home. (Her slave name is unknown.) From there, the newly named Eliza Harris moved to the town of Chatham, Canada. How did Harriet Beecher Stowe learn about the Black female crossing the Ohio River on ice floes? Miss Stowe lived in Cincinnati, Ohio, and had actually visited the plantation of the real-life Colonel Shelby, who was Simon Legree in the Uncle Tom novel. Most importantly, Stowe had met the real-life Uncle Tom, Josiah Henson, and he told her the story of the real-life Eliza. Both Josiah Henson and Eliza Harris spent their final years living in Canada.[5]

## The Underground Railroad Song

I'm on my way to Canada,
That cold and distant land;
The terrible effects of slavery,
I can no longer stand.
Farewell, old master,
Don't come after me;
I'm on my way to Canada,
Where colored men are free.[6]

# ❦ MARCUS GARVEY WENT TOO FAR ❦

Marcus Garvey, a Jamaican immigrant, came to the U.S. in 1916. Within four years, he had organized the Universal Negro Improvement Association, which attracted the largest number of people to any Back-to-Africa or Black economic movement in the history of the nation. Marcus Garvey crafted his movement around Black history, Black pride, Black economic development and a Black spiritual unity for the poor masses. These were the secret keys to his success. Like Paul Cuffee, who initiated an earlier Back-to-Africa movement, Marcus Garvey believed that Black Americans would never be respected until they had their own economy in America or returned to their own independent nation in Africa. Garvey and his various organizations were masters at raising money. On June 27, 1919, Garvey incorporated the Black Star Steamship Corporation. Selling stock for $5 a share, Garvey raised thousands of dollars and purchased three ships, the *Yarmouth*, the *Kanawha* and the *Booker T. Washington*, to begin taking Blacks back to Africa. His inexperience in running a shipping company and overextending his organization financially exposed him to his enemies, who only needed a justification and tool to bring Garvey down.

Racism often makes for strange bedfellows. The Black civil rights organizations, envious of Garvey's large following, rejected him. Garvey responded by seeking support from some of the nation's most racist White organizations. Since his Back-to-Africa and racial separation goals were similar to those of racist White organizations, Garvey believed they could be mutually supportive. Garvey communicated with the head of the Ku Klux Klan in Atlanta, Georgia, who pledged to support Garvey's goals and activities. Garvey also allied himself with the Anglo-Saxon Clubs of America, a vicious and sworn enemy of Black people. Garvey went over the top on October 28, 1925, when he invited John Powell, the Clubs' leader to speak at his Liberty Hall program in the Black community. Powell promised that his organization and the KKK would help Garvey ship his people back to Africa. This was the last straw for the NAACP and other Black civil rights organizations. Civil rights leaders signed petitions charging Marcus Garvey with a variety of criminal acts and then delivered the petitions to the Department of Justice. Selling stock in the Black Star Line had left Garvey vulnerable. He was found guilty of mail fraud, charged $1,000 and sentenced to five years in prison. In 1927, President Calvin Coolidge commuted his sentence, and he was deported back to Jamaica.[7]

## ❦ BLACK HEROES AT HARPERS FERRY ❦

On October 16, 1859, John Brown led 21 men in an attack on a Marine armory in Harpers Ferry, Virginia, to free and arm Black slaves. Of the 21 raiders, five were Black men. Two of these men would die in the attack, two would be captured and executed and one would escape to Canada. Who were these five brave Black men who accompanied John Brown on his Harpers Ferry raid when Frederick Douglass, the most popular Black leader in America, declined to join Brown out of fear? Dangerfield Newby and Lewis Sheridan Leary were free Blacks who died on the site in a shootout with United States Marines. Both were married, but their wives knew nothing about their plans to attack the armory. Shields Green, a fugitive slave, and John Anthony Copeland were both Black teenagers who escaped after the Harpers Ferry attack, but were later captured and hanged. On the gallows, John Copeland was heard to say: "If I am dying for freedom, I could not die for a better cause ... I had rather die than be a slave." Osborn Perry Anderson, the only Black to escape and remain free, enlisted in the Union Army during the Civil War. He published his eyewitness account of the raid on Harpers Ferry in 1861 and died in 1872. These five Black men are Black heroes.

*John Brown's battle at Harpers Ferry. (Library of Congress)*

Some of the lesser known heroes of John Brown's raid on Harpers Ferry were members of The Secret Six. John Brown's plan to liberate Black slaves was supported in principle and financially by this secret committee of Northern anti-slavery men. The Secret Six did not see their support for John Brown's raid as criminal. Just the opposite. They felt that the government's support for the institution of slavery, which ensnared millions of innocent Black victims, was criminal. They had given up on moral persuasion and were in a mood for direct action. The names of the members of The Secret Six — Thomas Wentworth Higginson, Samuel Gridley Howe, Theodore Parker, Franklin Sanborn, George Luther Stearns and Gerrit Smith — eventually emerged. It would have been The Secret Seven, but the name of the one wealthy Black supporter was protected and left off the list because he was a very visible businessman who had invested much time and energy trying to free Black people from slavery.[8]

## ❦ THE OLD WEST ❦

The show, *Gunsmoke*, one of longest running weekly television shows, featured Matt Dillon, a U.S. marshal who brought law and order to the Western frontier. Since over one-third of the cowboys in the old West were Black, were there any Black Matt Dillons? Yes! There were Black lawmen in the early West like Bass Reeves, a deputy United States marshal in the Indian Territory. He killed fourteen men during his career and died in 1910 at the age of 71. Grant Johnson, a former slave of the Creek Native Americans and a deputy marshal in the Indian Territory, was appointed by the White hanging judge, Isaac Parker. Johnson was loathe to use his weapon. He always tired to trick his target into being captured. He had been on the job 14 years before he killed his first man.

Robert L. Fortune, a deputy United States marshal, patrolled the area around Wilberton, Ohio. In 1916, he moved to Phoenix, Arizona, where he was a lawman for another twenty years and made an unsuccessful bid for the state legislature. Francis T. Bruce, a Denver policeman and civic leader, went by the affectionate name of "Daddy." He helped organize Denver's Black Masonic lodge and was appointed a bailiff for the municipal court. Ben Boyer was deputy sheriff of Coaldale, Colorado, from 1905 until 1910. A deadly shot, he carried a custom-made Colt .45 and could manage the roughest outlaw. Black lawmen existed in the West but do not seem to exist in television westerns.[9]

## ❦ Secret Protective Organizations ❦

Throughout American history, White society has hosted hundreds of legal and secret, extra-legal organizations that terrorized Black Americans to maintain the racial status quo. Centuries ago, the White Camellias, Black Horse Brigade, the Knights of the Rising Sun, the White Brotherhood, Constitutional Union Guard, the Ku Klux Klan and numerous similar organizations operated with near impunity to exploit, control and kill people of African descent. In modern times, the nation is riddled with secretive White hate organizations, such as the Ku Klux Klan, Neo-Nazi, Neo-Confederate, National Association for the Advancement of White People, Southern White Knights, Council of Conservative Citizens and Women of Aryan Unity. Controlling or eradicating these secretive hate organizations has not occurred. The government has not tried to do so because these hate groups have always had tacit approval and support from Whites in authority. Rarely have members of these terrorist organizations paid a price for all the property, wealth, votes, lives and hope that they took from Black people.

Only in a few instances have Blacks organized secret, nonsocial organizations to combat White terrorist organizations. To a great degree, meritorious manumission policies impeded Blacks from organizing and maintaining secrecy. Secret organizations such as the Masonic Lodges and Greek sororities and fraternities are permitted to exist in Black communities because they are non-Black in origin and social in nature. One of the earliest and truly serious protective organizations was created nearly a century ago. In 1921, Cyril Briggs posted the organization's mission in *The Crusader*, a Black publication, which said: "The African Blood Brotherhood is essentially a secret organization, though at present engaged in open recruiting in Northern states. We organized for the immediate protection purposes and eventual revolutionary liberation in Africa and other countries where Negroes constitute a majority of the population." Although there were numerous religious and social secret societies all across America, this was one of the few known groups that organized to physically protect Black Americans during the race riot periods before and after World War I. The Brotherhood was a prototype for the Black Panthers of the 1960s. However, the two primary barriers to Black people organizing secret, protective organizations has been their unwillingness to confront White terrorism and to value Blackness.[10]

## ❧ A BLACK "SHERO" ❧

Harriet Tubman is a Black "shero" who performed miracles while burdened by a number of handicaps. Every human is born into conditions that they must learn to adapt to and overcome, or otherwise perish. However, those who are born Black have extra burdens that go beyond class, ethnicity, religion and gender. Black people are forced to bear the burdens and handicapping conditions that are imposed on them simply because of their Black skin color. Yet, a few Blacks seem to find the strength to overcome their personal limitations, climb the extra mountains and lead their people to a better place. Harriet Tubman was such a Black leader and heroine. Harriet was born into slavery in 1820 and died in Jim Crow semi-slavery in 1913. As a child in slavery, not only was

Harriet overworked and denied an education, but she suffered a physical disability when she was struck in the head by a White overseer while trying to protect another slave. The blow was so horrific that it fractured her skull and caused lifelong episodes of narcolepsy, a sleep disorder that creates an uncontrollable sense of weakness and illusions. However, her medical disabilities did not weaken her determination to aid the millions of enslaved Blacks in the South.

Harriet eventually escaped from the brutal White overseer, but never forgot the painful experiences of slavery. She made over 19 trips into the South and led hundreds of slaves to freedom in the North. During the Civil War, she served as a Union scout, cook, spy and in at least one instance, she led Colonel Montgomery and his gallant band of 300 Black soldiers in a raiding party along the Combahee River in South Carolina. The raiding party destroyed millions of dollars worth of Confederate military supplies and rescued nearly 800 slaves. One Black woman who was being rescued brought along a pig, which Harriet Tubman named after Jefferson Davis, the president of the Southern Confederacy. After the Civil War, Tubman continued to work for the rights of Black people. In her retiring years, her health failed, but the United States government refused to give her military retirement, slavery reparations or physical disability payments. Harriet Tubman died as she had lived, in pain and poverty, but still in love with her people.[11]

## ❧ BLACK COAST GUARD HEROES ❧

A group of Black unsung naval heroes on Pea Island, North Carolina, were lifesavers on our coastal waters long before there was a U.S. Coast Guard. In the late 1800s, the U.S. Lifesaving Service manned coastal stations, patrolled coastal waters and performed rescue missions. In 1880, Richard Etheridge became the service's first African-American commander when he took charge of the Pea Island, North Carolina, lifesaving station. Etheridge, a Civil War veteran familiar with local waters, led an all-Black crew, whose predecessors had walked off the job in protest of Etheridge's appointment. In order to help his men pass the required civil service examination, he taught them to read and write. In a dramatic 1896 sea rescue, the Black lifesavers brought safely to shore all passengers and crew from the shipwrecked *E.S. Newman*. Almost a century later, the surfmen's public service was recognized when the U.S. Coast Guard presented Gold Lifesaving Medals to their Black descendants.[12]

## ❧ Black Detroiters Moved On Up ❧

In July 1831, Ruth and Thornton Blackburn escaped from slavery in Kentucky to settle and work jobs in Detroit, Michigan. Within a short time, they built a reputation for being a hardworking and honest couple. Two years later, a posse of Kentucky slave catchers rode into Detroit and had the Blackburns arrested. When Black men in Detroit got the word, they armed themselves with pistols while Black women planned less violent tactics to rescue the couple. A delegation of Black women visited Ruth Blackburn in her cell. One of the visiting Black women exchanged clothes with Mrs. Blackburn, who then walked out of the jail with the delegation. That very night, the Black delegation secreted her across the Detroit River into Canada. This was possibly Black America's first nonviolent victory.

The next day, the Black men put their plan into action. They armed themselves and began gathering around the jail. Whites did not pay very much attention to them because the Detroit newspaper had already reported that Black men near the jail were engaging in silly posturing and should not be taken seriously. When the local sheriff brought Thornton Blackburn out of the jail to turn him over to the slave catchers, the Black men swung into action. They grabbed Blackburn and spirited him away. When the sheriff intervened, he was beaten to the ground, his skull fractured and some teeth knocked out. Detroit's Mayor Marshall Chapin declared an insurrection and summoned federal troops. A few Blacks were arrested, but later released. The sheriff died from his injuries in what was called "the Blackburn riots." A few years later, in Canada, Thornton Blackburn became vice-president of the Canadian Mill and Mercantile Company in Buxton, Canada. By 1870, a Canadian paper reported that he was a wealthy citizen of Toronto, Canada. All is well that ends well.[13]

## ❦ CIVIL WAR "JANE BONDS" ❦

Whether it is a spy movie, novel or dramatization, the main characters in spying episodes tend to be males. However, there have been some real-life female Jane Bonds. Some of the more interesting female spying occurred during the American Civil War. Elizabeth Van Lew, a White female abolitionist, operated an elaborate spy ring for the Union Army. While the Southern Confederates rounded up suspected Northern sympathizers and abolitionists, Van Lew was establishing a tight-knit, twelve-member spy ring made up of wealthy Whites, government clerks and Blacks. Van Lew's top agent, or spy, was a Black female named Mary Browser, whose education at a Quaker School for Negroes in Philadelphia, Pennsylvania, had been paid for by Van Lew before the Civil War. When the Civil War began, Mary Browser was assigned to spy in the highest offices of the Southern Confederacy.

Van Lew successfully persuaded Varina Davis, the First Lady of the Southern Confederacy, to hire Mary Browser as a domestic aide. Once on the Southern payroll, Mary Browser began collecting and reporting information from within President Jefferson Davis' Confederate White House in Richmond, Virginia.

Thomas McNiven, another Union spy, reported that Bowser had a photographic memory and could recall and recite word for word from any notes, letters and military documents that she had read or any conversations that she had overheard. Browser's dark skin color was her best protection. Confederates assumed that most Blacks were loyal, illiterate, noncombative, happy people who were simply spectators of the war. In 1995, modern day Southerners were surprised when the Military Intelligence Corps identified Mary Bowser as a Black American and inducted her into its Hall of Fame.

Mary Browser was not the only Black female spy in the Civil War. There were hundreds. In February 1862, a free Black woman from Norfolk passed through Confederate lines and went to the Navy Department in Washington, D.C. Hidden inside of her dress was a letter from a Union sympathizer, who worked in the Confederate navy yard. The letter reported that the *Merrimac*, which had been scuttled earlier by the Northern forces, was being rebuilt and would soon be finished. Union military forces had fallen behind in their shipbuilding and did not know what progress the Confederate Navy was making. Since Browser's information confirmed that Richmond's Tredegar Iron Works was building a new *Merrimac*, which would be a warship with sides covered with metal armor, the Union hastily built a similar ironclad ship called the USS *Monitor*.

The Confederates launched the *Merrimac* and very quickly the ship made short work of several Union vessels in key ports. The Union accelerated construction and finished the *Monitor* just in time for it to confront and engage in a three-hour battle with the *Merrimac*. Though the winner of this great sea battle remained inconclusive, history is clear that had the Union Navy not rushed the building of the ironclad *Monitor*, the Confederate South could have controlled the seas during the Civil War. Thus a Black woman's smuggled information played a key role in determining whether the North or the South would rule the seas during the Civil War.[14]

## ❦ BLACK COOK BECAME A HERO ❦

The first time the United States military recognized and honored a Black cook as a national hero resulted from an act of heroism that occurred early Sunday morning, on December 7, 1941, when Japanese planes attacked Pearl Harbor, Hawaii. Dorie Miller, a cook's helper, who was stationed onboard the USS West Virginia, received the Navy Cross Medal for gallantry for dragging his wounded captain to safety and for manning a .50 caliber anti-aircraft machine gun he used to shoot down four Japanese planes. As a cook's helper, the nation was pleased that a Black man who had been denied combat training could have performed so heroically. Miller was honored and recognized in speeches and support-the-war posters; he remained a cook exempt from combat training. Two years later, on November 22, 1943, while serving White officers, a torpedo from a Japanese submarine sank the Liscome Bay, the escort carrier to which he had been assigned. This time, Dorie Miller was not so lucky. Miller and most of his crew went down with the ship. However, in the minds of older Black Americans, Dorie Miller will always be one of their Black heroes.[15]

## ❦ QUOTABLE NOTABLE ❦

Hugh Moss, a 19-year-old Confederate soldier who had just returned from the Civil War, said to one of his Southern friends: "I've been humiliated by Negroes who would no longer take orders. They are putting themselves on an equality with Whites. This makes my blood boil." His neighbor responded: "What the

North is sending South is not money but dynamite. This education is ruining our Negroes. They are demanding equality."[16]

## 🌿 FORGOTTEN WHITE HEROES 🌿

Nearly half a century after Rev. Martin Luther King Jr. was assassinated, it is now politically correct for White politicians to proclaim admiration for King and his integration dream. With White conservatives now professing their love and respect for a dead Martin L. King, the question that haunts many Black Americans is, where are all the White Martin Luther Kings? Throughout this nation's history, there has been a shortlist of Whites willing to fight for rights and justice for Black people. Of the few who did, they, too, paid a heavy price, usually with their lives. In a list of White heroes for Blacks, John Prentiss Mathews and his son ought to be at the very top, because they had the zeal and determination of the White abolitionist John Brown. John Mathews Sr. was born in Mississippi in 1840 to a wealthy family that owned 35 slaves. When the Civil War started, John believed so strongly in freedom and justice for Black people that he fought with the Union during the Civil War.

After the Civil War, radical Republicans helped John Mathews get elected to the office of sheriff in Mississippi. In his off-duty hours, he organized local Black voters into an independent party. A few White farmers who believed Black people were entitled to all the rights, privileges and immunities of American citizens also joined the independent party. When Mathews and his newly formed independent party outvoted local Democrats in local elections, they became the target of threats and violence. Black churches and homes were bombed and burned. White racists conducted "coon hunts" and warned John Mathews to stop politically aiding Blacks. He did not stop encouraging Blacks to register and vote in every election.

In 1883, on the morning of a major local election, John Mathews delivered ballots to polling booths in the town's Black community. But before he could drop the ballots, Ras Wheeler, a racist Southern Democrat, pulled out a shotgun and shot Mathews twice at close range, killing him instantly. An all-White jury found Ras Wheeler not guilty of killing John Mathews, and they appointed him to fill the then-vacant sheriff's position. Immediately upon assuming office, Wheeler posted a city ordinance that said: "In this town, no man or men shall organize the Negro race against the Whites in this county. Anyone who does, does so at their own peril." The members of the Black/While alliance took the hint and left town. The one exception was John Mathews Jr.

John Mathews Jr. was only fifteen when his father was murdered, but he tried to pick up where his father left off. Mathews Jr. began reorganizing local Blacks and liberal White Republicans and running them for political office on Black issues. John Mathews Jr. quickly became unpopular with Sheriff Wheeler and most Whites, who nicknamed him "coon." On Christmas day, in 1890, a week after his 22nd birthday, John Mathews Jr. was shot down by White racists in the street. He was buried next to his father in a Black cemetery. White Mississippians then enacted the infamous Mississippi Constitution of 1890, which kept Blacks out of politics for another 75 years. Except for the small, broken monument at their gravesites, it is apparent that few people, including Black people, remember John Prentiss Mathews and his son, and the personal sacrifices that they made.[17]

## ❧ BLACK HEROES IN ROMAN LEGENDS ❧

During the Black Civil Rights Movement of the 1950s and 1960s, Italian and Greek movies about Hercules filled the screens in theaters in Black neighborhoods. These movies paid respect to special Roman and Greek gods and the gifts they had bestowed upon a very special folk hero named Hercules, who stood head and shoulders above all others in Roman and Greek legends. Modern movies and literature present Hercules as a Greek with Aryan facial features. Movies and stories endow him with great strength, athleticism, virtue, masculine beauty, noble lineage and valor, but they fail to mention that Hercules was of African origin and was a Black man. The root of the name Hercules can be traced back to the people of ancient Ethiopia and Egypt, who conceived of a mighty savior named Heru. In some instances, Heru was a title bestowed upon Egyptian Pharaohs, who became known for their courage and pursuit of justice. Ancient Greeks who were students of African teachers adopted the words "Horus," "Hero" and "Heracles" as derivatives of Heru. Heracles, or Hercules, therefore are titles.

In his book, *Black Athena*, Martin Bernal points out that illustrations on ancient Greek paintings depicted the legendary Hercules as a curly-haired Black African. Hercules is shown as an enormous, muscular, black-skinned giant with obvious Negroid features common to people of African descent. In a battle scene with White Europeans and Black Egyptians, Hercules is depicted crushing the white-skinned assailants beneath his feet and striking the Black Egyptian attackers. In sculptures from early history, Greeks appeared to be descendants of Blacks and Whites. Would movie fans and readers of Greek literature still view Hercules as their hero if they knew of his Black past?[18]

## ❦ THE FIRST BLACK CONSTITUTION ❦

On May 8, 1858, legendary abolitionist John Brown and some of his White and Black supporters secretly convened in the Number Three Colored Fire Company in Chatham, Ontario, and drafted a Black National Constitution that they hoped would serve as the founding law of liberated Blacks and their community in the

Allegheny Mountains. The preamble to the Black Constitution read: "Whereas, slavery, throughout its entire existence in the United States, is none other than a most barbarous, unprovoked, and unjustifiable War of one portion of its citizens upon another portion; the only conditions of which are perpetual imprisonment, and hopeless servitude or absolute extermination; in utter disregard and violation of those eternal and self-evident truths set forth in our Declaration of Independence ..."

John Brown believed that slavery was nothing less than a crime against the most basic American principles. Rather than appealing to Whites for freedom and justice, John Brown felt that Black people needed to take up arms in their own self-defense. His plan was to capture the military armory at Harpers Ferry, free and arm slaves then retreat to an armed Black community in the Appalachian Mountains. Brown believed armed slave camps in the Appalachian Mountains which ran North to South across the eastern part of the United States would be like driving a stake into the heart of slavery. With the vision of a Black community in his head and a Black Constitution in his hands, John Brown and his interracial raiding party rode into Harpers Ferry and a special place in Black history. John Brown's raid on Harpers Ferry excited the nation and triggered a Civil War that led to the death of Black slavery.[19]

## 🌿 STRIP SEARCHING SOJOURNER TRUTH 🌿

During slavery, White male chivalry gave Black females freedom and access within mainstream society that Black males never had. Black females were nonthreatening to Whites, but they questioned the sex of aggressive Black women. Whites were often curious to know if an aggressive and outspoken Black woman really was a woman or was she a Black man impersonating a woman? To answer this question, White men often paid close attention to the bodies of Black women and sometimes demanded proof of their gender. White men never doubted nor challenged the gender of an outspoken and aggressive White woman associated with the Women's Movement.

Perhaps the best known incident of this sort of gender questioning of a Black female occurred with Sojourner Truth, the legendary Black female activist, in the 1800s. Sojourner Truth was asked to speak at a women's rights convention in Indiana. Upon arriving, Sojourner met the familiar charge that she was actually a Black man dressed up in women's clothing. A White doctor on the scene suggested that the gender issue be settled once and for all by having Sojourner bare her breast before the assembled White audience. The audience championed the doctor's suggestion. A witness to this spectacle retold the incident in a letter to William Lloyd Garrison, one of the nation's foremost slavery abolitionists. According to a witness: "Sojourner told them that her breasts had suckled many a White babe, to the exclusion of her own offspring, however all of them had grown into adulthood. Even though they had sucked her colored breasts, in her estimation, they were far more manly than those in the audience who were persecuting and embarrassing her." According to the witness, Sojourner quietly asked them, as she disrobed her bosom, if they, too, wished to suck! In vindication of her truthfulness, Sojourner told the White audience that she "didn't mind showing her breast to the public because it was not to her shame, but their shame."

Though she had no power or material resources, Sojourner Truth fought against Black slavery and gender domination. Unfortunately, she devoted her entire life to appealing to White morality and decency that evidently did not exist in race matters.[20]

## ❦ A BLACK INVENTOR TO THE RESCUE ❦

In 1914, Garrett Augustus Morgan, a scientist and inventor, constructed and patented a smoke inhalator protective hood and gas mask smoke protector that allowed the wearer to enter smoky or toxic environments without breathing contaminated air. His protective gear covered the wearer's head and shoulders and supplied clean air to the wearer through two tubes from a bag of air that hung on the back of the hood. Garrett Morgan's invention received national attention on July 25, 1916, when the Cleveland Waterworks exploded, entrapping more than twenty workmen inside a tunnel filled with poisonous smoke and gases and Garrett Morgan was called to the scene to rescue the men who were trapped about 228 feet below Lake Erie. Morgan and his brother put on their protective hoods, entered the tunnel and rescued the trapped workers. Morgan was proclaimed Cleveland's most honored and bravest hero.

Hoping to translate his newly acquired national popularity into sales of his invention, Morgan hired Whites to market and sell his inventions, especially in the South. When his customers discovered he was Black, his sales orders quickly dried up. Morgan discovered that rescuing twenty men and being recognized as a national hero was fine, but unfortunately, it did not wash off enough Blackness to allow him to compete and prosper in business.[21]

## ❦ THE LEGEND OF ST. PATRICK'S DAY ❦

Every spring, millions of Whites and Blacks alike celebrate Saint Patrick's Day by wearing green items of clothing or displaying the Irish shamrock. How many would continue to celebrate Saint Patrick if they knew they were honoring a Black man? In his book, *Nile Valley Contributions to Civilization*, Anthony T.

Browder tells how in 432 A.D., Pope Celestine I sent a former British slave named Patrick with an army into Ireland to convert the general population to Christianity. In the process of converting the local inhabitants, Patrick's army allegedly "slew thousands of Irishmen, founded more than 300 churches and baptized more than 120,000 persons."

The Vatican rewarded Patrick with sainthood and a feast day on March 17. According to Anthony Browder, what is not commonly known about St. Patrick is that the snakes he allegedly drove out of Ireland and into the sea were not the crawling kind but the walking kind. They were Druids, a religious group that worshiped snakes. The presence of Druids and their snake ideologies were a direct threat to the development of Christianity in Ireland and had to be removed. On the next Saint Patrick's Day, how many White people would proudly wear green and join St. Patrick's Day marches if they knew they were celebrating a Black man who freed Ireland by driving dreaded two-legged snakes out of the country and into the sea?[22]

## 🍂 BELATED RECOGNITION OF A BLACK HERO 🍂

Throughout this nation's history, Black men and women have fought in every war in defense of it, but have received little public recognition. Towards the end of the 20th century, things began to change. On January 16, 2001, President Bill Clinton awarded the Medal of Honor to Corporal Andrew Jackson Smith of the 55th Massachusetts Company, in the Union Army, for deeds performed at the Battle of Honey Hill in South Carolina on November 30, 1864. Corporal Smith distinguished himself by taking up his regiment's colors from the hands of a fallen color-bearer, then carrying the colors and exposing himself to enemy gunfire throughout the battle. President Bill Clinton's recognition of Corporal Smith is, without a doubt, a rare honor for a Black Union soldier in the American Civil War and the most belated military award in this nation's military history. However, it is always better late than never.[23]

# CHAPTER 3

# NAMES AND GAMES

*Naming is a power tool.*

## Mini Facts

◆ *In the 1800s, a Zip Coon was a real-life Sambo. A Zip Coon was an urban Black person who spent his time and money pretending to be high class.*

◆ *In the late 1850s, the U.S. State Department clarified its treaty with Mexico by declaring that, unlike Mexicans and American Indians, Negroes were not "people of color."*

◆ *In 1860, Blacks made up over 51 percent of the nation's prison population. One hundred and fifty years later, Blacks still make up over 51 percent of the nation's prison population.*

◆ *In the late 1890s, nearly 90 percent of the nation's hate crimes were against Black people. In the 1990s, FBI reports indicated that 68 percent of all hate crimes were against Blacks.*

## ❦ NAMING AND FRAMING A NATION ❦

This nation was named after slave-trading profiteers. It is debatable whether Columbus actually "discovered America"; however, there is no debate over the fact that Columbus carried slaves on his second voyage across the Atlantic Ocean and into the Caribbean Islands. Following in Columbus' footsteps, an Italian navigator named Amerigo Vespucci, who sailed West a few years after Columbus, saw the American coast line and lent his name to the North, Central and South American continents. It is an interesting fact that the Americas were named after a slave trader, Amerigo Vespucci.

Vespucci acquired more than two hundred slaves from another Italian slave trader, Antonio de Torres. Like Columbus, who promised his queen millions in slavery-generated profits, Vespucci envisioned earning millions in profits from slave sales. However, the financial dreams of these two men were never realized. The greatest irony is that both Columbus and Vespucci received international recognition for being identified with the Americas. Yet, neither one of them actually came ashore or even set foot on the landmass of North, Central and South America.[1]

## ❦ THE FIRST AMERICAN NAMES ❦

After European Whites came to America, they went through a litany of name changes. In order to set and maintain a proper distance from Blacks and Indians, who Whites called heathens, White colonists called themselves Pilgrims, then Puritans then Christians. The word Christian served well so long as Blacks and Indians could be called heathens. But when an increasing number of Blacks and Indians sought to be baptized in the 1700s, White colonists began to label themselves English, because Christian did not allow them to distinguish between a Christian White and a

Christian Black or a Christian Indian. The term Christian had become inadequate for maintaining distance between the groups. In the mid-1800s, a large influx of non-English European immigrants, including the French, Germans and Swedes, poured into America. This influx of Northern and Eastern Europeans overrode the term English, which was replaced by the unmistakable and unalterable term, White.

As slavery enriched the majority White society, White skin took on a value that was to be cherished and protected. Southern Europeans began migrating to America after the Civil War. These ethnic immigrants retained their White label, but built separate ethnic communities (Italian Americans, Greek Americans, Polish Americans, Arab Americans, Asian Americans, etc.). In the 1950s, Blacks protested for the right to leave their communities and socially integrate into White communities, institutions and businesses. In response to Blacks' integration demands, Euro-ethnics abandoned their ethnic enclaves and united into one, large "White community" to defeat the intrusion of Black Americans. By the early 1960s, there were few identifiable White ethnic communities. In the 1970s, Arabs, Mexicans and other Spanish-speaking people, who were classified and treated as Whites, began to stream into the country and build new ethnic communities. America entered the 21st century with a new White-Asian-Arab-Hispanic melting pot in formation. Black Americans remain outside and underneath the American melting pot.[2]

## ❦ THE WRONG THOMAS JEFFERSON ❦

On the 1st of July, 1800, newspapers across the country carried the report that Thomas Jefferson had died at his Monticello estate. Members of Jefferson's Republican Party did not believe the report and charged that it was a political trick. On the other side of the political aisle, the Federalist Party rubbed their hands in glee, secretly hoping the word was true and they could then take control of the national government. A week later, the public learned that Thomas Jefferson, the Founding Father was still alive. The rumor was not totally wrong. The Thomas Jefferson who died was one the distinguished Jefferson's old slaves with the very same name. Why Thomas Jefferson would give a slave his exact same name is unclear. Ironically, twenty-six years later, in the 1st week of July, death called again. This time, the real Thomas Jefferson did die.[3]

## PEOPLE OF COLOR?

Who are the people of color that the NAACP, the Urban League, Rainbow Push and other civil rights organizations have built their programs and policies around? Biologically, people of color could be all humans, since all humans, including Whites and albinos, have some melanin and skin color. However, over 140 years ago, the United States government defined people of color. In the Treaty of 1848, following the Mexican-American War, the United States government purchased the southwestern territory from Mexico for approximately $18 million. The treaty, negotiated by the U.S. State Department, stipulated that only Mexicans and American Indians qualified as people of color and were, therefore, entitled to citizenship rights.

Ten years later, the United States Supreme Court issued its infamous Dred Scott Decision that said: "No Black man has any rights that a White man is bound to respect." Again, Black people were singled out as different from those classified as White. In 1862, the U.S. Attorney General clarified the Dred Scott ruling, declaring that Black people: "... were not people of color and therefore they were ineligible to participate in the nation's homesteading, land granting or land rush programs." For the next forty years, only newly arriving Europeans, Mexicans, Asians and

Indians had people-of-color citizenship rights. Census data reveals these groups received special benefits not because they were people of color, but because they were classified as White. Since the 1862 homesteading and land grant policy ended in 1902, what benefits do Black people get today when civil rights organizations declare them to be people of color?[4]

## ❦ MEMIN PINGUIN, MEXICO'S SAMBO ❦

On Wednesday, June 29, 2005, the Mexican government issued a postage stamp series that depicted a dark-skinned, large, bubble-eyed, big red-lipped Jim Crow-era cartoon character, popularly known in Mexico as Memin Pinguin. These stamp images, which look like Little Black Sambo, infuriated Black Americans who saw them as racist. Black civil rights leaders demanded that President Vincente Fox of Mexico retract the stamps and apologize to Blacks. President Fox refused, insisting that the stamps were not racist because the Memin Pinguin is the most popular comic book character and a historically popular image in Mexican culture. This Memin Pinguin character regularly appears in the Sunday comic strip, along with Aunt Jemima.

The negative Black images in Mexico are not restricted to postage stamps and comic book characters. The most popular toothpaste in Mexico, and many Asian countries, has been Darkie Toothpaste. Although the company recently changed the product's name to Darley toothpaste in response to criticism, the signature character of the advertising remains. He is an extremely dark Black man with large white eyes, red lips and shining teeth, dressed in a black tuxedo. Negative images of Blacks are found not only in Mexico, but throughout Latin America, Asia and Europe. Advertisements for Kellogg's "Cracky Nuts" are built around pictures of Black Sambos in the jungle, with bones in their hair, holding spears and dancing around a pot in which Whites are being cooked. Pizza advertisements show Little Black Sambos eating pizzas instead of watermelons. The great irony is that Black civil rights leaders constantly seek to ally with Mexicans, minorities and people of color who show little respect or appreciation for Black people. Someday Black leaders will turn inward and ally with their own people first.[5]

———————❮◆❯———————

## In Honor of Black History Month

A Black man talks to a White man:
When I was born, I was Black,
When I grew up, I was Black,
When I'm sick, I'm Black,
When I go in the sun, I'm Black,
When I am cold, I am Black,
When I am scared, I am Black,
When I am sick, I am Black,
When I die, I'll still be Black.
But, you as a White person:
When you are born, you are pink,
When you grow up, you are White,
When you are sick, you are green,
When you go in the sun, you are red,
When you are cold, you turn blue,
When you are scared, you turn yellow,
When you are bruised, you turn purple,
When you die, you turn gray.
And you have the nerve to call me colored.

~ *Unknown Author*

———————❮◆❯———————

## 🍒 Racism in School Books 🍒

In the spring of 2004, the NAACP announced that it had finally convinced the Merriam Webster Company to remove the word "nigger" from future dictionaries. The NAACP believed that the less visible the word nigger to the general public, the less likely it would be used. On the other hand, does removing the word nigger from the dictionary solve the problem or remove the racial insult that the label connotes? Probably not. Ironically, the word is found throughout literature. No literary figure used the word more often than Samuel Clemens, best known as Mark Twain. Generation after generation of school children continue to be exposed to Mark Twain's classic stories of Huckleberry Finn and Tom Sawyer. Students might not be able to find the negative racial label, nigger, in the dictionary, but they can find it in most of Mark Twain's books.

Samuel Clemens was comfortable using the word nigger because he grew up in a slaveholding family in the Deep South. Samuel Clemens was thoroughly indoctrinated in White supremacy. He watched his father strip Black people of their humanity, religion, culture, dignity, families, rights and fruit of their labor. As a young child, he watched his father drag a Black female slave, Jennie, out of the house, tie and beat her. As a man, while traveling to New York for a personal appearance with abolitionists, Samuel Clemens said: "I reckon I had better black my face, for in these Eastern states, niggers are considerably better than White people." While all of the Mark Twain stories used the word nigger to show disrespect for Black people and keep them in their place, schoolrooms and public libraries have dutifully kept Mark Twain's books on their shelves. So, is it more important to erase the word or the concept that it stands for?[6]

## ❦ THE ORIGIN OF NONVIOLENT RESISTANCE ❦

Who gets the credit for originating the passive, nonviolent philosophy? During the Black Civil Rights Movement of the 1960s, the Rev. Martin Luther King Jr. attributed his passive, nonviolent philosophy to Ghandi of India. Ironically, Ghandi borrowed the philosophy from his readings about Frederick Douglass, an African American who believed that nonviolent political action was the best means to end slavery. The premise of the nonviolent resistance philosophy is that a person or group should be willing to sacrifice itself for a greater good. Frederick Douglass linked his passive resistance beliefs to the philosophy of William Lloyd Garrison, a White abolitionist, who believed that moral persuasion was the best way to end slavery. King, Ghandi and Douglass aside, the oldest and true origin of nonviolent resistance was Jesus Christ. In the New Testament of the Holy Bible, Jesus was "the lamb" who subordinated his godly powers and allowed himself to be brutalized and sacrificed to save the world. Now you know the real history and origin of the nonviolent, passive philosophy of the Black Civil Rights Movement of the 1960s.[7]

## ❦ INDIAN BLOOD WAS PRIZED ❦

In 1751, Benjamin Franklin, who had no use for Black people, counseled his compatriots to take measures to keep the country all White and Indian red. He lamented that "The number of White people in the world's population is proportionally very small," and that the slave trade could possibly "darken" America. He believed that American Indians were higher in the social order than Blacks and could easily mix with and expand the White population. He further believed the skin color of Indians would enhance the appearance of White skin, making the White man and the Red man true brothers and equals. Convinced that European Whites "discovered" North America and, therefore, they alone were entitled to enjoy the benefits of free land and free labor, Franklin believed that only American Indians were qualified to live with and interbreed with European Whites.

Benjamin Franklin was, however, known to be an abolitionist. What is not well-known is that he opposed slavery because he did not want Whites to interbreed with people of African descent. He once asked: "Why increase the sons of Africa by planting them in America, where we have so fair an opportunity by excluding all Blacks and Tawneys, of increasing the lovely White and Red?" Benjamin Franklin was one of the few Founding Fathers who opposed slavery, yet was fearful and opposed to mixing Black and White blood, because Black blood had the potential of dominating White blood. Old Ben wanted the nation to quickly end slavery and ship Blacks out of the country.[8]

## ❦ THE POWER OF A NAME ❦

For over 200 years, the name J.P. Morgan has signified wealth, power and greed. By 1912 in America, J.P. Morgan's House of Morgan and its associate companies were worth more than all the assessed value of properties in the twenty-two states and territories west of the Mississippi River. The wealth and power of the Morgan name was equally potent in Europe, where the mere mention of the name, Morgan, could open doors and provide worldly comforts. For instance, the servants at J.P. Morgan's London home nightly prepared his dinner and bath, turned down the bed and laid out nightclothes for master Morgan, even when it was known beyond a shadow of a doubt that he was a thousand miles away in America. The J.P. Morgan name has always been the proverbial 800-pound gorilla.[9]

# ❦ DOUBLE YOUR NAME OR NICK IT ❦

There is a saying that the most common identifying characteristics of a Southern "good ole boy" is his baseball cap, six-pack of beer, bluegrass music and a pickup truck with a dog and Confederate flag in the rear. There is another missing element to this stereotype — double first names. It was a part of early Southern culture for parents to give their offspring double first names, like Joe Joe, Billy Bob, Tommy Lee, Peggy Sue, Mary Ann, Jimmy Rob, Willie William, Bubba Junior and John John. Just a few generations ago, the worst thing that could happen to a typical Black person was to be approached by a Southern White male with a name like Bubba or Billy Bob. There are some historians who argue that the practice of double first names was a carryover from Scotland and Ireland, where people had the same first and last names. Once in America, they continued to use double names.

Black Americans also play with names. A generation or two ago, Southern Blacks routinely gave their children and acquaintances nicknames. These nicknames conveyed social relationships that grew out of close-knit families and communities. Nicknames tended to be based on physical features, behavior patterns or status in the family or community. For instance, the nickname of a person with a physical disability that caused a person to speak at a lower than normal volume might be Whisper. A person with a missing finger might be called Nub. In Black communities, nicknames like Chicken Monster, Gobble-Up, Broke Neck, Rat Man, Monkey Do, Two Head, Hambone, Bird Eye, Peanut, Tutti Fruiti and Dirty Red were not uncommon. Southern Blacks accepted and responded to their nicknames as readily as they did to their legal, given names because the nicknames were most often expressions of love and affection. After the Black Civil Rights Movement of the 1960s, double first names for Whites and nicknames for Blacks seemed to have decreased in popularity.[10]

## ❧ MADE IN THE USA ❧

The 13th Amendment to the Constitution abolished slavery, but allowed a slavery-like peonage prison system for former slaves duly convicted of a crime. According to Emerging Minds Did Your Know Web site, that slavery or peonage prison system is alive and well. Similar to the past, a large number of corporations make hefty profits from very low-paid prison labor. Even though Black Americans are only 12.3 percent of the national population, they make up over 51 percent of the local, state and federal prison population. While this nation is repulsed by slave labor operations in Asia and other countries, it appears there are few concerns that Black prisoners in this country are forced to work for slave labor wages that average 12 cents to 40 cents per hour. This is not volunteer work. The Federal Bureau of Prisons requires that all inmates must work if they are medically able.

Some of the nation's most recognized corporations are involved in profiteering from prison labor. Emerging Minds identified such corporations as Dell Computers, Microsoft, Starbucks, Honda, Toys-R-Us, McDonald's, Compaq, Texas Instruments, Pierre Cardin, MCI, 3Com, IBM, Motorola, Target, Revlon, Honeywell, Nordstrom, Nortel, Allstate, J.C. Penney, Kmart, Nike, Eddie Bauer and Victoria's Secret. Products produced by these majority Black prisoners generate billions of dollars in sales and profits. Criminalizing Black males who are a source of inadequately paid labor is big business.[11]

## ❧ RULES OF ETIQUETTE ❧

Rules of racial etiquette established and maintained a socio-political ranking between Blacks and Whites. These rules of etiquette were formally presented in the Slave Codes of 1705 and the Black Codes of 1866, and they remained in effect through the

Black Civil Rights Movement of the 1960s. The rules spelled out the relative position of Blacks and Whites, how they were to perceive each other and behave towards each other and most importantly, how they were to behave in race matters. One small but important aspect of the rules of etiquette involved names and titles. A White person was to address a Black person by his or her first name, and regardless of age, a Black person was never to be addressed by a title such as Mr., Mrs., sir or even ma'am. The rules of etiquette required that Blacks always address a White person by his or her last name, preceded by the title of Mr., Mrs., sir, or ma'am. Along with the titles, a Black man was required to take off his hat and look down when speaking to a White person and never argue with them or count change received from them after making a purchase. When approaching a White woman, a Black man had to step off the sidewalk and could never touch her under any circumstance.

Black and White children were introduced to these rules early in life. The rules demanded Blacks address White children by titles once they reached puberty or 12 years of age. While the rules required Blacks to treat White children as adults, they contrarily required Whites to treat Black adults like children. Violating rules of etiquette was considered an insult to Whites and could result in a Black person being beaten or killed. Even though these rules are no longer rigidly enforced in the South, Whites and Blacks continue to abide by them because the instructions were passed orally from generation to generation.[12]

## 🎜 THE KKK CLEANUP 🎜

Here's an unusual twist! Would you believe the oldest and premier racist organization in America had the gall to charge Blacks with racial discrimination during the Black Civil Rights Movement? In the mid-1960s, Black workers in a Black-owned laundry in Rocky Mount, North Carolina, refused to clean Ku Klux Klan robes. The Klan responded in protest. They picketed and threatened to sue the Black cleaners for discriminating. The problem wasn't discrimination. The laundry had two technical problems. First, the Black workers had lots of experience in washing White peoples' dirty sheets, but they lacked experience in ironing and starching "pin head" hoods. And secondly, they had a home delivery problem. While the Black drivers of the laundry trucks suspected or knew the identities of some of the Klan members, they were uncomfortable delivering hoods and sheets to Klan members' homes, businesses and government offices. The Black laundry knew the importance of providing high quality service and satisfying customers, especially if they were members of the nation's oldest terrorist organization.[13]

## 🍒 WHAT'S IN A NAME? 🍒

Many people, Blacks and Whites, wonder why Black people constantly change the labels that identify their group. First they were Black, then colored, then Negro, then African American and now they are Black again. Blacks change the names of the race for defensive reasons. Just like Whites changed the names of their heritage groups from hyphenated European Americans (for example, Irish-Americans) to White to maintain dominance and power, Blacks change their racial labels to shake off inferior status, powerlessness and disrespect that Whites consistently assign to people of African descent. However, all people of African descent do not necessarily identify with Black Americans or their adjusted group names. Black immigrants from the Caribbean, Africa, Central or South America tend to follow the naming patterns set by European, Arab, Asian and Hispanic ethnic groups. They usually refer to themselves by their country of origin and use hyphenated American names.

For instance, if people are from the Caribbean, they tend to see themselves as Bahamian-Americans, Jamaican-Americans or Haitian-Americans. People of African descent who migrate to America tend to prefer to be identified with their country of origin. Whether they are from Nigeria, Senegal or Ethiopia, they want to be called by their country of origin and feel insulted if they are mistaken for an American-born Black. Native Blacks respond defensively by labeling themselves African-Americans. Unfortunately, Africa is a continent and not a country of origin. When all kinds of ethnic and racial groupings migrate to America from Africa, the label African American signifies little. The most accurate label for any person of African descent who migrates to America is Black American. White Europeans unite and pool their collective image and resources. For Blacks who do not want to unite around their greatest commonality, their skin color, the best label for them would be "Need-to-Grows." This label, in and of itself, should speak volumes.[14]

## ❦ THE VALUE OF BEING AN INDIAN ❦

From the founding of the country, public policies and practices made clear distinctions between Blacks and Indians. While both groups were cast below Whites, Native Americans were preferred and ranked above Blacks in the nation's hierarchy of acceptability. Whites preferred Indian blood to Black blood; therefore, they chose Indian spouses to Black spouses. To elevate themselves, Blacks also identified with Indians. They found it easier to pass as Indian than White. Moreover, court rulings were especially encouraging for light-skinned Blacks to claim "Indian blood" over "White blood." One court ruling stated: "If a person appears visibly to be Black, then it is his responsibility to prove he is not a slave or inferior to Whites and Indians. But if the person appears to be White or an Indian, then he is considered to be free, and it is the obligation of his adversary to prove he is a slave and inferior." In other words, if a person appeared to be anything other than a Black, observers automatically perceived that person as free and above being sold into slavery.

Free Blacks had the option of proclaiming themselves to be White or American Indian. Claiming a blood link to Indians had inherent benefits. The children of a Black person freed from slavery on the basis of Indian ancestry were free at birth. This was certainly not true if the person was perceived to be Black or mixed with White. Blackness mixed with White carried little or no weight toward freedom. Few White slave owners were willing to set their slave children free, even when they appeared to be White. It was Black blood mixed with Indian Blood that was the license to freedom, even though the skin colors between Indians and Blacks were close.

Before the early 20th century, the average American Indian's skin was brown or bronze in color. Modern day Indians have become light-skinned or White due to changes in their social and economic status, brought about primarily by the Black Civil Rights Movement of the 1960s and the gaming industry. The government's minority polices and programs made American Indians eligible for benefits and showed them how to empower themselves under their doctrine of trust status. Indians found new economic opportunities which became an attraction, especially for Whites. In the twenty-year period between 1970 and 1990, when Indians acquired special rights to build and operate gaming casinos on their reservations, the American Indian population increased by over 300 percent, mostly from Whites who now claim Indian ancestors and the benefits of passing as an Indian.[15]

## ❦ BETWEEN A ROCK AND A HARD NAME ❦

Black Americans enter the year 2005 caught between a rock and some hard names. Arnold Schwarzenegger, a conservative Republican, was elected governor of California. While Lieutenant Governor Marty Bustamonte publicly called California Blacks "niggers" on two separate occasions, Governor Arnold Schwarzenegger's name, which is German, translated into English means "black nigger." President George W. Bush, an archconservative, came into his second term in the White House and began appointing his new administration. He selected John Negroponte as director of National Intelligence. The English translation of Negroponte is the "head nigger" in charge. These names alone signify that from coast to coast, Black Americans have a tough row to hoe in a conservative America.[16]

## ❦ TOO MANY GEORGE WASHINGTONS ❦

When public places are named after historical figures, it is some measure of the clout of the community that claims them. What historical figure has the most streets, schools, airports, parks and other public places named after him? Would you guess Abraham Lincoln, Martin L. King Jr. or Ronald Reagan? Conservative former President Ronald Reagan wins the contest over the last decade. However, if we look at a longer time period, back to the founding of the country, George Washington is the winner. George Washington has a state, seven mountains, eight streams, ten lakes, thirty-three counties, nine colleges, one hundred and twenty-one towns and villages and thousands of Black people and schools in their communities named after him. But the name George Washington and what it symbolizes are changing in some Black communities.

Before the devastating Hurricane Katrina struck, the city of New Orleans was sixty-seven percent Black. The Black city council initiated a public policy of removing the names of slave owners from schools and other public buildings. The first name the city council changed on buildings was George Washington. Blacks living in New Orleans are now setting their schools and public buildings free of reminders of slavery.[17]

## 🍂 BIG BROTHER IN SOCIAL SECURITY 🍂

Ever since the Social Security Administration was created, rumors have circulated in Black communities that social security numbers reveal more than a person's name, birth date, birth place and retirement benefit status. A rumor in Black communities posits that the $5^{th}$ digit in the social security number is coded to designate the race of the individual. Another rumor says that if the $5^{th}$ digit is even, it designates race as Black, whereas if the $5^{th}$ digit is odd, it designates the person as White, Asian, Hispanic or other. A random survey conducted by the authors of this book found that just as many Blacks had a $5^{th}$ digit that was an odd number as those who had even numbers. The rumor about the $5^{th}$ digit could not be substantiated. Moreover, it also defies logic that it would be possible to assign an even $5^{th}$ digit number only to the nation's 36 million Black people. So this is one big-brother-is-watching claim that is most likely untrue.[18]

## 🍂 BLACK HANGMEN NEED NOT APPLY 🍂

The position of a public executioner has always represented authority. As a subordinate class, Black Americans could neither represent nor exercise authority. Consequently, in only a few instances could a Black man hold the position of public executioner or hangman. One of the few instances occurred in New

Orleans, Louisiana, in 1768, when the French colony rebelled against the Spanish government. When the rebellion failed, the French leaders tried to save their own hides by promising no more rebellions and pledged their loyalties to Spain. The Spanish government did not accept their promises of loyalty. They held official trials and rebel French leaders were sentenced to hang. But there was a snag. In 1768, the official hangman for New Orleans was a Black man. Racial customs and laws forbade a Black man from injuring or killing a White man.

Out of respect for the rank and status of the convicted French leaders, Spanish officials felt obliged to find a White hangman to conduct the executions. They offered a monetary fee to attract a White hangman to come forth, but none did. So, rather than continuing to postpone the executions, the Spanish decided to change the punishment for the rebels from hanging from the gallows to being shot by a firing squad. Blacks were forbidden to own and carry rifles, so again, they were naturally excluded from participating in any firing squad. On October 25, 1768, the condemned French leaders finally met their fate. A Spanish commander named Alejandro O'Reilly organized a firing squad that shot all of the rebels in a New Orleans public square. A public shooting was so much more horrendous than a public hanging that the Spanish commander became known as "Bloody O'Reilly." Some members of the New Orleans community petitioned for a return of the quiet hanging by a Black executioner.[19]

## 🌵 WHOSE FOURTH OF JULY IS IT? 🌵

The Fourth of July is supposed to be a national holiday that symbolizes and celebrates freedom and independence for all citizens. However, from its inception, it was meant to be a national holiday for Whites only. The colonies knew that the idea of White slaveholders coming together with Black slaves to celebrate freedom and independence was utterly absurd. So when a few "Negroes" did attempt to join Whites in public celebrations, they were driven away by White mobs. Quasi-free Black people and slaves at a Fourth of July Independence Day celebration exposed the hypocrisy of the patriotic White enslaving class. They did not want their celebration of freedom to be ruined by racial realities.

After being chased away from the Fourth of July celebrations, free and bonded Blacks accepted the fact that they were outside of and underneath mainstream White society. Frederick Douglass pretty much summarized the feelings of Black people in a speech that he gave in Rochester, New York, on July 4, 1852. He said: "The Fourth of July is yours, not mine. Your sounds of rejoicing are empty and heartless, your shouts of liberty and equality, hollow mockery." In plain English, Douglass said clearly that Fourth of July celebrations were for Whites.[20]

## ❦ HEY, YOU GOT THE WRONG DAY! ❦

From the very beginning, the Fourth of July was the wrong day to celebrate independence from England, because the Declaration of Independence was not signed on the Fourth of July. Historical records indicate members of the Continental Congress declared America's independence in Philadelphia, Pennsylvania, on July second, not July fourth. On July second, the Pennsylvania Evening Post published this statement: "This day, the Continental Congress declared the United Colonies free and independent states." John Quincy Adams confirmed this date in a letter he wrote to his wife dated July third. He said: "The second day of July, 1776, will be the most memorable epoch in the history of America."

Contrary to popular myths, there was no unanimous signing of the Declaration of Independence. The representative for the New York colony and John Hanson, the Black president of the

Continental Congress, signed the Declaration of Independence on July 19. One of the signatories of the Declaration of Independence did not officially sign the document until five years later, in 1781. Clearly the nation is celebrating the wrong day. But regardless of what day the nation chose to officially celebrate its independence from England, the Declaration of Independence did not bring freedom and independence to Black people in America. They remained slaves and second-class citizens for another 200 years.[21]

## ❦ THE ORIGIN OF BLACK NAMES ❦

White slaveholders reserved the right to name Black adults as well as Black babies. Naming confirmed White authority and power. Contrary to popular history, there is no evidence that newly freed Black slaves chose to adopt the surnames of their former masters, some of whom had names like Pinckney, Randolph and Rutledge. In slavery, the names given to Blacks most often reflected their plantation job, status or geographical location. Other slaveholders gave Blacks names that reflected and mocked the slave's powerlessness and low status. Names such as Colonel, General, Senator, Caesar, Hercules, Captain, Sheriff, Socrates, Napoleon or Pompey were intended to be humorous and ridiculous. Auction house slave rolls were filled with insulting names like Sunshine Special, Sugar Bear, Pomp n' Circumstances, Sweet Liberty, Dick Freedom and Jump Free.

When Blacks were finally in a position to exercise some control over their lives, they used various methods to choose their names. For surnames, most chose innocuous, but common names, like Johnson, Jones, Smith or Robinson. Others chose colors, such as Brown, Green and White as last names. Only a few chose the color Black as a last name. A common practice was to use the name of the job they performed on the plantation, such as Tailor (Taylor), Carpenter, Wheeler (Wheel maker), Cooks, Woods or

Farmers. Equally as popular were names from the Bible and popular figures of the day such as George Washington, Abraham Lincoln, Thomas Jefferson or John Brown. When Black parents were able to pick their own names for their children, it was a real milestone.[22]

## ❦ TODAY'S BLACK NAMES ❦

Today's Black names are anything but simple and common. As a real-life example, how common is the name "Da' Brealla Da' ouin Lane Fudge"? This person is not an Asian, Hispanic, European or Arab immigrant. According to *The Daytona Beach News-Journal*, Black Florida parents gave this legal name to their baby girl. How far will Black parents go to fabricate names? During the Black power movement of the 1960s, the rise in Black consciousness spurred many Blacks to abandon Anglo names for Arab- and African-sounding names. While searching for a new racial identity and pride, the Black American psyche began to embrace the 1970s Black Is Beautiful movement, which generated a demand for different and exotic-sounding names. Black parents created new names by linking and repeating sounds and syllables for a rhythm. Within one generation, names like Zohnitha, Equilla, Lakeisha, Mishon, Nemonisha, Le Domona, De Andrean, Zanquisha, Shenene and Shamkrila became popular. These newly concocted names are hard to remember, cumbersome, unpronounceable, phonetically awkward and nearly impossible to spell.

Worse were the results that came from impact studies that were conducted because White society was curious about the Black name craze. According to Yolanda Young, in the *USA TODAY* newspaper (June 3, 2005), a study of 55,046 children by the University of Florida found that Black children with names that had prefixes such as "Lo," "Ta" and "qua" and suffixes such as "isha" or "ious" were more likely to have poor grades in school, have behavior problems and be associated with the lower socioe-conomic levels in society. Yolanda Young also reported in the same article that twice as many employers gave positive responses to job seekers with "White-sounding" names as they did to those who had exotic Black-sounding names. The new Black names are creative, flamboyant and distinctive. However, what might be exotic and ego lifting to some is apparently negative and nonsensical to others.

Therefore, a key question arises. Are some of the popular names that Black parents are currently giving their children allowing others to stigmatize them? Yes, says one academic survey. In January 2003, Harvard University issued a report on a national survey that indicated White employers and government personnel officers are 50 times more negative and turned off by Arab-, African- or Black-sounding names like Sanniquar, Shen-nay-nay and Shoshawana. Only time will tell what kind of names the next generation of Black parents will choose for their children.[23]

## ❦ WILL THE REAL DRED SCOTT STAND? ❦

Most Black Americans are familiar with the infamous 1857 Supreme Court Dred Scott case. Most would undoubtedly know that Dred Scott was a Black man. However, how many know Dred Scott's real name was Sam Blow? Why the mix-up? Apparently, there was a slave called Sam who was born in Southampton County, Virginia. Sam's master, Peter Blow, moved with a handful of slaves to St. Louis, Missouri, in 1826. Peter Blow died in 1831, the year of Nat Turner's revolt. Sam was sold to a new master, Dr. John Emerson, for $500. John Emerson joined the military and took Sam with him to live on federal property for two years. When Dr. Emerson died in 1843, a small group of anti-slavery advocates in St. Louis decided to use Sam Blow as a legal case against the

4$^{th}$, 5$^{th}$ and 6$^{th}$ amendments to the Constitution. When the legal case was filed, Sam's name was changed to Dred Scott.

Although Dred Scott, or Sam Blow, lost his case in the U.S. Supreme Court, he was eventually freed with the aid of White supporters. As a free man, Dred Scott became a hotel porter and a minor celebrity in the St. Louis area until he died a year later, in 1858. To the present time, the infamous Dred Scott decision has never been reversed in the U.S. Supreme Court.[24]

## ❦ WILL CRISPUS ATTUCKS STAND? ❦

Let's take a close look at another well-known Black name in history. Crispus Attucks was one of Black America's first Black heroes. Attucks was a runaway slave who acquired celebrity status and a place in history because he was credited with being the nation's first martyr of the Revolutionary War. On March 5, 1770, a Black man led a group of White colonists in revolt against British soldiers. The man who led the revolt was supposed to be Crispus Attucks. However, the people who picked up the body of the Black man who led the revolt did not address the dead man as Crispus Attucks. Instead, they called him Michael Johnson. Even John Adams, the president of the United States, later referred to the dead Black man as Michael Johnson. It appears that Crispus Attucks was using another name at the time of his death.

Some White historians have asserted that Crispus Attucks was an Indian or a free Black. He was neither. Crispus Attucks was a runaway slave. This advertisement ran in the Boston Gazette a year before his death:

"Ran away from his Master, William Brown of Framingham, on the 30th of Sept. last, a Mulatto Fellow, about 27 years of age, named CRISPUS, six-feet-two-inches high, short curl'd Hair, his knees nearer together than common ... Whosoever shall take us said Run-away and convey him to his aforesaid Master, shall have Ten Pounds Reward, and all necessary charges paid."

The runaway Attucks was never captured in Boston and the master, William Brown, never paid the reward because Crispus Attucks was killed while using the name Michael Johnson. In terms of leading a revolt, the name Crispus Attucks had more "ump" than Michael Johnson.[25]

## ❦ WILL SOJOURNER TRUTH STAND? ❦

The name Sojourner Truth is prominent in Black history as a preacher, lecturer and activist, but was this her birth name? No! Sojourner Truth's real name was Isabella Baumfree. The New York State Emancipation Act of 1827 granted Sojourner Truth the right of freedom from slavery. Even though illiterate, she became a powerful orator. Her account of slavery, freedom and women's rights stirred the hearts of many Whites and Blacks. She routinely drew large crowds as she traveled around the country preaching on a mission of truth. Both her social mission and her name were linked.

Sojourner Truth was born a slave in Ulster County, New York. Her Dutch masters gave her the name Isabella Baumfree. When slavery ended in New York in 1827 and she was set free, she decided to set her spirit free by changing her name. In search of a new name, Sojourner said she spoke to the Lord and asked for guidance. She reportedly told some friends that the Lord gave her the name Sojourner, because: "I was to travel up and down the land showing the people their sins and being a sign unto them. Later, the Lord gave me another name, because everybody else had two names; and the Lord gave me Truth, because I was to declare the truth to the people." So, the name Sojourner Truth came from the Lord instead of the slave master.[26]

## ❦ WILL FREDERICK DOUGLASS STAND? ❦

Here's another good one! How many Blacks know that the birth name of Frederick Douglass, the great Black orator and freedom fighter, was Frederick Augustus Washington Bailey? When he first escaped from slavery and moved to Baltimore, he simply called himself Stanley. Confused yet? Don't be! Later, while living in New York, he changed his name to Frederick Johnson. Years later, while living as a free Black man, he changed his name to Frederick Douglass. As a runaway slave and outspoken abolitionist, he constantly changed his name to protect his life as well as the lives of his supporters. As Frederick Douglass, he became a speaker of extraordinary power and was the best-known political activist in the 19th century. He debated slavery with President Abraham Lincoln, who added his name to the White House guest list. Since there was no such thing as a social security number, name changing made it difficult for slave chasers to catch runaway slaves.[27]

*Frederick Douglass (Library of Congress)*

## ❦ 'DE MASTER' IS GONE HUMOR ❦

The humor of Black folks differs from the humor of Whites because they have different group experiences, view points and cultural conditioning. For Blacks, centuries of slavery, Jim Crow segregation and racism shape how they react and emotionally protect themselves. Black humor is sometimes a therapeutic device to vent emotional frustration, anger and aggression. For a brief moment, humor liberates Blacks from the realities of being Black in a White-dominated society and flips the tables as demonstrated in this joke:

When a White slave master died, two Black slaves were told to dig his grave. After they had spent nearly half of day digging and preparing the burial site, a passerby inquired why the two slaves were digging the grave so deep and had gathered such a large boulder for a head stone. The two Black slaves admitted to the passerby that a typical grave should only be six to seven feet deep. However, they said: "Since da Massa was such a good Massa, we gonna make sure that he gets as close as possible to his permanent home. And to make sure that he stays there, we gonna put the biggest stone we can find on his grave." The nuance of their play on words made it difficult for anyone to really understand the true feelings of slaves. Pretending to love their White owner, these two clever slaves used a safe way to fight back. Black people appreciate this kind of Black humor because it alludes to the master getting his come-uppance.[28]

## 🌿 SATURDAY NIGHT LIVE RACIAL HUMOR 🌿

When *Saturday Night Live* first aired on national television as a new comedy program, it presented a Black and a White comedian speaking racial "unspeakables." The Black comedian was Richard Pryor, who appeared on the show with Chevy Chase, the White comedian. Chevy Chase played the part of a job interviewer giving a word association test to Richard Pryor. The test began innocently with words like "tree" associated with "dog." But soon it became an exchange of racial insults:

"White!" Chevy said. "Black!" Pryor answered.
"Negro!" "White!"
"Tar baby!" "What did you say?"
"Tar baby!" "Ofay!"
"Colored!" "Redneck!"
"Junglebunny!" "Peckerwood!"
"Burrhead!" "Cracker!"
"Spearchucker!" "White trash!"
"Junglebunny!" "Honkey!"
"Nigger!" "Dead Honkey!"

Audiences laughed, and this racial pairing became a water-mark in the history of television comedy.[29]

## ❦ INDIANS TOLD TO GET REAL NAMES ❦

For nearly two centuries, the federal government and American Indians have had a special guardian/client relationship that provided Indians on reservations with many of their basic necessities. American Indians did not have a written language, so parents did not have to write their children's names. According to Indian culture, names were supposed to tell stories and sometimes even give instructions. But the federal commissioner of Indian Affairs did not approve of this practice. He did not want Indians to use names like Tail Feathers Coming From Weeping Willow, or The Deer Who Walks With The Buffalo Herd, or He Who Knows Two Bones or The Ancient Arrow-maker On The Hill. Enough became enough. In 1903, the bureau issued an order that required all Indians on reservations to adopt plain American names. They especially encouraged them to use patriotic ones.

Indians began using European first names like George, Sam and Peter to stay on the Dawes Roll for public relief and tax-free status. They then shortened their last names; thus, names like Rolling Thunder became Ron Thomas. These shortened Indian names could more easily fit on public documents or an envelope, just like the Great White Chief in Washington wanted.[30]

## 🐛 QUILT, SONG AND SERMON MESSAGES 🐛

Despite laws that made it illegal to teach a slave language and math skills, enslaved Blacks used their innate intelligence and creativity to learn English, but they also established a national communication system of their own. Though most could not read or write English, Black slaves designed codes and methods to transfer information that was secret, yet public enough to guide runaways. Some of the most popular methods of communications were colorful patchwork quilts, slave songs and religious sermons employed by slaves, even though they were under constant surveillance by White masters, White overseers and Black informers.

The way slaves used patchwork quilt designs to provide instructions was particularily ingenious. If a monkey wrench quilt hung on a fence, the slaves knew to prepare to go north by wagon. If they saw a quilt with five square knots two inches apart, they knew the escape route would lead to Ontario, Canada. The quilt designs were a complex system of codes that gave voice to Black people's resistance to enslavement. Female slaves collected used pieces of cloth and sewed them together in colorful designs as a visual language. Scholars are examining how slaves escaping from Southern plantations read the messages in the quilt colors, patterns and even the stitching. The quilts served as signposts, maps, secret signals and visual speech that guided fugitives on their way to freedom. Any slave-produced patchwork quilts that survived to the present day are highly prized collectible folk art objects.

Black slaves were equally resourceful in their field songs and religious sermons. Most of their songs came from Biblical stories, but carried encoded messages. Besides longing for a better life, slave songs often communicated specific trails for slaves to take. The message was obvious in the words of popular slave songs, like "Steal Away to Heaven," and "Fly Away with Wings over Jordan." Other song phrases, like "Soon It Will All Be Over," signaled departing times. Black preachers sermonized to the slaves "to be ready when the day comes."[31]

# SEX AND SEXUAL TABOOS

*Like money, sex is hard to find
and gone too soon.*

## Mini Facts

♦ *In 1782, Deborah Gannett, a Black female, disguised herself as a male soldier and served in the Continental Army for 17 months.*

♦ *In 1808, slave states began offering monetary incentives to White males to impregnate female slaves and produce mulatto slaves who had high sales value.*

♦ *In the 1940s, the federal government built the Pentagon with twice the number of needed restrooms, because racially segregated Virginia required racially separate restrooms.*

♦ *In 1955, Emmett Till, a fourteen-year-old Black boy from Chicago, Illinois, was beaten and murdered by a gang of White men for whistling at a White woman in Mississippi.*

## ❦ A CONGRESSMAN WHO LOVED ❦
## BLACK PEOPLE

If any White person loved Black people, it was Congressman Thaddeus Stevens, the driving force within Radical Republicans who crafted the 13th, 14th, and 15th Amendments to the Constitution and the civil rights laws of the 1860s and early 1870s. Congressman Stevens had an obsession for Black rights and absolute equality for Black people. But his passion for Black people was not confined to the floors of Congress. Stevens talked the talk and walked the walk long before, during and after the Civil War. He publicly professed his hatred for Southern Whites and slavery. Newspapers taunted him by charging that Lydia Smith, his housekeeper, was really his Black mistress. She was a neat, kindly and pretty mulatto woman. There was no doubt that she was his housekeeper and devoted to his interests. She lived in the house with Stevens, a bachelor, and newspapers reported that he was the father of her children. One newspaper, the *Southern Union Springs Times*, printed that Congressman Stevens was "living in open adultery with a mulatto woman." Stevens never respond to the articles, nor did he ever threaten a lawsuit against any newspaper.

Congressman Stevens was a generous man who believed that absolute social and economic equality between the races included Black children. In the summer of 1867, Stevens was approached for a monetary contribution subscription to support the Home for Friendless Children in Lancaster, Pennsylvania. He offered to make a sizable contribution, but only if the solicitors could guarantee that Black children would receive equal benefits from his contribution. When no assurance could be given, Stevens refused to contribute and condemned the organization.

When Congressman Stevens went to Washington, D.C., or traveled any place in the country, Lydia Smith accompanied him.

She ran his households in Lancaster, Pennsylvania, and Washington, D.C. She planned and prepared parties, then received and entertained guests. In casual and formal discussions, Lydia spoke about herself and the congressman as "we." As Stevens grew older and weaker, Lydia became even more devoted and supportive of him. The most impressive display of his passion for Black people and unbending fidelity to their equality came out of a request that he made on his deathbed. Stevens had purchased a burial plot in a local cemetery, but upon reading the deed, he noticed the burial of Blacks was forbidden. Stevens returned the deed on the grounds that he preferred to be buried in a cemetery that did not discriminate. It is natural for a man to desire to sleep his last with those he loved in life. Congressman Thaddeus Stevens was laid to rest in a Black cemetery. When Stevens died, Lydia Smith, his Black mistress and beneficiary, was at his bedside. She wept.[1]

## ❦ FIRST TWO BLACK MISS AMERICAS ❦

For centuries, White women have been the American standard of beauty. In 1981, however, the nation was shocked when two Black women were crowned Miss America. For the first time in the sixty-two-year history of the Miss America Beauty Pageant, Vanessa Williams, previously Miss New York State, became the first Black woman to be crowned Miss America. In the very same Atlantic City pageant, the first runner-up to Vanessa Williams was Suzette Charles, Miss New Jersey, who became the first Black woman to win that state title. This double win for the Black female set a historic precedent, though Miss Williams was later forced to give up her crown following revelations that she posed nude for *Penthouse* magazine. Suzette Charles moved up and assumed the title of Miss America. It pays to have a spare beautiful Black woman, in case of an emergency.[2]

## WHATEVER HAPPENED TO SALLY HEMINGS?

Sally Hemings, an enslaved Black woman, became Thomas Jefferson's concubine at fifteen years old. Sally Hemings remained Jefferson's slave and mistress until she was freed by Jefferson's wife after his death. Hemings died in 1835, at the age of sixty-two. Through her intimate relations with Thomas Jefferson, she gave birth to two sons, Madison and Eston. Both of her sons, who were freed under Jefferson's will, moved to Ohio. Three decades later, one of Sally Hemings' grandsons, Thomas Eston Hemings, fought with the Northern Union Army in the Civil War. He was captured by the Southern Confederates and died in the infamous Andersonville, South Carolina, prison. Many of Sally Hemings' descendants are actively engaged in trying to prove that the blood of Thomas Jefferson flows through their veins. Since White blood symbolized value, possibly the Black descendants will receive some benefits.[3]

## GENERAL CUSTER'S BLACK MISTRESS

Military rank always has its privileges, and that was true in the American Civil War. Clearly, General George Armstrong Custer, the boy general of the Union Army, took full advantage of his military rank, especially in regards to a Black mistress. Military history revealed that he did not possess the clean-cut, high-principled character that this popular image suggests. Long before his last stand at Little Big Horn, General Custer had proven himself a racist, adulterer and a poor officer. During the Civil War battle at Trevilian Station in June 1864, Wade Hampton and some of his Confederate troops captured the Union Army wagon headquarters of General Custer. Among the items in Custer's wagon were assorted equipment, clothing, photographs of Custer's wife and a very special piece of camping and comfort "equipment" — General Custer's Black mistress.

According to the *Richmond Whig* newspaper, the Confederate troops who had captured General Custer's wagon heard Union soldiers approaching and decided to discard Custer's wagon and personal possessions. They cut the horses loose and in an effort to leave nothing for the approaching Union Army, they pushed General Custer's wagon, with his personal effects and Black mistress still inside, over the side of the cliff. Her screams could be heard by both Confederate and Union soldiers before the wagon hit the floor of the canyon. Some of General Custer's personal items were salvaged from the canyon floor and returned to him. Reportedly, General Custer was pleased to recover them; however, he expressed no concern for the loss and death of his Black mistress. She had been removed from the "Boy General's" life and legend forever.[4]

## ❦ STROM THURMOND'S BLACK OFFSPRING ❦

In the spring of 2003, Strom Thurmond of South Carolina, then the nation's oldest senator, Southern Dixiecrat and a self-professed racist, retired from the United States Senate at the ripe old age of 100. Strom Thurmond acquired his racist image the old-fashioned way. He spent decades earning it. In the 1948 presidential election, Southern Democrats, then called Dixiecrats, ran Strom Thurmond as their candidate for the nation's highest office. Thurmond lost the election, but switched from the Democratic Dixiecrat Party to the Republican Party, which had then become the official White Party in America. Election to the U.S. Senate gave Thurmond a national platform from which to promote South Carolina's brand of White hatred for Black Americans. While promoting White hate, Strom Thurmond established and maintained social friendships with safe Black conservatives.

An oft-quoted Biblical scripture is a warning to Strom Thurmond and others. It says: "That which is done in the dark will eventually come to light." In December 2003, Essie Mae Washington-Williams, a Black woman who lives in California, announced at a press conference that arch-segregationist Senator Strom Thurmond was her father. She informed the press that her mother, a maid in the Thurmond home, had been raped by Strom Thurmond when she was only 16 years old. Her charges recast the national icon of White superiority into not only a rapist, but a hypocrite and pedophile. Rumors had circulated for years that Strom Thurmond was overly friendly with Black women while publicly subordinating and marginalizing the Black race.

In their book, *Ol' Strom: An Unauthorized Biography of Strom Thurmond*, authors Jack Bass and Marilyn W. Thompson call attention to at least one of Thurmond's sexual escapades with Black women and his "colored offspring." In 1972, *The Edgefield Advertiser* reported: "Senator Thurmond is unprincipled with colored offspring, while parading as a devout segregationist." Strom Thurmond exploded in anger and called the *Advertiser's* accusation, "too scandalous" to even warrant a comment.

Death has a way of bringing out the truth. In 2003, *The Washington Post* and newspapers across the country ran front-page stories detailing how Carrie Butler decided to introduce her daughter to Strom Thurmond when she turned 16. Following the introduction, Strom Thurmond provided the daughter with limited financial support. However, considering how Senator Strom Thurmond publicly degraded and politically oppressed Black people, many people of African descent are puzzled and wonder why Essie Mae Washington-Williams wanted to identify with one of the nation's most ardent White racists and pedophiles.[5]

## ❦ BLACK PROTECTOR OF WHITE WOMEN ❦

The institutions of slavery and Jim Crow segregation prohibited a Black man from protecting himself, his children or Black women. However, Black men were programmed to be loyal and faithful protectors of White women. The psychological phenomenon known as identification with the oppressor generated a special bond between a White slave owner and his favorite Black slaves. When the White male was dead or off to war, even though he could not or would not protect his own, many Black males appointed themselves to protect the White woman and her children, as well as defend the master's house and plantation. These self-appointed protectors would lay down their lives to defend a White man and his property. Sometimes the master permitted faithful protective slaves to sleep in the "big house" during his absence.

Anyone who attempted to enter the house or to harm the master's young children or his wife during the night would have to first do battle with the Black male slave who slept by the door. It was a special honor for a lowly Black male to be so trusted by his White master. Many Black males, whether they are conservatives or liberals, continue to value protecting White females in the 21st century.[6]

## ❧ BENEDICT ARNOLD WAS SEDUCED ❧

Sex played a major role in the behavior of one of the country's most infamous historical political figures. Without a doubt, General Benedict Arnold was both infamous and famous. His name symbolizes treason, the most despicable form of political behavior. Benedict Arnold could have gone down in history as a hero instead of a villainous military traitor, hung for scheming to turn over to the British Army the American fort he commanded at West Point, New York, during the Revolutionary War. The question historians should ask is, why would a military general, twice wounded in gallant battles defending America, suddenly decide to sell out the country?

Benedict Arnold betrayed his country primarily for three reasons. First, he was embittered because he had been passed over for a promotion to a higher rank. Arnold felt his distinguished combat record entitled him to greater military recognition and rank. The second reason was possibly the greater one. Benedict Arnold was a womanizing widower who enjoyed the social set. He was known for throwing wild, lavish parties and chasing very young women. While recuperating from a wound received in an earlier battle and brooding about being passed over by his military superiors, he met and married a teenage girl who was half his age. She inflated his ego and was angry about him being passed over for a military promotion. She became the critical influence that led him to betray his country in the time of war. The third reason had to do with a Black spy and slave named James Armistead. Armistead won his freedom from slavery because he spied for both sides during the American Revolutionary War. He spied for Benedict Arnold against General Cornwallis of the British Army. General Cornwallis was so impressed with Armistead, that he recruited him to spy on Benedict Arnold and the American forces. Unbeknownst to either Arnold or Cornwallis, Armistead reported information from his clandestine activities to General Lafayette on the American side. Consequently, Armistead's reports and Arnold's own love life discredited his career and resulted in his death by hanging. When Armistead received his reward of freedom from slavery, he added "Lafayette" to his last name and became James Armistead Lafayette.[7]

## 🐛 NOT ENOUGH WOMEN 🐛

Both White and Black males outnumbered White females in colonial America. The first three boatloads of Europeans to arrive at Jamestown, Virginia, only had White men on board. White women began to trickle in after 1608, but they were still few in number. By the 1650s, the ratio of male to female immigrants was three to one. Women were in such short supply in colonies, especially in North Carolina and South Carolina, that the established governments shipped in boatloads of female prostitutes and encouraged White men to exercise privileges with any and all available women. Additionally, the government encouraged White males to marry Indian women, but outlawed marriage between White men and Black women. White men circumvented these laws by routinely keeping Black women as mistresses or concubines. These men did not perceive Black women as a threat to the White power structure.

Although Indians were classified as non-Whites, they held a special place in the White psyche. White males increasingly identified with Indian blood and culture, especially since Indian wives were legally acceptable. Intermarriage between Indians and Whites was so common after the turn of the century that black and dark-brown Indians became progressively whiter in skin color. White men taking Indian wives grew so numerous that the law of supply and demand increased the price for marriage licenses in some Indian tribes to as high as $1,000. The price of a marriage license for an Indian female was nearly the price for an attractive Black female slave. For $1,000, a White male could either get an Indian wife or buy a Black female slave and concubine.[8]

## 🍎 A CHASTITY BELT FOR BLACK MALES 🍎

Social myths have historically and untruthfully portrayed Black men as oversexed. Had it been true, it would have been the only thing that Black men were over. Both free and enslaved Black men had narrow options for marriage and sexual partners. Laws, public policies and social customs made it a capital offense for a Black man to sexually approach or propose marriage to a White woman. Black men were restricted to Black women and bonded Blacks had to have the approval of White authority. The government even dissuaded Indians from marrying, identifying with or accepting Blacks into their tribes or territory.

Until the American Revolutionary War started, Black male slaves outnumbered female slaves nearly three to one. Black female slaves increased in numbers after the United States Congress ratified the U.S. Constitution to prohibit the importation of slaves after 1807. This constitutional prohibition opened the doors to breeding slaves in Virginia, Maryland, Delaware and North Carolina. Slave breeding increased the value of female slaves. A few creative slave traders even began selling female slaves by the pound. In such instances, "fat was good" in both business and the bedroom.[9]

## ❦ BLACK WOMEN INVENTORS ❦

Despite the barriers of racism and gender, Black women invented and patented numerous useful commercial products. It is a twist of fate that any documentation exists at all, because for centuries, few public or private records indicated the race and/or gender of the inventors. However, even incomplete government records show some of the accomplishments of Black women inventors. Sara E. Goode was one of the first Black women inventors to receive a patent. She invented the folding cabinet bed in 1885. Ellen F. Eglin invented the clothes wringer in 1890. In 1888, Marian E. Benjamin invented the "gong signal system" that the United States House of Representatives adopted to summon pages. Sarah Boone, Claytonia Dorticus, Alice Parker, Archia Ross and Jane Wright were other Black women who held government-approved patents. Some of their inventions included:

| PRODUCT | INVENTOR | DATE | PATENT # |
|---------|----------|------|----------|
| Photographic Print Wash | C.J. Dorticus | April 23, 1895 | 537968 |
| Hose leak stop | C.J. Dorticus | July 18, 1899 | 629315 |
| Ironing board | Sarah Boone | April 26, 1892 | 473653 |
| Suspenders (trouser support) | A.L. Ross | Nov. 28, 1899 | 638068 |

The amount of money and recognition these Black women received for their various patents and inventions are unknown.[10]

## ❦ AN OFF-BROADWAY SPY ❦

Josephine Baker was a popular Black entertainer who became a spy and hero for the Allies during World War II. Josephine Baker was born in June 1906, in St. Louis, Missouri. By the time she was 16, Josephine was a popular entertainer recognized for her dancing and singing talents. Black musicians Noble Sissle and Eubie Blake were so impressed with her talent that they introduced her to a national American audience when they featured her in their all-Black musical, *Shuffle Along*. The show opened on Broadway in 1921. *Shuffle Along* introduced new kinds of Black dancing, singing and chorus lines that revolutionized Broadway musicals and threatened White entertainers. The White entertainment industry responded as it has throughout history. It quickly began emulating Black entertainers while using political and economic power to force them out of Broadway musicals.

Rather than fighting racism within the American entertainment industry, Josephine Baker formed her own troupe, as so many Black entertainers did, then moved to Europe, where she felt they would be respected and appreciated. Ms. Baker guessed right. Europeans were dazzled by the Black musicians, singers and dancers. Josephine Baker became the hit of the European continent for the next 20 years. Her *Follies Bergere* was so popular at the Casino de Paris that she chose to make Paris her home. When the Germans invaded France in the 1940s, they, too, were so attracted to Josephine Baker and her Black troupe that they allowed her shows to continue under Germany's military occupation. The highest ranking officers in the German Army regularly attended her shows and socialized with her. They never realized that Josephine Baker was gathering secret information from them and conveying it to America and the European allied forces through the French underground.

After World War II, Josephine Baker was inducted into the French Legion of Honor for her work as a spy. She died on April 15, 1975, from a cerebral hemorrhage in Paris, France. Baker risked her life for America, as well as for France. However, only France honored and expressed its love for her.[11]

## ❦ NOTABLE QUOTABLE ❦

Slave masters promoted White female superiority over Black female inferiority by saying: "White women were for marriage; mulatto women were for sex; and Black women were for work."[12]

## ❦ SOUTHERN INCEST WAS COMMON ❦

In popular culture, there are numerous jokes about Southern kissing cousins and the practice of marrying "one's sister." The Jerry Springer television show, known for illuminating modern society's dark secrets, has opened the eyes of America to unimaginable practices. The Southern practice of incest, however, especially across racial lines, is as old as the country itself. Though White males had openly indulged in sex with Black females, the practice increased in the early 1800s when international slave trading was officially scheduled to end. Some masters mixed sexual pleasures with their business. Monetary incentives encouraged slave masters to breed their females with male slaves or to personally impregnate the female slaves, then sell the offspring into slavery.

Mulatto and mixed children demanded a higher price in slave markets. The typical buyer purchased them for artisan jobs, domestic service, or to fulfill sexual fantasies. Mulatto concubines were status symbols and White males were not too particular about lineage. Incest was common on slave plantations. J.A. Rogers, in his book, *Sex and Race*, said: "White men had children not only by their mulatto daughters, but by their quadroon grand-daughters." It was also common for the slave owner to offer up his female slaves to White male guests. J.A. Rogers quotes remarks made by Calvin Fairbanks, who encountered this practice while visiting a plantation in Montgomery County, Kentucky. After the slave master offered access to any and everything on the planta-tion, Fairbanks said: "I became interested in a young slave girl of fifteen, who was the fifth in direct descent from her master being the great-granddaughter of a slave whom he took as his mistress at the age of fourteen, five being his own daughters, and all were slaves." However, Fairbanks learned that it was standard fare for this White master to make mistresses of the daughters of his mistresses. No Black woman or her daughters were safe from the lust of White males. Mothers who tried to protect their daughters were often brutally treated or killed.

There are an endless number of stories about White males who engaged in sex with their daughters, including stories about Judge John G. Cocks, a New Orleans judge who J.A. Rogers says had a child by his own fifteen-year-old daughter. Even White males in the highest levels of society and government took advan-tage of the sexual accessibility of their own kin across racial lines. During the Civil War, Jefferson Davis, president of the Southern Confederacy, had as his mistress his mulatto niece, the daughter of his own brother, Joe Davis. The practice of incest across racial lines continued long after the Civil War ended.[13]

## 🐛 FEMALE SLAVES IN THE MIDDLE PASSAGE 🐛

In the 1820s, approximately 20 percent of the population of countries such as Iran and Iraq were identifiable Black slaves. African Blacks have been enslaved and sexually exploited by Arabs from the mid-700s into the 21st century. In January 2004, *The Washington Post* printed a front-page story about modern-day Arab slave trading. Arabs were still kidnapping and selling young Black girls and boys to be sexual objects for an average of $500 apiece. For over a thousand years, Arabs have captured and shipped Blacks out of Africa along three slave tracks — the Atlantic Ocean slave track, the Arab-Red Sea track and the Indian Ocean track. The Atlantic Ocean slave track is erroneously referred to by many people as the Middle Passage. It just ain't so. The true middle passage was the Arab Slave route that ran directly up from sub-Saharan Africa into what is presently called the Middle East (see photo). That route was the most brutal and horrendous of all the routes and continues active in our the present day. The Arab-Red Sea track and Indian Ocean track were feeder systems for the European slave trade in the Western Hemisphere and contributed to "colorizing" people in the Far East and Pacific area. Slave seekers within the two tracks went into the African continent and sought out Black Africans based upon the market demands of European countries for size, strength, gender and tribe. The institution of African enslavement was also based upon market demands and the perceived work capabilities of African Blacks, who were sold into slavery to be field laborers, domestic servants, soldiers of war and harem guards for the wealthy.

The Arab and Indian Ocean slave traders placed greater importance on sexual potential, such as youthful and physical attractiveness for both the female and males. Non-European slave traders wanted Africans in a ratio of two women for each man. They wanted sexually exotic Black females for domestic servants, harems and concubines. Arabs preferred Black slaves from certain tribes for a variety of reasons that ranged from looks to temperament. Of all African females, Ethiopian women commanded the highest prices for their exotic looks and sexual attractiveness. This was especially true for Ethiopian girls between the ages of 11 and 15 years of age, even into the 21$^{st}$ century.

*African slave routes. (Library of Congress)*

In exercising sexual privileges and power, Arab men were no different from White men in the Western world. They used Black females as concubines while protecting their own women, especially from Black males. To protect their women from even casual contact with males, Arab culture imposed a strict code of conduct and dress on Arab women that eradicated their sexual attractiveness, made them sexually inaccessible and protected their virginity. Arabs routinely castrated enslaved Black men to prevent sexual contact with Arab women. Arab slave owners castrated hundreds of thousands of Black men, turning them into eunuchs. Castrated Black males were then assigned to watch over and protect Arab females.

A study conducted in Basara, Iraq, as late as the early 1900s, reported that there were as many as 40,000 Black eunuchs present. Castrated Black males could safely be assigned to Arab homes or to the military as day warriors and substitute sex partners. Wealthy Arab families would frequently assign Black slaves to their young sons at birth, thereby creating a master-partner relationship that required slaves to follow and protect the Arab sons until death.[14]

## ❦ A FEMALE TUSKEGEE PILOT ❦

Mrs. Mildred Carter was among the first women to earn a pilot's license from Tuskegee Institute's Civilian Air Training School, which became legendary with the success of its airmen in World War II. Female pilots of any race were prohibited from flying in combat. However, after she received her license in 1941, Carter felt she could find a flying career in civilian aviation. But it was not to be. Her flying career ended before it began. She received a letter from the Women's Air Force Service Pilots that stated she was ineligible to fly because of her race. Carter continued to fly and rack up flying hours in her private time at her own expense.

In 1943, the Women's Auxiliary Ferrying Squadron and the Army Air Force Women's Flying Training Detachment were formed. These women pilots ferried planes from the factories to their point of embarkation. Mrs. Carter again applied to join these female flying groups. Her dream of flying for her country again was shot down by the head of the program. According to some historians, at least two Asian and several Hispanic women were accepted into the flying program. Apparently, Black female pilots were on the lowest rung of the preference ladder. They were just below Black male pilots. The program was already tenuous because female pilots were not socially accepted. The program administrators hinted that the addition of female pilots who were Black would drive a nail in the coffin of the flying program. The sky was the limit, except for a female Black pilot.[15]

## ❦ HORATIO ALGER, A GAY PEDOPHILE? ❦

Myths of the mid-1800s have shaped America in important and crucial ways. Some have buttressed racism and even led Black Americans to engage in inappropriate behavior patterns. The tale of Horatio Alger is such an example. Generations of Americans, both Blacks and Whites alike, have heard the mythical tale of Horatio Alger, a hero who rose from rags to success by his own bootstraps. Horatio Alger tales were designed to convince the working class of the blessings of diligence and hard work, to accept a specific set of values and to behave in certain ways. Black ex-slaves were to learn to appreciate the advantages of being America's core labor force, even if it meant working for their former masters at low or no-wage sharecropping jobs. In 1866, the country admonished nearly five million newly freed Black slaves to forget about the promised "forty acres and a mule," work hard and model their lives after Horatio Alger. Since most newly freed slaves were barefoot, it was unclear how they could pull themselves up by their own bootstraps. How could people, who for centuries had been forced to work themselves to death, possibly profit from more hard work at poverty-pay rates. Most importantly, it was unclear why Black people, who had been stripped of their culture and mores, ought to replace their values with the social values of Horatio Alger, who was rumored to be a gay pedophile.

Historical records indicate that Alger engaged in sex with several young boys while he was the pastor of the Unitarian Church in Brewster, Massachusetts. In the late 1860s, Horatio Alger was accused by his congregation of using his authority in the church to lure young boys into sexual relations. When an angry community threatened to lynch him, Horatio Alger secretly moved to New York, where he established friendships with poor Blacks and some homeless people. He began his new life, in, of all things, writing children's books.

So for both common sense and moral reasons, Horatio Alger and the myths of his life, which were generated to show the value of hard work, did not qualify as a sensible model for Black Americans. Even Michael Jackson, who is Black and, without a doubt, one of the most popular entertainers in the world, is aware of the moral and legal dangers of close alignment with young boys.[16]

## ❧ AFRICAN PRINCESS HAUNTS A PLANTATION ❧

Anna Madgigine Jai Kingsley was an African princess and one of the most intriguing characters in 19th century Jacksonville, Florida. According to local folklore, the mysterious African woman was a White slave trader's wife and lived with him on the Kingsley Plantation on Fort George Island, near Jacksonville. The legend goes that Anna Madgigine was the captured daughter of an African king. She was an exotic woman, who later enchanted the heart of the White slave trader who married her. As the wife of the slave trader, Anna became a slave taskmaster who was just as cruel in using the whip as any White slave driver.

Anna Madgigine used her slavery-generated wealth to travel the world. After her husband died in 1843, she returned to Jacksonville, Florida, and lived on the plantation with her two daughters. It took a Civil War to change the way she treated Black people. After the war, she established settlements for newly-freed slaves and their families. She quickly spent most of her once great plantation fortune. She died in 1870 and was buried in an unmarked grave in the old Clifton Cemetery. Centuries after her death, legend has it that her spirit continues to walk the rooms of the plantation mansion, rearranging the furniture at night and, like so many Blacks who still wait for their ships to come in, Anna Madgigine's ghost keeps watch for her White husband's ship to return from a slave-trading trip.[17]

## ❦ A Transvestite Union Spy ❦

Americans are familiar with 20th century spies, like Mata Hari, a seductress, and Ethel Rosenberg, a traitor and communist sympathizer. But how many Americans know of Miss Sarah Emma Edmonds, a young Canadian White nurse who was a resourceful and skilled spy during the American Civil War? Miss Sarah Edmonds became known as the famous "federal soldier girl." What made Miss Edmonds such a unique spy was the fact that in the early 1860s, she successfully disguised herself as a Black man. In her disguise, she was known as Franklin Thompson, a male nurse, in the Union Army, 2nd Michigan Regiment. In the early years of the Civil War, Miss Edmonds confined her spying to the eastern South. She worked the Confederate camps and battle lines, penetrating rebel headquarters, securing secrets on military strength and strategies, then delivered detailed plans and charts to officials in the Union Army. While passing as a Black man, her cover was never broken. This was quite a feat for a White woman at a time when being a Black man, in and of itself, was extremely risky.

Prior to the end of the war, the Union Army relocated her to a military unit in St Louis, Missouri, that reportedly was running over with Confederate spies. Believing in the old adage that it takes one to know one, the Union Army asked her to play the role of a "spy detector." She succeeded in discovering and exposing a Confederate spy ring operating among Union troops. After the war, Sarah Edmonds received a big thanks and a monthly pension of $12 from the federal government. Her adventures are recorded in the book, *Unsexed*, or *The Female Soldier*. The real significance of her story is the fact that her accomplishments occurred while she pretended to be a Black male at a time when White women were supposed to be aloof, dainty and fragile.[18]

## ❦ SPANISH MEN PREFERRED BLACK WOMEN ❦

Once upon a time, Spanish men were known for their desire for Black women. In 1442, fifty years before the discovery of the Americas, Spain had a high population of African Blacks. Portuguese slave traders had transported many Black slaves to Spain. Also, because of the physical closeness of Spain to Africa, Black Africans had freely migrated to and spread throughout Spain. In the early 1500s, Spaniards were noticeably changing from blond and blue-eyed to Black hair and brown-eyed. African women stimulated a new appetite in the Spanish men. Both free and bonded Black women became exotic items. There was a cry for "La morena," the brown-skinned woman with jet-black eyes. At the same time that the Black woman was becoming the symbol of beauty and the target of sexual desires in Spain, nature was taking its due course to a lesser degree between Spanish women and Black men. The sexual evolution changed hair texture, skin color, and eye color throughout Spanish-speaking societies. Ironically, the modern-day image of bronze-skin, hot-blooded Hispanics and Latinos are never associated with the genes of their African ancestors.[19]

## ❦ RIDING A JACKASS OF SHAME ❦

Though crime is never a laughing matter, at times in our history, crimes and punishment have been humorous and sometimes even ridiculous. This was especially true in White male and White female relationships. For instance, when Black slavery officially began in the mid-1400s, some European societies had a practice of publicly shaming women who mistreated their husbands. Women who were found guilty of beating or "henpecking" their husbands had to ride the back of a jackass through town facing backwards. If the husband shouldered any of the blame for having failed or refused to defend himself against his wife, he was subject to equal embarrassment. The husband had to personally lead the jackass, with his wife riding and looking backwards, through the city streets. Historical records do not show a similar punishment for a man who browbeat or abused his wife. Consequently, social biases defined gender roles. At that period in European history, chivalry entitled women to ride an ass and weak men were qualified only to lead an ass.[20]

## ❦ SEXISM SMOTHERS RACISM ❦

In the late 1960s, conservative social forces used Title IX in the 1965 Civil Rights bill as a platform to effectively stymie the Black Civil Rights Movement, shift the nation's attention away from racial justice and Black rights and refocus attention to sexism and gender rights. When women's issues were placed in the same category with slavery and structural racism, the move gave the ruling White male an alternative to eradicating racism. Refocusing on women's issues and giving them a minority preference was a win-win situation for the ruling class. White males knew their wives, daughters, sisters, mothers and any other female member of the White race would outrank Blacks in affirmative action programs. Moreover, equating gender issues to racism makes White women eligible for double or triple benefits. White women are a majority group that gets additional benefits for being female, displacing Blacks and masquerading as a minority while continuing to enjoy the advantages of being White.

Ironically, the Civil Rights Act of 1964, a landmark piece of legislation, was originally intended to forbid racial discrimination against Black Americans. The Title IX amendment that added "gender" to the Constitution was successfully passed into law as a joke to sidetrack civil rights legislation for Blacks. Representative Howard Smith, a Virginia Democrat and White racist, added the gender issue to the 1964 Civil Rights bills in the belief that it would kill the bill. Representative George William Andrews of Alabama supported the gender amendment because he believed White women were members of the White skin color team. Rep. Andrews said: "Unless the amendment is adopted, the White women of this country would be drastically discriminated against in favor of a Negro woman." Nearly all White males rose and supported the gender equity amendment. With confusion sufficiently sowed, a vote was held. The odd coalition of White racists and pro-feminist liberals prevailed. The derailment of the Black Civil Rights Movement succeeded in shifting this nation's attention and resources to women, minorities and children.

Immediately, women's issues began to totally supplant race issues. For example, in the state of Florida, when the 69 school counties were surveyed to find out how they preferred to spend their schools funds — desegregating schools for Blacks or Title IX for women — all 69 school districts voted to spend their funds on Title IX for women. Within one generation, the number of civil rights lawyers who would accept racial discrimination cases dwindled to very few. Nearly 99 percent of all discrimination litigation focused on gender or sexual orientation issues. Most public and private affirmative action programs had results similar to the state of Texas, where White women received 78 percent of all contracted services and goods. Similar figures appear in the affirmative action programs in the private sector corporations, like Coca Cola, where women received as much as 68 percent of contracted services and goods. Title IX has done its job.[21]

## 🍒 Women Boxers 🍒

Although the public seems to have mixed feelings about female boxing, Laila Ali, the beautiful daughter of Muhammad Ali, has done a lot to popularize boxing as a women's sport. Like her father, Laila Ali is strong, skilled and confident in her abilities to meet and defeat female opponents. According to *Jet* magazine, in March 2003, Laila Ali, the 25-year-old boxer, held all three middleweight titles. Her professional record was 14–0, with 11 knockouts in her four-year career. However, Laila Ali was not the first Black female professional boxer. Historical records indicate Emma Maitland, a lightweight, and Aurelia Wheeldin, a bantamweight, were two earlier Black female fighters, though they never actually entered a professional boxing ring in America. Instead, they accompanied vaudeville acts and boxed on stage rather than in rings. Both fighters toured and fought in Europe, Cuba and Mexico during the mid-1920s. They were noted dancers and singers, but achieved their greatest notoriety from professional boxing. At the pinnacle of their boxing careers, they earned a whopping $100 an hour. That was a lot of money in those old days, especially for Black women. In September 2005, Laila Ali announced in Jet magazine that she was retiring from boxing while she was still undefeated, and while she did not say it, "still beautiful."[22]

## ❦ A BLACK WOMAN IN THE WILD WEST ❦

Black women who went West had to be just as strong and self-reliant as men. One such free Black woman was ex-slave Elvira Conley. She was a tall and strong Black woman, who, after being freed from slavery in St. Louis, decided to move further west to Sheridan, Kansas. Like most of the West following the Civil War, Sheridan, Kansas, was a wild town filled with reckless spirits and lawlessness. The slavery experience had conditioned Elvira Conley for any and everything. She was not intimidated by threats resulting from her sex or skin color. She was unafraid of the town's assorted racists, gamblers, prostitutes, crooks and killers. Elvira's skin was deep ebony black. She was Black and proud. She knew who she was. One person who knew her said: "The majesty of her bearing, her great pride, always commanded respect." She was so well received by the town that she experienced little difficulty in opening a laundry that soon became a thriving business.

The quality of her work and personality helped her laundry draw customers and some of the town's leading characters. Two of her most famous customers were Wild Bill Hickok and Buffalo Bill. In her later years, she told some of her friends how these two famous persons would walk into her laundry in their broad-brimmed hats, carrying "their shirts, which were made of a fine dark flannel and needed special care." As a result of the special treatment that she gave their laundry, the three became close friends who shared stories and jokes. Their friendship provided some protection for Elvira, an unattached woman, in a rough town. Their reputations may have been dubious, but Elvira kept a high opinion of both Wild Bill Hickok and Buffalo Bill.

As usual with Hollywood, when the television series *Deadwood* aired in 2004, Wild Bill Hickok, the central character, was surrounded by Whites, Indians and Asians, but no Elvira or Black men who actually made up nearly one-third of the cowboys in the real Wild West. Eventually, the Wild West ceased being wild. After years of operating her laundry, Elvira met a wealthy White family, who persuaded her to give up her laundry business and become their governess. For the next 60 years, she lived well, traveling with the family around the world. But, she never lost her Wild West spirit or her Black pride.[23]

## 🍂 BENJAMIN FRANKLIN'S ILLEGITIMATE SON 🍂

Benjamin Franklin was strongly opposed to the enslavement of African Blacks. Without a doubt, Benjamin Franklin was also one the most famous men in the world during his time. Children learn early in elementary school that Benjamin Franklin invented the printing press and foolishly discovered electricity by flying a kite with a key on a string in a lightening storm. But few have heard about his sexual transgressions and even fewer about the relationship he had with his illegitimate son. Although not formally married, Benjamin Franklin had a common-law wife named Deborah Franklin. This common-law marriage did not stop Benjamin Franklin from openly and notoriously courting a variety of young ladies of his day. Eventually one became pregnant. Since he was such a well-known person, he felt obliged to do the right thing by his son, so he accepted the child and took him home to live with him and his common-law wife, Deborah.

Some would say Benjamin Franklin's decision was outrageous. Deborah was understanding of Franklin's dilemma and agreed to raise the child, who they named William. To make the situation more family-oriented, Benjamin brought the illegitimate child's White mother into his house as a maid. As William grew into manhood, the father-son relationship was good. William helped Benjamin write and publish *Poor Richard's Almanac*, a handbook of practical advice for productive living. When Franklin conducted his experiments to draw lightening from the clouds with a kite and key, he asked William to be a dutiful son and to run around the cow pasture holding the kite while lightening was flashing. Had the boy known more about lightening strikes or inherited his father's good senses, he would not have risked his life to please his father.

However, the good father/son relationship did not last. William disagreed with Benjamin over the writing of the Declaration of Independence and the Revolutionary War. When the war broke out, Benjamin broke with his son and had him arrested and imprisoned in a solitary cell containing only old straw and human waste. William was denied writing paper, clean clothes and even bathing or toilet facilities. During his three years of imprisonment, William lost his hair, his teeth and his wife, who died. When William was finally released from prison, Benjamin asked him to sign over all property rights in repayment for money that he had spent on him as a child and then exiled him to England. Benjamin Franklin died alone in his bedroom. He never said goodbye to William, his illegitimate and only son, who he had spent years punishing for disagreeing with him.[24]

## ❦ Red Color Was Used to Trick ❦

Black people have always had a thing for the color red, which has a highly symbolic history. In the scriptures, red or scarlet, was associated with sin. In modern times, the color red became associated with sex and prostitutes in the red-light districts. According to Louis L'Amour, the Western fiction writer, the red light was associated with prostitution and red-light districts, because in the late 1800s when train conductors visited houses of ill repute after dark, they often left their red lamps hanging outside. Whether a person was riding or walking, the color red or a red light has always signaled a person to stop. From its association with sin, the color red or scarlet evolved to signal danger, stop or don't go there.

Red has also been associated with American farming. By the 1800s, farmers across America were painting their barns red. European farmers, who traditionally painted their barns white, changed when they migrated to America during slavery and began painting their barns red. Some paint merchants claimed Americans painted their barns red because red paint was invented during slavery and it was cheaper than white paint. Others claim that barns were painted red because excitable and dangerous horses and bulls were housed in barns and the color red signaled "dangerous, keep out."

When all is said and done, the color red had a special significance to people of African descent. Red cloth was used to entice and capture African Blacks into slavery. Estaban Montejo, an African who ran away from a Cuban slave plantation in the 1800s, told abolitionists how White slave traders used the color red. He said: "Slave traders carried lots of scarlet cloth that they used to attract and capture Blacks in Africa. Blacks were attracted to the bright red colors. Hoping to get some of the red cloth, both the kings and the Black villagers came to the slaveholders without even a struggle. When the African kings saw Whites holding and waving red handkerchiefs, they told their people to go on and get a scarlet (red) handkerchief. Black tribesmen were so excited by the scarlet (red), that they ran down to the ships like unwary sheep to the slave traders and their slave boats."

In the 20th century, African and Black nationalists used red, green and black in their designs and flags. The red color in the flags and designs symbolized blood that was shed by the millions of Blacks who were tricked, enslaved and colonized.[25]

## 🐝 A LEWIS AND CLARK DISCOVERY 🐝

Every American history book talks about the Lewis and Clark Expedition that explored the American Northwest between 1804 and 1806. While Lewis and Clark are credited with having discovered various mountain passes, waterways and Indian tribes, nothing is said about York, their Black slave, guide and interpreter, whose diplomacy with the various Indian tribes made the expedition possible. York married an Indian woman and sired numerous mixed-blood children. While nothing is said about York's role in the discovery of the Northwest territory, nothing is said either about how the men in Lewis and Clark's party discovered venereal diseases in the wigwams of the Chinook Indians. Perhaps it was only fair that the Indians repaid the White man for first introducing syphilis onto the North American continent. Fair or not, the Chinook Indian chief introduced members of the Lewis and Clark expedition to the tribe's women and to the world of syphilis.

Lewis was a little wiser regarding Indians who came bearing gifts. He gave strict orders that his men were not to behave in any manner that would expose them to venereal diseases. But, other than a verbal order, there were no attempts to stop them from indulging with Indian women. Though Lewis and Clark wrote in their logs that: "To prevent this mutual exchange of good offices on the part of our young men whom some months abstinence have made very polite to those tawny damsels," they themselves did not abstain from relations with Indian women. Mercury was the cure for VD in the early 1800s, and it was reported that the expedition spent many an hour rubbing the medication directly into the skin or swallowing a mercury derivative in pill form. Either treatment was guaranteed to prove the truthfulness of the popular adage: "A night with Venus; a lifetime with Mercury."[26]

## ❦ EQUALITY IN A BOX ❦

Henry "Box" Brown made a daring and difficult escape from slavery by concealing himself in a small box and having it shipped to friends in a Northern city. With little food and water, Henry "Box" Brown was fortunate. He arrived uninjured and a free man in the North. Hearing of his daring exploit, a Black female slave decided to replicate the stunt. But, things went wrong. The female was in the box too long and spent too much time upside down in the box. She arrived in freedom-land with "brain fever," another name for brain damage. She emerged from her box gray-headed and appeared ten years older than her actual age. Even though she had suffered permanent physical damages, she preferred living with her new handicaps in Jim Crow societies in the North to living under the handicapping conditions of slavery in the South. Apparently brain damage was a small price to pay for freedom from slavery.[27]

## ❦ WHITE WOMEN SUPPORTED SLAVERY ❦

White women supported and benefited from Black slavery just like White men. White women co-owned, co-controlled, co-influenced and inherited nearly 100 percent of everything that White men gained from slavery. In a plantation field or in the home, White women's power was second only to that of the White male. Moreover, the female mistress or wife could be just as cruel as the male master. They lived together in the same home, slept in the same bed, went to the same church, put their feet under the same table, lived in the same community and raised the same children. Even single, White females could legally own slaves and dominate any Black person. When George Washington married Martha, she brought 153 slaves that she owned into their marriage.

A point that is rarely made is that White women held the responsibility for disciplining the Black domestics. The White wives and White mistresses were cruel to Black women, who they suspected of having sexual relations with White males, especially the masters. Besides severely beating female slaves, White female slave owners sometimes inflicted cruel physical punishments, like having a breast cut off, fingernails pulled out or faces disfigured. There are recorded instances where female slaves were thrown down steps or embankments to induce miscarriages. White female slave owners did not want their own children to have half-White sisters and brothers.

White female writers usually used their profession to defend and support slavery. In the early 1800s, Susan Petigru King, a novelist, defended slavery, stating: "Black slaves have as much contentment in slavery in their way as we (Whites) have." Louisa S. McCord, a poet, dramatist and essayist on social matters, who wrote under her initials in influential Southern journals, argued that it was the Christian duty of Whites to enslave Blacks. When the Civil War broke out, she used her money to support her beliefs. She purchased clothing and weapons for an entire Confederate company. This history seems to be forgotten today when feminists proclaim that throughout history, women have been as exploited and deprived as Black people. If that is the case, and since White women benefited from and supported centuries of Black enslavement, then when did Black people ever enslave and benefit from exploiting White women? It never happened. Consequently, there is nothing more unequal than treating White women and Blacks as equals.[28]

# ❦ THE WOMAN'S VOTE: ❦
## THE NON-DISNEY VERSION

The 19th Amendment to the Constitution was passed in 1920, supposedly to give women the right to vote. However, in fact, landowning White women have voted for centuries. As early as 1776, White women who owned property routinely voted in Massachusetts, New York, New Jersey, Rhode Island and Pennsylvania. A century later, with the opening of the Western frontier, White women were allowed to vote in Kentucky, Kansas, Wyoming, Utah and Washington. In the rest of the country, White males deprived White females of the right to vote in the belief that they were protecting them. Viewing White women as angelic and above all other women, White men placed them in a protected class that, along with children, would have to be defended at all costs. Politics and voting were perceived as dirty business that White women ought to remain above.

When the 19th Constitutional Amendment was ratified, giving the right to vote to some women, White women already had the right to vote in 15 of the 48 states. The 19th Amendment simply made adjustments that extended voting rights in every state to White women, regardless of their class status or property ownership. White males had a compelling reason to extend voting rights to all White women. Following the new Black consciousness that World War I gave Black soldiers and Black Americans, White society needed the women's vote to maintain the nation's racial status quo, especially with Black Americans' increasing demand for access to voting booths. While White women got full voting rights and privileges in 1920, the Black female did not get the right to vote for another half century, because her race was more disqualifying than her gender. The 19th Constitutional Amendment was only for White women and only for the White race.

A half-century after the enactment of the 19th Amendment, the myth of a women's voting bloc evolved. In reality, there has been no separate women's vote. Only in the presidential elections of Eisenhower (in 1952) and Bill Clinton (in 1992) did the White women's vote differ even marginally from the White man's vote, and that difference was less than 2 percent. White female voters have kept the faith with White men. Similarly, Black women, like White women, tend to vote like their male counterparts.[29]

## ❦ BLACK WOMEN OVER BLACK MEN ❦

According to the Joint Center for Political and Economic Studies, over the past 30 years, Black females have increased their quality of life and life chances over Black males. For example, Black females are elected to public office by a rate of 5-to-1 over Black males. While over 51 percent of the nation's prisoners are Black, 96 percent of those Black prisoners are Black men. Black female births outnumber Black male births two-to-one. Black women have a higher rate of survival, income, employment, job stability, business ownership, college attendance and wealth accumulation. Black women fall victim to fewer catastrophic illnesses, criminal incarcerations, homicides and outlive Black men by nearly twenty years. For years, studies have shown that Black females outlive both White men and Black men. Apparently, when James Brown sings "It's a Man's World," he is not singing about Black men.[30]

## ❦ BLACK WOMAN MADE A FREAK ❦

The *Los Angeles Times* newspaper, on May 4, 2002, carried a story of Saarjite Baartman, a South African Black woman, who was born in 1789 and died in poverty in 1816. Baartman lived her short life as an international circus freak. She was a Black woman with a physical abnormality — a very large protruding butt. In 1810, a British Navy doctor in South Africa convinced her that if she accompanied him to London, she could make a fortune displaying her body to curious Europeans. In London, she was dubbed the "Hottentot Venus" at circus side shows, museums, bars and universities. Public promotions proclaimed her to be part animal. She was kept in a cage and made to sing and dance in public. When a large number of males expressed curiosity about sexual abilities, Baartman's promoters took her to Paris and introduced her into prostitution. Eventually, the physical exploitation of her body took its toll and she died.

Upon her death, French and British scientists began using parts of her anatomy to perpetuate vulgar stereotypes about race and African sexuality and to support claims that Blacks were inferior. Later, and for over 150 years, a French museum publicly displayed her preserved brain, sexual organs and skeleton. Not until the 21st century did a combined act of the French and British governments order Baartman's remains returned to her home in South Africa for burial. Baartman's epitaph could read: "My short life provided wealth, learning, pleasure and public entertainment for those who despised me."[31]

## ❧ THE LAYING-ON OF HANDS ❧

In 1812, the Quarterly Conference of the Baltimore Circuit of Baptist and Methodist Ministers held a special meeting for the specific purpose of relieving Reverend John Chalmers of his ministerial duties. Why? Because two Black female members of his congregation had charged Rev. Chalmers with making unacceptable sexual advances. At first glance, this does not appear unusual, but it was. The two Black women were slaves and Reverend John Chalmers was White. Now that was real Black power, especially since in the early 1800s, White women had no voice in church proceedings, nor did they have any authority to challenge a White male minister or his laying-on of hands.[32]

## 🐦 ROOTS OF CATHOLIC PRIEST 🐦 HOMOSEXUALITY?

In recent years, the Catholic Church has been racked by revelations of widespread sexual abuses by its priests — pedophilia, homosexuality and adultery. On February 16, 2005, the *USA TODAY* newspaper announced that the courts had sentenced a priest from 12–15 years for repeated sexual abuses of young boys. A shocked world entered the 21st century with the pope and top officials within the Catholic Church hierarchy apologizing for the behavior of Catholic priests who had sexually abused scores of young victims. The media and the public at-large blasted the church for harboring and protecting pedophile priests. But sexual abuse of young boys by and within the Catholic Church is not new. It began centuries ago in the early formation of the church.

In 1589, the Catholic Church officially sanctioned the practice of castrating young boys within the church to prevent puberty. For what purpose? Because the church valued its soprano choirs and needed high-pitched male voices. The church couldn't use female voices because its own traditions prohibited gender mixing. Therefore, choirs made up of young boys were an alternative that could provide the angelic music the church sought, if puberty could be halted to prevent their voices from deepening in their early teens. Church leaders knew that if a young boy was castrated, his voice wouldn't deepen. Besides a music contribution, castration offered additional benefits to the church. Without sex organs, boys would be less likely to get into trouble, while their bodies retained youthful, female-like characteristics.

The church's practice spread into mainstream European society and a castration industry evolved. Barbers performed castrations as a sideline business. Signs in their shop windows read: "Boys castrated here." Farmers, who had experience in castrating animals, made a little money on the side performing castrations on young boys. These operations were performed without anesthesia. Historians estimate that three out of ten castrated boys died because of hemorrhaging or infections from the surgery. In some instances, the castration was for naught because it did not guarantee that a boy would always sing soprano. After castration, many young boys were taunted as freaks. Famous composers like Handel and Rossini composed music specifically for these young boys. The practice of castrating young boys in the Catholic Church eventually came to an end. However, were there any similarities of anticipated outcomes in castrating young boys to produce sopranos in the Church and the historical psychological and physical castration of Black males that produced falsetto voices in songs and emotional moments? If not, why did Black male singers abandon the falsetto voice after the Black Civil Rights Movement?[33]

## 🌱 COLONIAL SEXUAL MORES WERE LOOSE 🌱

Today, a popular goal of political conservatives is to reestablish traditional American values and sexual mores in all segments of society. Conservatives charge that loose sexual constraints and premarital sex are un-American and cause deterioration of moral values which is destroying the country. They hope to recapture the good ole days of Puritan ethics and the mores of the Founding Fathers. Contrary to conservative propaganda, the Founding Fathers were not shining moral role models. From the very beginning, the Europeans who supposedly came to America in search of religious freedom openly indulged in premarital sex. Between 1720 and 1740, one out of ten White wives gave birth within the first eight months of marriage. During the next twenty years, almost one out of every two newlywed couples had a baby before their marriage was nine months old. In Massachusetts, a third of all babies born in the 20 years before the Revolution were conceived out of wedlock. In modern times, conservative public office holders are far from paragons of sexual mores. In the mid-1990s, when conservative Republicans attempted to impeach President Bill Clinton for indulging in sexual behavior with a young intern in the Oval Office, publisher Larry Flynt, of *Hustler* magazine, researched the bedroom activities of some to the most well-known political conservatives, including George W. Bush, and found that most of them were not practicing the sexual mores that they preached. Conservatives live in glass houses, but still enjoy throwing bricks at others.[34]

## 🐝 AFRICA'S AMAZON WOMEN 🐝

The fictional Amazon woman called Wonder Woman was immortalized in post-World War II comic books and a 1970s television series. The story goes that Wonder Woman and her sister Amazons were attractive, skilled warriors from a fictional island who devoted their lives to fighting crime and corruption around the world. These female warriors were stronger than the average man. While most admirers accepted Wonder Woman and the Amazons as nothing more than fictional characters, there is evidence that Amazon women really existed over a century ago.

In 1892, French Legionnaires fought with and learned to respect what Europeans called African Amazons. These Amazon were tall, strong Black women. They were professional fighters and soldiers from the kingdom of Dahomey, which is now known as the Republic of Benin, in West Africa. There are enough similarities between the African women of Dahomey and the comic book Amazon women to conclude that the original Wonder

Woman comic book character was probably inspired by real Black African women.[35]

## 🌱 PROSTITUTES IN THE YELLOW PAGES 🌱

Whether it was the American revolution of the 1770s or the sexual revolution of the 1970s, prostitutes were conspicuously available, but customers sometimes preferred to let their fingers do the walking through the *Yellow Pages* to find them. During this nation's fight for independence from England, there were more houses of prostitution in the colonies than churches. When the American Civil War started, elected officials in several Northern cities considered giving prostitution and houses of ill repute legal status. By 1867, the New York Police Department endorsed a plan to regulate prostitution. In other cities, guide books to red-light districts were very popular. In one instance, *The Gentlemen's Directory* explained the personal services offered by most of the brothels and provided directions. When the *Gentlemen's Directory* was attacked by local ministers, the publishers of the directory countered criticism by pointing out that the information regarding locations and personal services offered by upscale ladies helped strangers to the city avoid low-class neighborhoods and thugs.

Though there was no reliable or precise way to determine how many people actually patronized the brothels or how much money they spent, some estimate that in New York City there were no less than 10,000 working prostitutes in 1870. Twenty years later in 1890, the number of prostitutes had increased to nearly 40,000. Apparently, the South had a smaller number of identified prostitutes. From 1901 to 1915, the *Blue Book*, a directory like the *Yellow Pages* that was printed annually, listed some 2,000 prostitutes working in New Orleans' Storyville. Based upon the popularity of brothels and the continual presence of prostitutes, there must have been some truth to the saying that its pays to advertise.[36]

## ❦ MOJO BEFORE VIAGRA ❦

"There is nothing that she can do, Lord, when I use my High John the Conqueror Root," said blues singer Muddy Waters. He and many other Blacks apparently believed in the ability of John the Conqueror Root dust to bring luck and enhance sexual prowess and also to give the user power and control over members of the opposite sex. High John the Conqueror was pivotal in African-American folklore and until the recent development of Viagra, High John the Conqueror Root had no equal in the minds of many Black folk. However, few Blacks actually knew who and what John the Conqueror was, and where he came from.

Folklore has it that John the Conqueror, mojo and voodoo came to America with slavery. John the Conqueror was the son of an African king. He was enslaved, but while in captivity, cleverly tricked his master and gained power over him with root portions, which became popularly known as High John the Conqueror. The Conqueror's life became an inspiration to other slaves who wanted to rebel against their masters, but were afraid to do it openly. So they incorporated mojo and hand-me-down medical practices into voodooism. Through the use of incantations, powders, "pieces" and roots, it was believed that a voodoo practitioner could heal the afflicted, bring bad luck or raise the dead. During slavery, some believed they could cause harm to a White slave master by chewing certain kinds of bitterroot and spitting towards him. Voodoo practicing slaves also believed that if they created a doll that represented the master, whatever the slaves did to the doll would actually happen to the master, whether the slaves stuck the doll with pins or did other physical harm to it.

Even Black women began to seek mojo psychic control over men or their enemies through voodoo rituals and various root dusts. According to J.A. Rogers, one of the most successful users of mojo and root dust was a Black woman named Mammy

Pleasant, who was born in New Orleans, Louisiana. After the Civil War released her from slavery, Mammy Pleasant moved to San Francisco, California, and established a voodoo practice through sales of her love charms. Reportedly, she made a fortune from selling love charms and portions to enterprising young ladies desiring the favor of wealthy gentlemen. Before she died at eighty-six, she reinvested much of her acquired wealth into mining stock and was a powerful political figure. In the 21$^{st}$ century, fortune tellers and incense shops still manufacture and sell High John the Conqueror Root to Black men and women more now as a spiritual supplement.[37]

## ❧ WHITE PEEPING TOMS ❧

The Rev. Henry Rurner, pastor of the all-Black Israel Beth Congregation in Washington, D.C., put aside his clerical garb to recruit a Black regiment for the Union Army. As chaplain of an all-Black unit, and most likely the only Black person who could write in his outfit, Rev. Rurner kept detailed records of his regiment's activities. Once while marching through coastal North Carolina in search of enemy combatants, the all-Black regiment ran into to a sizable stream at the edge of an all-White town. The Black soldiers prepared to cross the wide stream by taking off their uniforms and underwear and attaching them to their bayonets so they would be dry after they waded across the stream.

According to Rev Rurner: "Dozens of White women in the finest attire imaginable," got the word and hurried down to the stream to watch the first naked Black men they had ever seen. Some of the White women fainted while others fanned at the sight. Upon seeing a full regiment of naked Black men, the White women who were watching began singing: "My eyes have seen the Glory of the coming of the Lord."[38]

## 🐛 DRESSING IN THE GOOD OLE DAYS 🐛

The constant in women's fashion is change, yet one thing remains the same. In the 1990s, Monica Lewinski's tryst with President Bill Clinton popularized the female undergarment called a thong. It has become fashionable for the top part of the thong to show above the waistband and to be color coordinated with the rest of the young lady's outfit. While a thong covers little, women believe what it does cover is preferable to going around with bare bottoms. Yet, that is exactly what fashionable women did nearly two hundred years ago. Ironically, women did not wear panties in public until the late 1830s. Prior to that time, pants of any form were considered too masculine. Under all those billowing petticoats pictured in magazines and movies of the 1800s, respectable women from Marie Antoinette to Betsy Ross to Martha Washington were most likely bare underneath.

Underwear came about with the advent of the hoopskirt in the mid-1800s. The stiff frames that gave the hoopskirts their shape were a problem and created much social disturbance in high winds. The dresses acted like kites. So fashion designers created a solution. Instead of thong panties, they designed pantaloons or balloon bloomers. Pantaloon was an English word for extra-large pants. And like today's thongs, in high or low winds, young ladies of centuries ago were known to show off their pantaloons in public.[39]

## 🐛 A RACIST GOVERNOR AND SEXUAL MANIAC 🐛

James Hammond was a slaveholder, congressman and governor of South Carolina in the 1850s. He was known for his brutal treatment of slaves and general hatred for all Blacks. Governor Hammond believed Blacks were inferior human beings and slavery was an appropriate means to control Blacks' otherwise untamed carnal or sexual instincts. Hammond, like most Whites, generally characterized Blacks as oversexed, immoral animals.

But here is the catch. His castigation of Blacks is laughable when viewed against the governor's own sexual escapades. Even though he was South Carolina's governor and chief executive officer, historians relate that Governor Hammond not only had sex with his wife, but with his wife's four nieces, with Sally Johnson, his slave mistress, and her twelve-year-old daughter Louisa, at least two gay White men and a number of female and male slaves. Whether his sexual partners were homosexual or heterosexual was of little importance to Hammond. In many respects, Hammond's uncontrolled and insatiable desire to indulge in sex with anybody, anything at anytime typified the sexual hypocrisy of White males in power.[40]

## 🍎 JIM CROW BLACK HUMOR 🍎

A very powerful and wealthy Southern landowner gave a party at his political estate. He invited all the powerful and influential White gentlemen to attend. He had his staff of Blacks on hand to cater every wish. After dinner, the host decided to impress his guests with entertainment, and he invited them to join him at a pond located in the rear of his Southern mansion. When all the male guests had assembled, the host announced that the pond was filled with alligators. To see who was the bravest guest, he said: "Gentlemen, I am a billionaire and am willing to give up most of my money and my daughter's hand in marriage to any man who is brave enough to swim the length of this pond that is filled with hungry alligators."

Within a matter of seconds there was a loud splash. The guests were shocked to see the Black butler swimming with amazing speed to the other side of the pond. He reached the other side safely then walked around to confront his White master. As he approached, his master said: "Willie, I don't believe in the mixing of the races, but I am a man of my word." The Black butler responded: "I don't give a damn about your money or your daughter's hand. I want to know who in the Hell pushed me in the pond!"[41]

## ❦ COMBINING SISTERHOOD AND SLAVERY ❦

Rumors sometimes do reveal little known secrets. Rumor has it that two of the most notorious White slaveholders in the city of New Orleans, Louisiana, were White females. They owned and traded Black slaves, then used their profits to build a restaurant that became very popular. Even more interesting is the fact that these two female slaveholders were thought by many to be notorious lesbians, well-known in the highest levels of society. They gave lavish parties with their profits from slavery and provided personal entertainment in a house of ill repute that they owned and operated. Even though it remains undocumented, it is rumored that the establishment they opened, Two Sisters Restaurant, became a major tourist site in the New Orleans French Quarters.

## ❦ ART DEPICTS LIFE ❦

Monuments, paintings, statues and other art produced by White artists during slavery and through the period of Jim Crow segregation usually reflected the relative position of Blacks to Whites. White women were most often placed up high, overlooking the surrounding landscape or depicted with status and reverence. Statues, like the Statue of Liberty, generically depicted women as virtuous, representing the state, liberty, angels of peace or bringing comfort to mankind.

Images of Blacks were just the opposite of White females. The dominant trend in Black portraiture from colonial times to the present has depicted Blacks in a low status in society. Whether a painting, drawing or monument, Black images appeared beastly, humble, cowardly or comical. Black caricatures routinely appeared in consumer advertisements, newspapers, magazines, figurines and greeting cards.

# CHAPTER 5

# PRESIDENTS AND THEIR SCANDALS

*Power corrupts. Absolute power attracts
women and money.*

## Mini Facts

◆ *On January 30, 1835, President Andrew Jackson escaped
the first known attempt to assassinate a president of the
United States.*

◆ *In 1840, President William Henry Harrison gave the
longest inaugural speech ever. During the one hour-
and-forty-five-minute speech, he caught a cold that
eventually killed him.*

◆ *In 1856, James Buchanan was the first bachelor ever
elected president of the United States. With a male as a
constant companion, it was speculated that President
Buchanan was gay.*

◆ *In the 1860s, as a result of his military victory at Fort
Donelson, General Ulysses S. Grant's supporters sent
him 10,000 boxes of cigars. He died of throat cancer.*

# ❧ NOSTRADAMUS' PROPHECY ❧ AND PRESIDENT BUSH

Nostradamus, who lived in the mid-1500s, is considered by many to have had the ability to predict future events. Though many of his predictions were wrong, a large number of people believe Nostradamus hit the nail on the head with at least one of his predictions. In 1555 A.D., Nostradamus said: "Come the millennium, month twelve, in the home of the greatest power, the village idiot will come forth to be acclaimed the leader." In December 2000, after a plethora of election fraud and partisan politicking that split the nation, the U.S. Supreme Court unconstitutionally intervened into the presidential election and proclaimed George W. Bush the new president of the United States. Activist Dick Gregory thinks George W. Bush fulfilled Nostradamus' prophesy. George W. Bush, with a reported I.Q. of 95, was appointed president of the United States in December 2000. During the first four years of his administration, he consistently demonstrated limited verbal ability and marginal intelligence.

Nostradamus' prophesy picked up an unexpected confirmation from President Fidel Castro, the leader of Cuba. In an internationally televised speech in October 2004, President Castro devoted a major portion of his public address to President George W. Bush. Castro called him dumb and politically incompetent. Further, Castro questioned President Bush's reading ability, speculating that Bush may have a learning disability that needed to be addressed using special education teaching methods. Dick Gregory's and Fidel Castro's comments about President George W. Bush suggest Nostradamus was close, if not right on the money[1]

## ❦ NORTHERNERS KILL THE 40 ACRES BILL ❦

After the Fugitive Slave Act was passed in 1850, Mary Bowen, the wife of a future mayor of Washington, D.C., wrote a letter to the U.S. Congress stating that: "No sane-minded man acquainted with the Black population in the South could wish them liberated and allowed to remain in the states." Seven years later, on the eve of the Civil War, a national opinion poll indicated that 98 percent of all White Americans opposed ending slavery and freeing Black people. They knew it would be nearly impossible for nearly five million ex-slaves to survive, much less prosper without some land, money, tools, shelter, animals and weapons.

*Cartoon about status of Blacks in political parties.*
*(Library of Congress)*

After the Civil War ended, Black ex-slaves received nothing, even though a few radicals encouraged Northern Republicans who controlled both houses of Congress and the executive branch of government, to enact a bill that authorized ex-slaves to receive forty acres, a mule and $100. Congressmen Thaddeus Stevens, Charles Sumner and other Radical Republicans filed a bill to give ex-slaves some economic foundation. But, conservatives with both political parties would not allow it. Contrary to popular beliefs, it was not racist Southerners who denied Blacks the 40 acres and mule. Instead it was Northern racists who argued, "It is not right to take White people's land and give it to Blacks." Northern and Southern Whites wanted newly freed Blacks to remain a cheap and available labor force for the rebuilding of the South. So they allowed the South to enact Black Codes which replaced the old Slave Codes and locked Black Americans into peonage, sharecropping and Jim Crow segregation.[2]

## 🐝 WHIPPINGS CAN BE THERAPEUTIC 🐝

On June 22, 2005, Senator William Byrd, a Democrat from the state of Virginia, publicly apologized to Black Americans for his support of Jim Crow segregation and other racial acts. The William Byrd family of Virginia had a long history in race politics and slavery. In the ante bellum Civil War period, the Byrds were one of Virginia's most prominent landowners. Besides a good life, they apparently enjoyed whipping their slaves for any infraction or illusive reason. For instance, William Byrd once whipped one of his wife's favorite slaves to get back at her after she had whipped one of his slaves after he had warned her not to. The whippings went back and forth with both Bryd and his wife using slave beatings as therapy to achieve some personal satisfaction by besting their spouse. Neither of them expressed any concern for the hurt, pain and injuries they were inflicting on the helpless slaves. Maybe the Bryd family believed beating powerless Black slaves improved their image as a slave masters. Or maybe whipping Black slaves was simply good for the soul.[3]

## ❦ THE EMANCIPATOR OPPOSED ❦ EMANCIPATION

In 1861, President Abraham Lincoln voluntarily signed the 13th Amendment to the U.S. Constitution which would have made it unconstitutional for the United States Congress to enact any laws to free Blacks from slavery. This 13th Amendment that President Lincoln rushed to sign was the first of two versions of the 13th Amendment enacted by Congress in the 1860s. The 36th Congress enacted this first version of the 13th Amendment in sympathy with and support of the South's slaveholding class. Had this version of the 13th Amendment been ratified by two-thirds of the member states, Black Americans would still be bearing the lash and picking cotton in the 21st century. It is ironic that President Lincoln, who became known as the Great Emancipator, went out of his way to sign a Constitutional Amendment to prohibit the federal government from emancipating five million enslaved Black Africans. With friends like President Lincoln, Black Americans did not need any enemies.[4]

## ❦ A BLUE-BLOOD RACIST QUOTE ❦

After resigning from the Ku Klux Klan of America in 1944, Senator Robert Bryd of Virginia said: "Rather I should die a thousand times and see Old Glory trampled in the dirt never to rise again, than to see this beloved land of ours become degraded by race mongrels, a throwback to the blackest specimen from the wilds." As of 2005, Robert Byrd was still a Democratic senator from the state of Virginia.[5]

## ❦ A PRESIDENT'S RIVER BATHTUB ❦

The first presidents of the United States were the nation's Founding Fathers and leading citizens, but they were far from models for personal hygiene by today's standards. They might have been wealthy and politically powerful people, but they were constrained by the technological conditions of their time. Modern plumbing has made the practice of regular baths possible. In the first two centuries of this country's history, there were no bathrooms and no bathtub facilities, not even in the executive mansion or the White House. The first presidents bathed when it was convenient or when they were going to be in the company of others and knew a bath would be appreciated.

John Adams, the second president of the U.S., was the first president to actually occupy the White House. The White House had a wooden outhouse in full view of the passing public. The outhouse did not have a bathtub, but neither was there a bathtub in the White House. Although he routinely washed himself in a face bowl, John Adams did, however, enjoy taking a bath in the Potomac River just before sunrise when most of the citizens of the District of Columbia were still asleep. However, one morning while he was bathing nude, someone stole his clothing. Adams shouted for help until he attracted the attention of a young Black boy, who rushed to the White House and returned with clothes for the president. Ironically, in the mid-1970s, the District of Columbia posted signs discouraging swimming in the Potomac and cautioned all to scrub with soap after making contact with water from the river.[6]

## ❦ WHITE HOUSE AND WHITE SHEETS ❦

All the white sheets in the White House were not on the beds. The Ku Klux Klan, this nation's oldest terrorist organization, has drawn members from the highest to the lowest ranks of government. In the mid-1920s, the Klan bragged that its national membership had topped four million. The large membership had members from all levels of government and business, and to some degree, this explains why it has been so difficult and taken so long for Blacks to find racial justice in America. How can our society provide freedom and equal opportunity when thousands of teachers, preachers, lawyers, law enforcement personnel, mayors, governors, legislators, congressmen and even presidents held membership in the Klan and similar hate organizations?

Even Warren G. Harding, who many suspect had Black blood, was a member of the Klan. Once he was elected to the Office of President of the United States in the 1920s, Harding could not wait to be sworn into the Klan. Just before he took the presidential oath, the Klan held an induction ceremony, complete with robes and masks, in the Green Room of the White House. After pledging to obey the edicts of the Imperial Wizard, President Harding presented the Wizard of the Klan with a War Department license plate for his limousine as a token of esteem.

In the 1920s, the Klan staged a rally and march through the streets of Washington, D.C., that demonstrated its numbers, affiliation with the White House and the highest levels of government. The D.C. march promoted public acceptance for their organization. Klan membership included not only the highest levels of the executive branch of government, but also at least five U.S. senators, some of the most popular ministers and nearly half a million White women. These women were assembled into "ladies" auxiliaries that occasionally visited the White House. In the 1920s, Harvard University boasted in its venerable newspaper, the *Harvard Crimson*, that it had its own chapter of the Ku Klux Klan, affectionately known as "the Harvard Clan."[7]

## 🐝 A SELF-HATING BLACK PRESIDENT 🐝

President Andrew Jackson, whose face appears on the $20 bill, was often attacked by his opponents as a "blood-thirsty military tyrant" who had "Black blood" in his veins. In the 1820s, the *Cincinnati Gazette Herald* said: "General Andrew Jackson's mother was a common prostitute bought to this country by the British soldiers. She afterwards married a mulatto man with whom she had several children, of which General Jackson is one." Another issue of the paper revealed that President Andrew Jackson's older brother was sold as a slave in the Carolinas. Andrew Jackson responded to his critics by being a slaveholder and racist, who went out of his way to prove he had no love or affection for people with "Black blood."[8]

## 🐝 THE TOUGH LIFE OF LINCOLN'S SON 🐝

President Abraham Lincoln devoted his administration to healing a divided country; however, his own family was just as divided as the country. Robert Lincoln, the only surviving son of President Abraham Lincoln, took care of his parents in ways that few can imagine. Robert endured repeated attempts of graverobbers to steal his father's body. In 1876, the Secret Service and Pinkerton detectives foiled an attempt by "Big Jim" Kinnelly, a counterfeiter, and his gang to steal President Lincoln's body from its initial resting place in the National Lincoln Monument at Oak Ridge, Tennessee. The gang intended to hold the body and demand a ransom from the federal government. Lincoln's grave was moved several times because of the constant threat from graverobbers. Finally, Robert Lincoln decided to put an end to it once and for all. In 1901, he ordered that his father's body be buried deep inside the tomb and covered with nearly two feet of concrete to seal it forever.

Robert Lincoln then turned his attention to his mother, Mary Todd Lincoln, who had begun to act strangely. Unlike his father Abe Lincoln, who tolerated his wife's lavish spending, emotional tirades and offensive behavior, Robert did not want to indulge her. He was tired of her attempts to turn his wife against him and her use of mediums to communicate with her dead children. So Robert decided to put an end to that, too. On May 19, 1875, Robert made charges in court that his mother was crazy. He appeared as the star witness against her in a jury hearing and hired a long roster of people to testify against her. His all-male kangaroo court ruled that Mary Todd Lincoln was insane. She was then confined to Bellevue Place, a private asylum outside of Chicago, for three months. While she was confined, Robert took total control of her financial assets. Robert did not throw mommy off the train; he just locked her away.[9]

## 🌿 A CURSE ON THE WHITE HOUSE 🌿

A curse is a misfortune or harm that comes upon someone or something as if via willful retribution. Has someone cast a spell or curse on the Office of President of the United States and the White House, the primary residence of the president? If not, how do you explain that beginning in 1840, nearly every candidate elected to the presidency of the United States in a year that is divisible by 20 died in office or was the target of an assassination attempt? Is it a curse on the American presidency? Look at the pattern below, then you decide.

| DATE | PRESIDENT | NATURE OF CURSE |
|------|-----------|-----------------|
| 1840 | William Henry Harrison | Died in office |
| 1860 | Abraham Lincoln | Killed in office |
| 1880 | James A. Garfield | Killed in office |
| 1900 | William McKinley | Killed in office |
| 1920 | Warren G. Harding | Died in office |
| 1940 | Franklin D. Roosevelt | Died in office |
| 1960 | John F. Kennedy | Killed in office |
| 1980 | Ronald Reagan | Wounded in office |
| 2000 | George W. Bush | Still in office |

Curses can become effective immediately or they may plague a person, family or thing for generations. In either regard, the challenge of all curses is to break them. Will the curse on the White House, if there is a curse, eventually be broken by our current president, George W. Bush, before he leaves office in 2008?

## ❦ SLAVERY ENRICHED ROYALTY ❦

The Catholic Pope's endorsement of the commercial enslavement of African Blacks in the late 1400s to enrich the Catholic Church and Portuguese royalty birthed capitalism and today's banking system, and it revived the European continent, which was sweltering under massive poverty, crime, famine and disease. Capitalism and modern banking were built upon the slave industry. In 1503, the governor of Hispaniola asked King Ferdinand and Queen Isabella of Spain to put an end to the exportation of Black slaves to his colony. However, they turned a deaf ear, ignoring his request. Both the king and queen had a self-interest in Black slavery. They collected a tax of two ducats for each slave sold, as well as an export tax.

English royalty was just as involved and self-interested in this business venture. John Hawkins, an Englishman, made three trips to West Africa in the 1560s for the sole purpose of buying Black Africans, who he then sold to Spaniards in the Americas. On returning to England after the first trip, his handsome profits from slave trading caught the eye of Queen Elizabeth, who decided to participate directly in Hawkins' next slave-trading venture. Queen Elizabeth provided Hawkins with money and a ship named, The Jesus. On his second trip, Hawkins sold so many slaves and paid Queen Elizabeth such a tremendous profit that she made him a knight. The Barclay Banks were established in the Caribbean Islands to enrich and laundry slavery-generated wealth and income.[10]

## ❧ WOBBLY WARREN AND HIS MISTRESSES ❧

Warren G. Harding was attacked by politicians and newspapers that claimed he was a Negro passing for White. While it was inflammatory in the 1920s to be charged with having "Black blood," it did not stop Warren G. Harding from being elected president of the United States or dissuade him from being a devoted gambler and womanizer. A broom closet tryst with Carrie Fulton Phillips became an infamous love affair. Why? Because Carrie Phillips was the wife of one of his oldest and best friends. The affair lasted for nearly fifteen years. The second known affair was with Nan Britton. Since Ms. Britton was thirty years younger than Harding, a married man, the Secret Service spirited her in and out of the White House. Eventually Britton became pregnant and bore Harding a child.

While President Harding had a roving eye, he did not want the public to know of all of his private sexual pursuits. Pornography had not come into its own in the 1920s, but President Harding was a regular visitor to the neighboring burlesque theaters. To afford President Harding more privacy at one of his favorite hangouts, the management of the Gaiety

Burlesque Theater in the District of Columbia, built a private box just for him so he could watch the female performers without being seen by others attending the shows. Harding loved the night life. Living fast, President Warren Harding died early. But by the public and women, he was a well loved national figure.[11]

# 🍃 Ike Wasn't Right 🍃

Dwight D. Eisenhower was an international military leader and hero before he became the president of the United States. He was a quiet and reserved man who enjoyed playing golf, practical jokes and, according to rumors, had at least one mistress. Rumor has it that while he was stationed in England and his wife, Mamie, was confined to the United States, Eisenhower spent most of World War II being taken for a ride by his attractive female chauffeur named Kay Summersby. She accompanied Eisenhower around the world when he was serving as the supreme commander of the Allied forces in Europe. Eisenhower's reputation as an effective military hero overshadowed most of the infidelity rumors and aided him in being twice elected president of the United States.

In May 1979, the American Broadcast Company presented a six-hour mini series that focused on Ike's love life with Miss Summersby. Mamie Eisenhower, who was still alive at that time, claimed that there was no truth to the rumor. Miss Summersby reportedly told her friends that she was disappointed by the pressures that World War II had placed on Eisenhower.

Eisenhower may have faced pressures in WWII, but he surely did not identify with or respond to the pressure to treat Black troops with fairness and compassion. Although it is rumored that Eisenhower's mother, Ida Stover Eisenhower was Black, as commander-in-chief of the Allied Forces, Eisenhower opposed integration of the military and ignored the underlying racial causes of disputes with the British government and violent riots in the military. In Britain, many White British women chose to date Black American soldiers. That sparked a dispute between the British and United States governments. British military officials asked U.S. officials to send more Black women in the armed forces to Europe to serve as social companions for Black soldiers. General Dwight D. Eisenhower refused, apparently because he did not think Black soldiers needed the same kind of companionship he did. Eisenhower's behavior made him a hypocrite and a racist. Shame, shame![12]

## ❦ QUOTABLE QUOTE ❦

In the 1960s, President Richard Nixon gave backhanded support to affirmative action policies saying: "With Blacks you can usually settle for a dumb one, because there are not enough smart ones to go around."[13]

## ❦ ELEANOR ROOSEVELT'S BLACK CABINET ❦

Though President Franklin D. Roosevelt was known as a "poor man's friend" and was deeply loved by Black Americans, he was totally indifferent to structural racism and its negative impact on the lives of Black people. His wife, Eleanor Roosevelt, continuously pleaded for him to use the powers of his office to stop the daily lynchings that were occurring in the South at the rate of at least one Black man a day. Roosevelt refused, arguing that he could not afford to aid Blacks and risk offending White Southerners and losing their Congressional support.

Eleanor Roosevelt identified and sympathized with Black Americans. She selected a number of nationally visible Blacks to come to the White House and advise her on racial issues and to help her push for greater social equality and opportunities for

Black Americans. Those who attended Eleanor Roosevelt's meetings became known as her "Black Cabinet" or "Kitchen Cabinet." This term grew out of a practice that evolved after slavery when White and Black White House workers were not permitted to eat together. Only Whites were permitted to eat in the dining room. Blacks had to eat in the kitchen. By the 1930s, Blacks in the White House became associated with the kitchen.

In 1943, Eleanor Roosevelt's political opponents attacked her through rumors and innuendoes about her Kitchen Cabinet. One rumor claimed that Eleanor Roosevelt and her cabinet of Black women were planning a social revolution to change the social order and to reverse the roles between Black women and White women and make White women servants instead of Black women. The rumor eventually died, but so did Eleanor Roosevelt and her Black Cabinet of advisors. However, the term "kitchen cabinet" remains alive and well as part of today's politics.[14]

## ❦ THE OLD SOUTHERN POLICY ❦

Post-election television coverage of the 2004 presidential election used maps of the U.S. that colored states red or blue based on the political party that received the majority of popular votes. The red states represented a win for the Republican candidate and blue represented a win for the Democratic candidate. What the national color-coded map, possibly unintentionally, indicated was that very little had changed racially over the last 50 years. With two exceptions, the blue and red states in the 2004 presidential election results reflected the Southern policy on Black people before the 1960s Black Civil Rights Movement. The red states that supported George W. Bush and gave the presidential victory to the Republican Party were nearly identical to the states that formed the Southern Confederacy 150 years ago. Conservatism, racism and the Southern Policy are alive and well.

In his book *Southern Policy*, V.O. Key Jr. defined the Southern Policy on Blacks after slavery as hardball politics. Key said: "Politics of the South revolves around the position of the Negro. It is at times interpreted as a politics of cotton, as a politics of free trade, as a politics of (rural) poverty, or as a politics of planters ... in the last analysis, the major peculiarities of Southern politics go back to the Negro." Howard Dean, the chairman for the Democratic National Committee, created an uproar when he labeled the Republican Party as the White Christian party in America. Although Dean was roundly criticized by members of both political parties, he was right. As it was a century ago, national politics and the political parties revolve around Black people, or Negroes.

The Republican Party, as the new and official White party, is yesterday's Democratic Party. Whites switched national party affiliations to avoid Black issues and Black people. In the 2004 presidential elections, Black Americans were an invisible and forgotten people. Neither national political party or any of their high-level representatives have taken action to directly eradicate the historical structural inequalities that render Black Americans noncompetitive. The Southern Policy is alive and well in America.[15]

## PRESIDENT GARFIELD FORESAW HIS DEATH

Annihilation of nearly a half million Civil War soldiers and the assassination of President Abraham Lincoln transfixed the nation on death for over a generation. Four months into his term of office, President James Garfield became preoccupied with the possibility of his own death. He called Secretary of War Robert Todd Lincoln to discuss the assassination of his father, Abraham Lincoln. Garfield asked questions about how it must have felt to be John Wilkes Booth, Abraham Lincoln, or a member of Lincoln's family. Robert Todd shared his feelings with Garfield, then departed. This meeting between Robert Todd and President Garfield took place on June 30. On July 2, Charles Guiteau fired two shots at President Garfield and mortally wounded him, only two days after President Garfield had openly expressed concern about his death. Garfield was shot at the very same Washington railroad station where Robert Todd Lincoln had met and was saved by John Wilkes Booth's brother. Was this an instance of predestination?[16]

## ❦ BOOTH'S BROTHER SAVED LINCOLN'S SON ❦

During the Civil War, trains were used as a primary mode of mass transportation, even though they were slow, late and over-crowded with military personnel and equipment. Robert Todd Lincoln, the son of President Abraham Lincoln, who had just completed some business for his father in New Jersey, had gone to the train station to catch a ride home. When he arrived at the station, he noticed that there were a lot of important people waiting for the very same train. One person in the group was a famous actor that Robert Lincoln recognized from several stage plays. Lincoln was tempted to approach and introduce himself to the actor and tell him how much he enjoyed his performances. At the sound of the approaching train, people began to press forward on the railroad platform in their eagerness to get one of the few beds left on the incoming Pullman sleepers. As the train got closer, the crowd surged and pushed Robert Lincoln off the platform and down onto the tracks, right into the path of the train. Robert struggled to get back up onto the platform, but there was no room and nothing to grab onto.

At the very last minute, he felt a hand grab him by the collar of his coat and pull him back onto the platform. He was saved from sure death. When he turned around to thank his rescuer, he recognized the famous actor he had noticed earlier. It was Edwin

Booth. He and his brother John Wilkes Booth were probably the most famous actors in Washington, D.C. It is ironic that nearly a year and a half after the train station incident, Edwin's brother, John Wilkes Booth, shot Robert's father, Abraham Lincoln, in the head in the Ford Theater. Robert Lincoln was the only remaining son of President Abraham Lincoln and Mary Todd Lincoln.[17]

## 🐦 BLACKS IN RECONSTRUCTION POLITICS 🐦

Black Americans elected to national and state offices during Reconstruction after the Civil War were a novelty and their power was mostly symbolic. They exercised little power or control and produced no significant legislation to benefit newly freed slaves. At best, they helped some Black people get jobs in the postal service as process servers and sheriffs in a few all-Black towns. Although hundreds of Blacks, most of them former slaves, served in state legislatures, only a few served as judges. No Blacks were elected governor, though Blacks were the majority population in six Southern states. In the state of Louisiana, Pinckney B.S. Pinchback, a Northern Black and former Union soldier, won the office of lieutenant governor and served as acting governor when the White governor was indicted for corruption. Several Blacks were elected to the office of lieutenant governor, state treasurer and secretary of state. Two Blacks became senators in Congress, Hiram Revels and Blanche K. Bruce, both Mississippi natives who were educated in the North.

During the ten-year Reconstruction period, Blacks elected to public office did not have the benefit of a quality education, political experience and an economic base, but they did the best they could with what little they did have. They were, however, locked into an implied public policy that stipulated that Black-elected officials must: 1) avoid a group or Black agenda; 2) focus on *individual* merit and achievement; and 3) never hold Whites accountable for centuries of Black slavery. These same policies remain in effect in these present times.[18]

## ❧ TWO OF A KIND ❧

For nearly half a century, J. Edgar Hoover used the Federal Bureau of Investigation (FBI) to spy on and discredit elected officials, gays and Black leaders. But Hoover was not the first to use the power of the federal government to spy on, harass and punish those that he did not personally like. Much earlier, in the late 1800s, Teddy Roosevelt did the very same thing. President Roosevelt used his office to spy on and blackmail members of Congress. Whenever he anticipated close votes on an issue, Roosevelt would dispatch the Secret Service to dig up dirty information about members of Congress. He was always interested in finding out which members of Congress frequented the capital whorehouses, red-light districts, or picked up prostitutes off the streets. He then used this information to force the Congressional member in question to vote the administration's position on any issue.

Before Roosevelt assumed the office of president, Congress passed an amendment requiring the Secret Service to limit its investigations to the activities of the executive branch of government. President Roosevelt, who was fearful of the growing number of communist cells in America, asked for an appeal of the amendment and lobbied to have the Secret Service investigate any individual or organization whose political ideologies were inconsistent with mainstream American thinking. A generation later, when federal officials established the COINTELPRO and the King Alfred Plan to monitor and harass Black Americans, they were simply following a model of government intimidation that President Roosevelt had put into place much earlier.[19]

## 🐞 A NATIONAL MYTH TOO MANY 🐞

A famous painting hangs in the White House that preserves forever one of the nation's biggest myths. The painting depicts Teddy Roosevelt and his Rough Riders gallantly charging up San Juan Hill, defeating Cuban forces in the 1890s. History books describe the Rough Riders as "a motley mixture of cowboys, adventurers and odd characters raised and led by Theodore Roosevelt to fight in the Spanish-American War." What really happened at San Juan Hill is different from the accounts in history books and the images captured in the painting. It is a dirty little secret that a large number of the Rough Riders, or those individuals that the history books refer to as "cowboys, adventurers and odd characters," were Black Buffalo soldiers.

If the truth be known, Teddy Roosevelt did not lead the Rough Riders in a charge up San Juan Hill. He led his troops up Kettle Hill, a smaller hill in front of and to the right of San Juan Hill. Teddy Roosevelt used Kettle Hill as an observation post while his soldiers assaulted San Juan Hill. By the time Roosevelt had descended Kettle Hill and followed the rest of the American Army up San Juan Hill, the Cubans were long gone. Yet, Teddy Roosevelt rode the San Juan Hill myth and image of only White soldiers at San Juan Hill into the United States presidency and history. Neither the painting nor the myths include the role played by the Black Buffalo soldiers who had been reassigned from the American West to help Roosevelt in the fight with Cuba.

The sin is of omission. According to Frederick Remington, a star football player from Yale University who accompanied Roosevelt into battle, Teddy Roosevelt was an incompetent leader and a hindrance in the battle. Remington said the relocated Black Buffalo soldiers were the real heroes of the San Juan Hill battle. Remington's conclusion about the San Juan Hill battle was supported by other White officers. Lt. John J. Pershing publicly confessed that: "We officers of the Tenth Cavalry could have taken our Black heroes in our arms." Another White officer in the Rough Riders openly agreed saying: "If it had not been for the 10th, the Rough Riders would have been exterminated. I am not a Negro lover. My father fought with Mosby's raiders and I was born in the South, but the Negroes saved that fight and the day will come when they will be given credit for their bravery." The story of the Black troopers was also preserved in a popular song of that day entitled, "Hats Off to the Boys Who Made Good."

While accepting credit and glory for something that he did not do, Teddy Roosevelt never publicly acknowledged his indebtedness to Black soldiers. This story about heroes and myths is just another one in the long line of examples that show that Black soldiers throughout this nation's history have been consistent and unwavering warriors, but have never seen a painting, news release or statute that said: "Thank you. We are indebted."[20]

## ❦ LINCOLN'S BLACK BLOOD ❦

The first Dirty Little Secrets book raised a question about President Abraham Lincoln's race. Before and during his administration, his political opponents referred to him as a Black man and a Black Republican. They frequently used the name "Africanus Lincolnus." Had Lincoln's political opponents taken the time to read Lincoln's autobiography which he wrote a year before running for the office of president of the United States, they would have found some hints of his race. In 1859, Abraham Lincoln wrote in his autobiography: "If any personal description of me is thought desirable, it may be said, I am average in height, six feet, four inches, nearly; lean in flesh, weighing, on an average, one hundred and eighty pounds; **dark complexion, with coarse black hair, and gray eyes** — no other marks or brands recollected." (Emphasis added)

In 1860, according to public policies and social customs, a Black person was anyone who had 1/16th of Black blood. How many pure Whites had dark complexions and coarse black hair? This is about as good of a confession as one could expect in a race-conscious, slave-holding nation. As disturbing as it might be to the nation's psyche, the evidence strongly suggests that Abraham Lincoln, the great emancipator, and sixteenth president of these United States, had Black blood, whether or not he or the country knew it.

Despite the strong visual evidence of his racial lineage, Lincoln would do nothing to aid his Black brethren. He reluctantly issued the Emancipation Proclamation in January 1863. Early in his administration, Simon Cameron, the secretary of war, and a member of Lincoln's cabinet, had pressed Lincoln to free and arm Black slaves to fight in the Civil War. President Lincoln not only disagreed with Cameron, but fired him for even suggesting that Black slaves should be free and armed.[21]

## ❧ COINCIDENCES OF TWO PRESIDENTS ❧

Both Presidents Abraham Lincoln and John F. Kennedy are remembered for their human rights efforts, even though in reality neither president intentionally did anything to directly and specifically aid the nation's underserved Black population. It is amazing that Black people loved and identified with Lincoln and Kennedy more than all other American presidents because both presidents were indifferent to Black people and their problems. There are a number of unsettling similarities and strange coincidences involving these two tragic figures. For instance, how do you explain:

◆ *Abraham Lincoln was elected to Congress in 1846; John F. Kennedy was elected to Congress in 1946*

- ◆ *Abraham Lincoln was elected in 1860; John F. Kennedy was elected in 1960*

- ◆ *Both were trapped in the civil rights of Black people; both wives lost children while living in the White House*

- ◆ *Both were shot on a Friday; both were shot in the head*

- ◆ *Lincoln's secretary was named Kennedy; Kennedy's secretary was named Lincoln*

- ◆ *Both were assassinated by Southerners; the successors of both were Southerners named Johnson*

- ◆ *Andrew Johnson, who succeeded Lincoln, was born in 1808; Lyndon Johnson, who succeeded Kennedy, was born in 1908*

- ◆ *John Wilkes Booth, who assassinated Lincoln, was born in 1839; Lee Harvey Oswald, the alleged assassin of Kennedy, was born in 1939*

- ◆ *Both assassins were known by their three names; both names are composed of fifteen letters*

- ◆ *Lincoln was shot at the theater named "Ford;" Kennedy was shot in a "Lincoln car" made by "Ford"*

- ◆ *Both Booth and Oswald were assassinated before their trials.*

What do you think? Coincidences from playing with words? Or is this a really weird historical phenomenon? (Source unknown)

## 🐚 WHICH EMANCIPATION PROCLAMATION? 🐚

Increasing numbers of Black Americans are celebrating Juneteenth. This was the date, in 1865, that a Union soldier rode into Galveston, Texas, and announced that an emancipation proclamation had been signed by President Abraham Lincoln and Black slaves were free. Celebrating Juneteenth is very important to Black people because after centuries of every sort of human deprivation, they were hungry for some cultural celebrations which were peculiar to Black people. Such a reaction is normal and appropriately needed. However, Blacks need to be clear on what they are celebrating. Over the course of two centuries, there have been at least four different emancipation proclamations for Black people and none of them actually freed Blacks from slavery.

The first emancipation proclamation was issued by Lord Dunmore, the British royal governor of Virginia, in November, 1775, on the eve of the American Revolutionary War. In response to the threat of war, Lord Dunmore declared martial law and promised to free any Black slave who took up arms against and fought with the British against the American colonies. Within the first few months, nearly 6,000 slaves ran away and took Lord Dunmore's emancipation proclamation offer. Out of fear for what the Black slaves would do to White colonists, the British government pressured Dunmore to withdraw his emancipation proclamation offer of freedom to Black slaves.

The second emancipation proclamation was drafted in response to Nat Turner's slave revolt. In 1832, Nat Turner led a slave revolt in which slaves killed 57 Whites. The thought of 4 million angry Black slaves revolting sent fear through every White in the South. Virginia legislators quickly offered an emancipation proclamation proposal to abolish slavery. When nearly half of the legislators voted to abolish slavery, Virginia, the birthplace of slavery, came just a few votes short of ending slavery and preventing the Civil War.

The third emancipation proclamation was reluctantly offered by President Abraham Lincoln. His emancipation did not free a single slave. That is the reason the 13th Amendment to the Constitution had to be enacted. Lincoln's emancipation proclamation was little more than a publicity device to excite slaves to take up arms against the Southern Confederacy.

The fourth emancipation proclamation was proposed by the Southern Confederacy in the closing months of the Civil War. In hopes of maintaining their independence from the Northern Union, General Robert E. Lee and Jefferson Davis, the president of the Southern Confederacy, announced their emancipation proclamation and willingness to free their slaves in exchange for official recognition of the South as an independent state or territory. One Mississippi newspaper said: "Let not slavery prove a barrier to our independence ... If it is found to be in the way ... away with it. Let it perish." The South finally decided to set Black slaves free, but by then it was too late. They had lost the Civil War. So, which emancipation proclamation should Black Americans celebrate? At this late date, it's best to go with what you already have going ... Juneteenth.[22]

## THE FATHER OF THE COUNTRY

George Washington, who is commonly addressed as the father of the country, fathered more than the country. During his lifetime, George Washington held more Blacks in lifetime bondage than any other president or public official. But, more importantly, Washington was heavily involved in breeding Black people for the slave trade. Anecdotal records suggest that Washington fathered a number of the children himself and even allowed his guests to seek comfort with his female slaves, especially the mulatto females.

George Washington's adopted son, George Washington Parke Custis, reportedly had fifteen children by Black women. The fact that George Washington had slave children and grandchildren was not a big secret, especially for his neighbors. According to anecdotal records, one neighbor reported that he saw George Washington and his interracial family members regularly ride pass his house. The neighbor said: "I see Washington's grandchildren every day. They are of a dark yellow. They are mixed race mulatto children." Apparently, Washington's plantation was populated with slaves that had a rainbow of skin colors that reflected Black and White ancestry. Could this explain why George Washington is called the "father of the country" and the Washington monument is a phallic symbol?[23]

## ❦ In George Wallace's Doorway ❦

In 1963, Governor George Wallace of Alabama opposed school integration by blocking federal marshals in the doorway of the University of Alabama and screaming the memorable lines: "Segregation now. Segregation tomorrow. Segregation forever!" George Wallace's defiant declaration served as a ten-year platform for White Southern resistance and violence against Black Americans, who were simply seeking their inalienable Constitutional right as taxpayers and citizens to attend Alabama's public schools. After he was shot in Laurel, Maryland, became paralyzed and confined to a wheelchair, George Wallace recanted those memorable words and apologized to Alabama's Black citizens. Many Black Americans became sympathetic and forgave him for his vicious racist attitude.

But there is a dirty little secret about George Wallace's school door speech. George Wallace did not write his unforgettable words. The author was Asa (Ace) Earl Carter, a right-wing terrorist with close ties to the violent Ku Klux Klan organization. Earl Carter helped organize new chapters of the Ku Klux Klan throughout the country. After penning the memorable lines for Governor George Wallace, Carter went on to become a successful, self-taught writer and author. Carter also wrote a best-selling novel, *The Rebel Outlaw: Josey Wales*, which became a popular

Civil War motion picture starring Clint Eastwood. Clint Eastwood and Black moviegoers may not have known that the author who wrote the novel for the film also wrote the hateful words spoken by Governor George Wallace in the 1963 doorway speech.[24]

## ❦ OUR DRUG HERITAGE ❦

A prevailing myth about drugs suggests they are new and peculiar to Black Americans. For several generations, this nation and its media have conducted a war on drugs primarily in Black neighborhoods, resulting in a disproportionate number of Blacks filling the nation's prisons. Contrary to popular myths and media images, Black Americans are the last people in a line of drug users, a trend that started centuries ago with celebrated historical American and international figures. Columbus is credited with discovering America, but it is not well-known that when he set sail on his voyage to the East Indies, his supporters were depending on him to bring back some of the best opium. When he failed to find opium in the Americas, Columbus, instead, took tobacco back to Europe. His supporters accepted tobacco as a substitute and became addicted to nicotine.

A century or so later, some of America's colonial elite, like George Washington, were growing marijuana. George Washington, the father of the country, grew it on his farm at Mount Vernon, Virginia. Washington was in constant pain because of ill-fitting dentures. He tried to ease the pain by taking laudanum, a mixture of opium with a hint of cocaine. Thomas Jefferson, the drafter of the United States Constitution, not only raised and smoked marijuana, but he reportedly invented a machine to make fiber from marijuana, also called hemp plants. Old Benjamin Franklin, a sage and inventor of the modern printing press, was discovering opium at the same time he was discovering electricity. Franklin died addicted to opium that he took for gout.

According to historian Henry Pratt, on October 12, 1860, Abraham Lincoln walked into the drugstore and purchased a bottle of cocaine for 50 cents. In 1862, President Lincoln had a toothache and visited a Dr. G.S. Wolf, whose dental office was near the White House. As Dr. Wolf prepared to insert forceps into Lincoln's mouth to do a tooth extraction, Lincoln waved his hand saying: "Just a minute, please." Lincoln took a small bottle of chloroform from his vest pocket and took a deep sniff. Chloroform was a recreational drug at that time in history. It's funny that modern-day conservatives, who advocate the values of the Founding Fathers, adamantly oppose medicinal use of marijuana by cancer patients. Are Black Americans the original drug pushers, or are they the beneficiaries of an American legacy?[25]

## ❦ SLAVEHOLDERS RECEIVED REPARATIONS ❦

President Abraham Lincoln believed in paying reparations, but not to Black ex-slaves. Before the Civil War began, Lincoln believed the federal government should pay reparations to slave-holders for any losses they incurred as a result of ending slavery. Lincoln requested Congress to enact legislation to pay slave-holders for losses they would suffer in freeing their slaves. Congress denied Lincoln's request, primarily because the federal government did not have the approximately $6 billion required to cover the total market value of Black slaves. Since Washington, D.C., was popularly known as the nation's slave capital, Congress did approve funds to pay slaveholders in the District of Columbia $325 for each slave that they freed.

Since the U.S. Constitution legitimized and the federal government supported the "peculiar institution," some Congressional members believed the government had a moral and contractual obligation to compensate slaveholders for a loss of their investment. This being the case, the reverse was also true. Didn't it mean the federal government had an even greater moral and legal obligation to compensate the Black slaves and their descendants for the injuries they suffered under slavery? Slavery was approved in the Constitution and maintained by the actions of all levels of government. Government codified slavery, enacted fugitive slave laws and used its military power to put down slave revolts. Had not government abetted slavery, there is little likelihood that it would have lasted more than a few weeks. Consequently, all levels of government have a moral obligation to intervene into today's growing Black reparation movement, and for the first time, side with the descendants of slaves in their quest for justice.[26]

## ❦ WHAT WAS THE FREEDMAN'S BUREAU? ❦

The Freedman's Bureau, both in name and purpose, was a misnomer. The bureau was an initial attempt by Radical Republicans, the liberals in Congress, to repair some of the economic, political and educational damage inflicted on Black people by centuries of slavery. However, the Freedman's Bureau did not achieve the initial purpose that the bureau's name implies. Instead of focusing on newly-freed slaves and assisting them in adjusting to their newly-granted, quasi-freedom, the Freedman's program was intentionally expanded and misdirected to include everybody — old slaveholders, ex-Confederate soldiers and newly-arriving ethnic immigrants. The bureau's economic, political and health focus was immediately shifted from Black slaves to Southern Whites. Homestead lands and the bulk of the food, clothing and federal funds were used to rebuild the Southern White caste system, which locked ex-slaves into share cropping peonage. The federal government established Freedman's Banks with White administrators, who stole Black depositors' life savings within a decade. Except for the establishment of the nation's public school system, which marginally educated Black children for another 100 years, Blacks received practically nothing from the Freedman's Bureau. The Freedman's Bureau served and protected everybody, except newly freed Black men and women.[27]

## 🐦 COLOR AMERICAN PATRIOTS BLACK 🐦

Considering the popular zeal for honoring and revering this nation's Founding Fathers, how well-known is it that those who screamed the loudest about liberty, freedom and no taxation actually avoided fighting in the Revolutionary War? With rare exception, the Founding Fathers were brave only behind the battle lines. Most of the political patriots and members of the wealthy class bought their way out of the army or hired substitutes to do their fighting. What was even more hypocritical was the fact that many of the "patriots" promised their Black slaves freedom if they served as replacements in the army and served in battles. George Washington, one of the few patriots who clamored for freedom and went to war, felt that the outcome of the Revolutionary War between the British and American colonies depended on "Which side can arm the Negroes the faster." The American patriots and British loyalists offered incentives to free and bonded Blacks to join their side. The fear of slaves on one hand, and the military potential of mobilizing slaves on the other hand, created a major dilemma for both groups of Whites.

During the Revolutionary War, Blacks made up nearly 34 percent of the nation's population. Yet, with the rare exception of Crispus Attucks, they are conspicuously absent from Revolutionary War activities. It is virtually impossible for that many people not to have played a role in the "total war" of that day. There is no dishonor in revealing an enslaved peoples' participation. The dishonor occurs from the conscious omission of their deeds. One day, the truth about Black people fighting for their own life, liberty and the pursuit of happiness in America will be recognized and accepted by all Americans.[28]

## ❦ HITLER, A FAST LEARNER ❦

The treatment of Blacks by Whites in America served as a role model for Hitler's persecution of Jews during World War II. Throughout the 1930s, Blacks were treated brutally throughout the nation, but especially in the South. Eleanor Roosevelt, the wife of then-President Franklin D. Roosevelt, was very concerned that a Black man was being lynched every day. Eleanor Roosevelt urged her husband to use the powers of his office to get the United States Congress to enact an anti-lynching law. Regardless of how much she pressured him, President Roosevelt refused to support anti-lynching legislation, fearing it would offend members of his own Democratic Party and Congressional legislators from the old Confederate states. President Roosevelt's indifference to Black Americans came back to bite him. While Roosevelt was not concerned about Black Americans, he did become alarmed when he learned Hitler and his Nazi Party were exterminating Jews across Europe.

Roosevelt, incensed over the persecution and extermination of "innocent human beings," contacted Hitler and criticized his treatment of Jews. Rather than promising to back off, Hitler rebuffed President Roosevelt saying: "How can you tell me about how I should treat Jews when I learned how to treat Jews by watching how you and the rest of White America treat Black people?" Even though President Roosevelt did nothing to stop the lynchings, Black Americans admired and supported him. When Roosevelt died, a line in a popular Black song said: "Tell me why you like Roosevelt, everybody knows he was a Black man's friend." Did they really?[29]

# 🌑 WOODROW WILSON SET A VOTING PATTERN 🌑

Following the enactment of the 15th Amendment, generations of Black Americans have grown up hearing that the Black vote and voter turnout is pivotal, especially in a presidential election. In at least one instance, the popular belief about the Black vote proved true. In the early 1900s, Woodrow Wilson was a candidate in a heated presidential race in which the odds were against him. Needing every vote to win, Woodrow Wilson contacted Black leaders and civil rights organizations and promised he would help Black Americans, if they helped him win the election. Woodrow Wilson was one of the first White presidential candidates to openly seek the Black vote. Black voters responded in full strength, giving him the margin of victory in a close election.

Once elected to the nation's highest office, President Wilson showed his true colors. Instead of remembering and rewarding Black Americans with quid quo pro benefits, President Wilson did just the opposite. He issued executive orders that kicked Blacks out of federal employment, cut off access to public programs and resources, appointed openly racist judges and government officials and supported new segregation laws.

*1925 Ku Klux Klan march in Washington, D.C. (Library of Congress)*

Possibly the worst thing that President Wilson did was to actually use his presidency and the White House to encourage racism and terrorism against his Black supporters. During Wilson's presidency, the Ku Klux Klan of America tripled its national membership and staged its largest march ever down Pennsylvania Avenue in the nation's capital. Wilson's administration approved violence against Black people and demonstrated it when the White House hosted the premiere of Birth of a Nation, the most hateful anti-Black film ever produced. This film generated angry White mobs that attacked, beat and lynched Blacks across America.

President Wilson refused to call out the National Guard or other military forces to protect the outnumbered, unarmed, defenseless Black minority. The treachery and deceit of President Wilson established a model of political betrayal that remains a strategy until the present time. In close elections, White political candidates rally Black leaders to turn out a large number of Black voters. Black voters deliver a block vote to political candidates who promise much and deliver nothing to Black Americans. Black voters remain loyal and ignored until the next election.[30]

# CHAPTER 6

# CONSERVATIVES AND SAMBOS

*"Negras are docile and forgiving. They love their White Masters better than they love themselves."*
*~ A White preacher*

## Mini Facts

◆ *In 1676, a faithful Black slave named Jethro saved the lives of Whites in the town of Taunton, Massachusetts, by warning them of an attack by Chief King Philip and his Indian tribe.*

◆ *In 1710, the governor of Virginia freed Negro Willis, a slave, for exposing a slave Revolt. Willis became the first slave to win freedom under a new Meritorious Manumission policy.*

◆ *Between 1710 and 1865, there were over 265 reported slave revolts. None of them succeeded because fellow slaves revealed the revolt to the slave masters or White authorities.*

◆ *In 1822, Denmark Vesey planned an elaborate slave revolt in Charleston, South Carolina. Two Black slaves who betrayed him were found poisoned to death a few days later.*

## ❦ A FOOLISH AFRICAN KING ❦

Did you ever wonder why Arabs and European Whites collectively decided to venture onto the unfamiliar continent of Africa and why they were so well received? Initially, gold was the biggest motivating factor. In 1350, sub-Saharan Africa had two-thirds of the world's gold supply. But it was Mansa Musa, the ninth king of Mali who reigned from 1312 to 1337, who advertised Africa's gold supply, then threw the doors of the Malian empire wide open. He invited the world to come take whatever resources Africa had. Musa's political and religious naivete set the stage and provided the entree for an economic and religious invasion of Africa, as well as the commercial enslavement of African Blacks.

When Mansa Musa became king of the Malian Empire, the people were rich in spirit and material wealth. They were unified in their culture, religion and, most importantly, they were feared and respected by other nations. But Mansa Musa wanted international recognition and commercial acceptance from Arab and European nations. Even though he was not a Muslim, he organized a lavish promotional pilgrimage to Mecca. Musa's entourage of over sixty thousand people and eighty camels ladened with gold, threw gold at spectators in every city en route and convinced Arabs that Mali's streets were paved with gold. Musa's promotion succeeded so well that in 1375, the first European maps labeled Musa "the king of gold" and showed Mali as a thriving international trading market.

The Arab nations were so impressed with Musa that they began migrating into sub-Sahara Africa in search of the three G's: God, Glory and Gold. The Malian empire and Arab nations established international trading partnerships based upon the willingness of Chief Musa and his administrators to convert from ancestor worship to the Islamic religion. Islam allowed the Arabs to stick the camel's nose inside the African tent. Within two generations, Arab immigrants used Islam to invade the breadth of Africa and seize control of Mali's material resources, economy, educational institutions and cultural heritage. After Arabs caused the fall of Timbuktu, they used their mosques to establish Islam as the official and required religion. When scholars and historians describe Mansa Musa's administration, they establish the myth that Arabs and the Islamic religion benefited African Blacks. However, the benefit was for the Arabs, for within a short period of time, the Arabs discovered Black gold — African slaves — which had a greater market value than yellow, metal gold. The Gold Coast of Africa was named not after the metal gold, but after the Black gold.[1]

## ❦ A BLACK GUARDIAN OVERCLASS ❦

Black America has an overclass that is charged with the responsibility of maintaining the racial status quo. This Black overclass is typically made up of Black athletes, entertainers, ministers, civil rights leaders and elected officials who are financially, politically and institutionally wedded to the White structure of power and are, therefore, opposed to any independent thoughts or actions which might unite Black America. The overclass is commissioned by White organizations and governments to keep Black Americans disorganized, dependent and economically powerless by allying externally with other groups rather than allying internally with members of their own race.

The Black overclass concept originated with captains of slave ships. To reduce and prevent rebellions, ship captains picked "slave guardians" from among every boatload of slaves. The primary purpose of the guardians was to control the other slaves with feel-good rhetoric until they could be managed by a sufficient number of armed Whites. The other slaves viewed the unarmed guardian overclass as a harmless, visible source of hope that one day, they, too, would do better ... if they cooperated in their own enslavement and exploitation and refrained from revolting. The guardians succeeded and few revolts occurred. In return, the guardian overclass received a little better treatment while onboard the ship. However, when the slave ship docked, special privileges for the guardian overclass ended and they were sold into slavery just like the other Black slaves, i.e., the under-class. Centuries later, both the guardian overclass and the under-class appear to have learned very little from their experiences.[2]

## ❦ SOONER DOG POLITICS ❦

Did you know that the politics of "sooner dogs" and Blacks in politics have some similar characteristics? They both use politics of defeat. A sooner dog, for instance, would sooner lay down and roll over on his back to get along rather than to hunt and fight to defend himself and his turf. In contrast, a security dog or hunting dog is always ready to hunt, fight and give it his best shot. He will show in his behavior his readiness to defend himself and his turf. When approached by a larger dog, a security dog or hunting dog will spread his legs in a defensive stance, stiffen his back, curl his tail, perk his ears, show his teeth and growl to signal he is ready to fight — win, lose or draw.

But when a larger dog approaches a sooner dog, or he senses a larger dog is near, the differences are clear. A sooner dog bends his back legs, tucks his tail between his legs, lowers his ears, lays down on his belly, rolls over on his back, folds his front legs, stretches and exposes his throat then urinates on himself. The sooner's behavior declares his weakness and begs the bigger dog not to hurt him. A dog or group, regardless of size, that will stand up and fight for itself commands respect. Beginning with slavery, Black people practiced the sooner dog politics of defeat. Had the first load of captured Africans simply said: "No, we will fight and die before allowing you to strip us of our lives, culture, language, religion, families, dignity, humanity, self-respect and of the fruit of our labor," and had African slaves taken such a stance, rather than Rodney King's, "Why can't we all get along philosophy?" it is highly unlikely that slavery would have lasted two weeks or become a peculiar institution. With millions of Black Africans just saying "No" and demonstrating a fighting dog determination, slave owners would have realized the implications of blinking, going to sleep or eating food prepared by Black cooks. Unlike hunting or security dogs, Black people chose the path of nonviolent resistance and have paid dearly across six centuries for that decision.[3]

## ❦ RUSSIAN PREMIER AND ❦ CONSERVATIVE BLACKS

In the late 1960s, while visiting the United States, Premier Nikita Khrushchev of Russia expressed an interest in touring some urban cities and visiting Disney World. Since the Black Civil Rights Movement was well under way, the State Department briefed Khrushchev on both the status and impact of the movement on prevailing racial ideologies. To explain and yet minimize the political impact of the Black Civil Rights Movement, the State Department blamed the political and social disruptions on Black militants and White liberals. Further, the State Department hastened to assure Premier Khrushchev that: "All Blacks are not militant activists. As a matter of fact, many are contented Black conservatives." Upon hearing that some Blacks were contented conservatives, Khrushchev reportedly broke into laughter and asked: "What are Black conservatives conserving?" Nearly fifty years later, neither the United States government, a political party or conservative Blacks themselves have offered a sensible answer to Premier Khrushchev's pointed question.

In his book, *Slavery in the Cities*, Richard C. Wade includes a quote by Samuel Cartwright that may shed some light on the mind-set of conservative Blacks today. Cartwright was an infamous racist social commentator, generally considered as the spokesperson for those who justified slavery. He made these remarks in the mid-1800s after observing free Blacks and slaves:

"There is no office which the negro or mulatto covets more than that of being a body servant to a real [White] gentleman. They are delighted to be at the elbow, behind the table, to brush the coat or black the shoes, or to perform any menial service which may be required, and to hold out the open palm for a dime. This innate love to act as a body-servant or a lacquey [for Whites] is too strongly developed in the negro race to be concealed."

The motives of conservative Blacks today are often attributed to a desire for White approval, White acceptance or simply to be White. However, Cartwright's observation of Blacks would indicate that what conservative Blacks are conserving is perhaps their positions as accommodating flunkies or lackeys for Whites. The attitude Cartwright describes may also be part of the reason Blacks seem to only evaluate individual success and race progress in relation to the closeness they have achieved to Whites. Whether the issue is desegregation, moving up the corporate ladder or the degree of how color-blind and conservative they are, Blacks who are "body-servants" for a White agenda usually find themselves opposing their own people. This psychology surely had its roots in slavery, but sadly, it survives and is still alive and operative. Simply look at the behavior of Blacks today, whether they are high-level elected officials, in corporate boardrooms, in religious institutions or the entertainment realm, one cannot simply dismiss the truth that might be contained in Cartwright's offensive words.

## ❦ SAMBOISM BACKFIRED ❦

Strange things do happen. One of the strangest racial incidents occurred on November 3, 1988, on Geraldo Rivera's television talk show. The topic was race. To present the different perspectives, Rivera invited a Black man, Roy Innis, from the Congress of Racial Equality (CORE), and John Metzger, a White man and member of the Neo-Nazi Party. Apparently Rivera was not aware that since the civil rights movement of the 1960s, CORE had evolved into a right-wing conservative organization that functioned as an extension of the Republican Party. Confusion reigned from the outset of Rivera's program as Roy Innis, the conservative Black man, repeatedly agreed with and supported the racist statements of John Metzger, the White Nazi. Roy Innis and CORE's ideologies had become just the opposite of the NAACP and most other civil rights organizations and were more similar to racist hate groups, like the Ku Klux Klan and the neo-Nazi groups.

Near the midpoint of the program, John Metzger, the White racist, could no longer stand Roy Innis, a Black man, agreeing with him on race matters. Metzger screamed at Innis: "I am tired of you trying to support the Nazi positions on race. We don't need a nigger Uncle Tom helping us." John Metzger's remarks must have touched a raw nerve in Roy Innis. Innis immediately jumped up from his chair, ran across the stage and began choking Metzger. Fists were flying all over the stage and other guests joined the fight. Geraldo Rivera was injured when he rushed in to break up the brawl, and someone threw a chair that struck him in the face and broke his nose. This free-for-all was televised and possibly for the first time in history, the nation witnessed a member of a White racist organization rebuffing a conservative Black for being a Sambo. What in the world is going on when even a White racist cannot tolerate or be publicly associated with a conservative, or Sambo Black, who is equally devoted to keeping Blacks in the ditch?[4]

## ❦ QUOTABLE NOTABLE ❦

Movie producer and director Spike Lee, commenting on the nation's only Black Supreme Court Justice, Clarence Thomas, said: "He is a handkerchief-head, chicken-and biscuit-eating Uncle Tom."[5]

## ❦ A PURVEYOR OF SELF-HATE ❦

Dr. Walter Williams, a conservative Black professor at George Mason University in Virginia, advocates that Blacks should take pride in the fact that both free and bonded Black slaves fought with the Southern Confederacy during the American Civil War to maintain Black enslavement. Williams does not point out the pathology and insanity of Black slaves taking up arms against Union soldiers who were fighting to free them. Instead, Williams recites the story of a group of White slave owners and their loyal slaves, who were prisoners of the Union Army. Union officers offered the Black slaves freedom if they would take an oath of allegiance to the United States. Williams quoted the indignant reply of the slave who said: "I can't take no oath as dat. I'm a black nigger." Upon learning that his White master had refused to take the oath, Williams further quoted the slave as saying: "I can't take no oath dat Massa won't take." In another recited instance, a White slave owner took the oath, but his slave didn't. When the Black slave was returned to Virginia under a flag of truce, he expressed disgust at his White master's disloyalty, saying: "Massa had no principles." In citing these utterances as examples of laudable behavior, Williams solidifies his credentials as a conservative, or what Black Americans are increasingly calling, a Sambo. Dr. Williams choose to highlight the behavior of Blacks who were clearly emotionally disturbed, lacked a group self-interest and were identifying with their oppressors. Moreover,

Dr. Williams failed to point out as *Harpers* magazine did in the 1860s, that the few Blacks who did take up arms to fight for the Confederate South often did so because they had loaded guns pointed at their heads.

Dr. Walter Williams provided other examples of slave/master role reversals and inappropriate behavior. In his book, *Black Confederate Soldiers*, Williams recited how after the battle of Seven Pines in June 1862: "Two Black Confederate regiments not only fought, but showed no mercy to the Yankee dead or wounded, whom they mutilated, murdered and robbed." Dr. Williams underscored his support for conservatives and racist Whites by saying: "Black civil rights activists and their White liberal supporters who're attacking the Confederate flag have committed a deep, despicable dishonor to our patriotic Blacks ancestors, who marched, fought and died to protect their homeland from what they saw as Northern aggression." In both his writings and personal appearances on conservative radio talk shows like Rush Limbaugh, Dr. Williams, a Black arch conservative seeking meritorious manumission, appears unable to see the Confederate flag as the symbol of the nation's first traitors and oldest terrorist group.[6]

## 🌿 A BRILLIANT, COLOR-BLIND SCIENTIST 🌿

George Washington Carver was, without a doubt, one of this nation's greatest scientists and botanists. Carver was born the son of slaves in 1860 in Diamond, Missouri. When the public school system was established after the Civil War, Carver aggressively pursued an elementary and secondary school education. Continuing his education, he graduated from Iowa State Agricultural College in 1894. He was then prepared to do what he liked best — teach agricultural sciences and biological research. Carver began his career teaching at Tuskegee Institute in Alabama, where he headed the agriculture department, a position he held until his death.

Carver was a pioneer in agricultural research and plant chemistry. He quickly amazed local governments and major corporations with creative uses of farm products. He discovered a new method of organic fertilization, conservation and crop rotation to restore soil. Whites were astounded that a Black man could produce more than 350 products, such as soap, shampoo, insecticides, vinegar and wood stains, from peanuts, sweet potatoes, pecans and other plants. Carver's crop rotation system saved the Southern agricultural industry. However, Carver's great research and achievements produced practically no economic benefits for him personally or for any other descendants of slaves. Nearly 100 percent of the recipes, formulas and production techniques that Carver's research produced were passed on, not to Tuskegee Institute, Black students or Black people, but instead, they became the property of Alabama's White universities and White-owned businesses.

Just like during slavery, everything that a Black slave produced belonged to the slave owner. Why weren't Black people offered the opportunity to commercially develop some of Carver's chemical formulas, agricultural systems and commercial products? Carver justified not using the fruits of his labor to enrich and elevate his race by publicly proclaiming that: "They belong to the world. My work, my life, must be in the spirit of a little child seeking only to know the truth and follow it." George Washington Carver was a brilliant man, but with a childlike attitude about the realities of the world. Like so many Black Americans, he ascended to the top of his field, then hid behind race-neutral, color-blind philosophies and used them as excuses to do practically nothing for long-suffering, poor Black people. At best, Carver's lifetime achievements earned him a place on bulletin boards in Black schools during Black History Month.[7]

## ❦ CIVIL WAR HUMOR ❦

The American Civil War, which is frequently referred to as the war that pitted brother against brother, was the background for some racial humor. The phrase brother against brother was not restricted to Northern Whites fighting Southern Whites. It also included loyalty conflicts between free Blacks and slaves, as well as conservative Sambo Blacks and the Black masses. For example, in the midst of a major battle between Union and Confederate troops just outside of New Orleans, Louisiana, a Black Union soldier shot and killed a Black who was fighting for the Southern Confederacy. A White Confederate officer who witnessed the shooting turned to a fellow Rebel soldier and snarled: "Did you see what that nigger did to our Colored boy?"[8]

## ❦ FEMALE SAMBO REWARDED ❦

By the mid-1700s, meritorious manumission policies of the South had been adopted as far North as Charlestown, Massachusetts. Just as in the South, meritorious manumission policies personally rewarded slaves who informed on slave conspiracies. In one instance, Mark and Phyliss, two Black slaves, had been slipping arsenic into the food of John Codman, a prominent White slaveholder and their owner. Their plan was to poison him, then escape to Canada. However, another Black female slave named Phoebe noticed that before White master died, his body had turned progressively black. Suspecting that her master had been poisoned, Phoebe revealed what she felt was a slave plot to neighboring White slaveholders. The neighboring slaveholders moved quickly. They grabbed Mark and hung him. Phyliss was strangled and burned at the stake. And Phoebe, the loyal slave, was fittingly rewarded. She was sold to a new slaveholder in the West Indies, where the life expectancy of a Black slave was much shorter. Is that poetic justice?

## ❦ THE IMMORTAL UNCLE TOM ❦

Perception is influenced by he who pays the bill and owns and controls the channels of communication. Two publications released in 2002 — *Savoy* magazine and the *1st Millennial Edition: The American Directory of Certified Uncle Toms* — make the point. Both publications featured their take on Black leadership in America. The first publication, Savoy magazine, was "aimed, at those successful, affluent and educated Black men and women" that are the Black overclass. Savoy, owned by Vanguarde Media, a company whose investors were predominately non-Black corporations that profited from Blacks as a market, touted its list of the "100 Black Leaders and Heroes" with authority and bravado. Who topped *Savoy's* list?:

| | | |
|---|---|---|
| Colin Powell | Condoleezza Rice | Clarence Thomas |
| Oprah Winfrey | Ward Connerly | Stanley Crouch |
| J.C. Watts | Alan Keyes | |

The second publication, *The American Directory of Certified Uncle Toms*, is a book written by Blacks to evaluate the progress of the race and to identify "race betrayal" behavior by visible Blacks, or the overclass. The purpose of *The Certified Directory of Uncle Toms* was to hold visible Blacks accountable for their actions. It used the term Uncle Tom synonymously with Sambo, Aunt Jemima and the House Negro to label a Black person who sought personal gain by acting in ways that benefited Whites and injured Blacks. *The Directory* ranked Uncle Toms in descending order, based upon the amount of damage each had inflicted on Black people. What did the Savoy list of 100 Black Leaders and Heroes have in common with the Uncle Toms? Almost everything. Here are some of the names that *The Directory* certified as Uncle Toms:

| | | |
|---|---|---|
| Colin Powell | Condoleezza Rice | Clarence Thomas |
| Oprah Winfrey | Ward Connerly | Stanley Crouch |
| J.C. Watts | Alan Keyes | |

Many of the same people were on both lists, but under different headings. How did that happen? One's point of view is colored by expectation, conditioning and where the money comes from. Blacks whose livelihoods depend on White support and approval and Blacks who live with racial realities are wearing different glasses. Savoy folded in bankruptcy in 2003 after a three-year run. The reader may find interest in some of the other names that appeared on the Directory's list of certified Uncle Toms:

| | |
|---|---|
| Armstrong Williams | Ken Hamblin |
| Vernon Jordan | John Lewis |
| Julian Bond | Tiger Woods |
| Laurence "Larry" Elder | Morgan Freeman |
| George Foreman | Henry Louis Gates |
| Whoopi Goldberg | Mary Frances Berry |

The authors of the *Directory of Certified Uncle Tom's* promised an updated list in the near future. There is a chance that some of the above individuals may no longer be viewed as Uncle Toms. Then again, perhaps they will.[9]

## 🐝 A KEEPER OF THE FAITH 🐝

Adam Clayton Powell Jr., the pastor of Abyssinian Baptist Church in Harlem, New York, was a brash, bold and unapologetic pro-Black leader and political role model for Black Americans during the Black Civil Rights Movement of the 1960s. Powell's signature phrases were: "Keep the Faith, Baby" and "Stay Black." Powell was such a forceful and skilled politician that he rose to become chairman of the powerful Ways and Means Committee in the United States House of Representatives. As chairman, Powell moved approximately $6 billion to fund President Lyndon B. Johnson's Great Society and War on Poverty Programs. Powell aggressively used his congressional powers to take care of Black Americans, regardless of White resistance.

"Yet, the political attitude of Congressman Adam Clayton Powell Jr. was just the opposite of his father, Adam Clayton Powell Sr., who built and pastored the largest church in America. The Senior Powell was a model racial accommodator, whose racial docility was nearly identical to that of Booker T. Washington. In the 1940s, Adam Clayton Powell Sr. advocated that Black Americans adopt a "meekness of Jesus" attitude and become even more compromising. The senior Powell told White America that: "Each race has a contribution to make to the other. My race needs the White man's courage, initiative, punctuality, business acumen and aggressiveness. The White man needs the Negro's meekness, love, forgiving spirit and the emotional religion expressed in his folk songs." Why the senior Powell thought Whites should adopt characteristics that had not served Blacks very well is unclear.

Ironically, in 1896, at the Cotton States and International Exposition in Atlanta, Georgia, Booker T. Washington expressed nearly the exact same sentiment, saying: "Blacks are the most patient, faithful, law-abiding, and un-resentful people that the world has ever seen. As we have proved our loyalty to you in the past, in nursing your children, watching by the sick bed of your mothers and fathers, and often following them with tear-dimmed eyes to their graves, so in the future, in our humble way, we shall stand by you ... ready to give our lives." The conciliatory attitudes of Booker T. Washington and Adam Clayton Powell Sr. brought much comfort to White Americans and much pain to Black Americans. Being Black and proud, Adam Clayton Powell Jr. admonished his people to simply "Keep the Faith" while he delivered the goods.[10]

##  BOOKER T. WASHINGTON'S MONUMENT

Some Black Americans view Booker T. Washington and his social philosophies with mixed emotions. Most Black Americans appreciate the role Washington played in developing educational and business opportunities for Blacks in Alabama. However, an even greater number of Black Americans feel Washington betrayed them in the Uncle Tom role that he played in national politics. Black Americans often express mixed feelings towards Booker T. Washington, especially when they view the monument to Booker T. Washington that stands at the entrance to the Tuskegee University campus, in Tuskegee, Alabama. The inscription on the sculpture reads: "Removing the veil of ignorance from the young Black American man who kneels before him." Washington is standing over a kneeling student, holding a piece of cloth above the student's head. Black Americans who found Washington's compromising and passive racial attitudes offensive gaze at the monument and semi-jokingly ask: "Was Washington taking the veil of ignorance off, or was he putting it on?" The answer varies, depending upon whether the inquiring mind belongs to a Black realist or a Black conservative.[11]

## ❦ The Loyal and Protective Slaves ❦

Throughout the history of this nation, both free and bonded Blacks have demonstrated an overwhelming commitment to protect White lives and property. This behavior was especially conspicuous during slavery and the American Civil War. For instance, in the fall of 1864, a free Black named Goler, whom other blacks shunned as a mean cuss, betrayed a group of Union soldiers after they took shelter in his home. The Union soldiers felt comfortable in Goler's home since, in large measure, they were fighting Confederate soldiers to free Black slaves. However, once the Union soldiers had settled in for the night, Goler excused himself to fix food for them. Instead of fixing food, he secured some Confederate soldiers, who captured the Union soldiers.

Another Black slave, Burrell Barret, of Cold Harbor, Virginia, behaved in an equally unfitting manner. Burrell Barret was the classic loyal and faithful slave prepared to die for his master. Beginning with and throughout the four years of the Civil War, Barret slept on the floor outside of his master's bedroom with an ax. He swore to kill anyone who he thought might even attempt to harm the master's family. Yet, Barret's own wife and children remained unprotected and struggled to survive. How long would Black enslavement have lasted if loyal Blacks like Burrell Barret had demonstrated similar intense interest in protecting their own homes, families and race?

## ❦ America's New Nazi Party ❦

In his book, *Old Nazis, the New Right, and the Republican Party*, author Russ Bellant describes how after World War II, the United States government gave special immigration status to hundreds of former Nazis from Germany, then imported them into the United States to apply their skills to develop America's technology sector, especially the flagging space program and military defense. These German scientists were Nazi fascists who were anti-Jew and anti-Black and had just fought a war based upon racial superiority. German scientists began entering America in the late 1940s and early 1950s and infused themselves into the most right-wing, conservative political organizations. Nazis began to enter the country just as the Democratic Party was becoming the liberal party and the White racists were moving into the Republican Party. With their German past and racist agendas buried in neo-conservative rhetoric and ideologies, they identified with a new, emerging Republican Party and its affiliated political think tanks and educational institutions. With their help, the Republican Party became the official White political party in America by the late 1970s.[12]

## ❦ A QUOTABLE NOTABLE ❦

After suffering extensive internal injuries and numerous broken bones at the hands of White Los Angeles policemen who beat and kicked him for over an hour, Rodney King exited a Los Angeles Hospital and said to the media: *"Why can't we all just get along?"* What hint did the police give King that they were trying to get along with him?

# CHAPTER 7

# BUSINESS AND BUFFOONERY

*The Founding Fathers believed slavery
was a necessary economic evil.*

## Mini Facts

◆ *In the 1920s, Black Americans had five times more businesses per 100,000 Blacks than they have today.*

◆ *In the 1920s, Tulsa, Oklahoma, was so racist and segregated that it was the only city in America that could boast of segregated telephone booths.*

◆ *According to the 2000 Census, approximately 54 percent of Black businesses had revenues of less than $10,000 per year.*

◆ *In the year 2004, Black America exported nearly 98 percent of its collective $700 billion annual disposable income out of its own pockets and into non-Black businesses.*

## ❦ MAKING BRICKS WITHOUT STRAW ❦

In 1866, nearly a century before the U.S. Supreme Court's, Brown vs. Board of Education desegregation decision, George T. Downing, a successful Black businessman, forced the public schools in several northeastern states to integrate. Instead of lawsuits and court rulings, Downing used his business skills, acquired wealth and political contacts. Downing was one of the few free Blacks who had become wealthy from operating a profitable business in the North during slavery. Not only was he was rather unique because he was a free Black and a successful businessman, but also because he was a politician who was a militant crusader for racial justice for Black people. He made money while fighting for his people.

In 1845, when he was only twenty-six years old, Downing established a successful restaurant and catering business in New York that served the cream of the crop of White Broadway society. In 1846, he opened another restaurant in Newport, Connecticut. He also had a thriving real estate business in Providence, Rhode Island. After the Civil War, Downing took over the restaurant that served the House of Representatives in Washington, D.C., and used some of his profits to fight structural racism in other parts of the country. He launched a drive to break down racial barriers in Rhode Island's public schools by appealing to the governor and state legislators. His strong and determined efforts paid off. Rhode Island's legislature outlawed school segregation and several other Northern states quickly followed Rhode Island's lead.[1]

## ❦ BLACK RICE IN SOUTH CAROLINA ❦

Black rice was a name that a growing number of historians are giving to white rice in an effort to credit its existence in the Western world to African slaves. The introduction of both slavery and rice were essential to the survival of the South Carolina colony. White farmers had experimented with cotton, tobacco, sugar cane, silk and ginger, but failed. They needed a cheap labor force to raise a stable cash crop. Black slaves who had grown up in Africa taught White masters how to plant and harvest rice in the low coastal areas of the state. Ironically, when they shared that knowledge, they locked themselves into slavery, as well as one of the harshest, most labor-intensive farming industries that has ever existed. White planters repaid the slaves by forcing them to work under horrendous conditions in the swamp lands, which were infested with mosquitoes. Black men and women died in alarming numbers from malaria and a wide range of other infectious diseases. Many fell, disabled from exhaustion and poor diets. When the slave population fell too low, the plantation owners simply imported more Africans, finding it cheaper to buy new slaves than to maintain the ones they had.

By the 1730s, rice plantations covered the tidal and inland swamps of South Carolina and had begun to spread into other Southern lowlands. Rice continued to be an important crop after slavery. By the early part of the 20th century, America's rice industry was supplying millions of pounds of rice to Europe and the Far East. Rice today continues to be one of the world's basic foods, especially in Third World nations. It is ironic that centuries after African slaves introduced rice into the American colonies, millions of sub-Saharan Blacks are now starving. Perhaps there is a way to return Black rice to Black Africa and save a starving race of people.[2]

## ❦ BLACK LIGHT ❦

According to Joan Potter, in her book *African-American Firsts*, Lewis Latimer, a Black man, was a member of the famed "Edison Pioneers," who brought electric light to a dark world.

Lewis Latimer was born in 1848 in Chelsea, Massachusetts, to parents who had escaped slavery. When he was fifteen, Latimer joined the Union Army to help free nearly five million Blacks who were in bondage. After the Civil War, Latimer got a job in the office of a White patent attorney, where he learned how to prepare mechanical drawings. He was rewarded with a promotion to draftsman and assigned to prepare drawings for Alexander Graham Bell's application for his telephone patent. Bell received an approved patent in 1876. Shortly afterwards, Latimer left the patent office and took a job with an electric lighting company in Connecticut. There he improved the incandescent light that Thomas Edison had invented one year earlier.

It was Latimer's invention that improved the quality of Edison's invention and gave us our present-day incandescent lighting. In 1882, Latimer gave us the long-lasting carbon filament for electric light bulbs. In recognition of his invention, Latimer was asked to install his lighting systems in the cities of New York and Philadelphia, as well as in some cities in Canada. By 1918, he was nationally recognized as one of the twenty-eight charter members of the Edison Pioneers, a prestigious group. Latimer died in 1928.[3]

##  BLACK BUSINESSMAN OF THE 20TH CENTURY

Arthur G. Gaston could easily qualify as the role model Black entrepreneur of the 20th century. Gaston started his business career in 1923 by establishing a funeral home in Birmingham, Alabama, to ensure that Black people could receive decent burials. A decade or so later, with a successful funeral home as an economic foundation, Gaston started the Booker T. Washington Business College, whose primary goal was to teach economics and build a Black entrepreneurial business class. Next, he built the Brown Belle Bottling Company, which capitalized on the popularity of the World's Heavyweight Champion, Joe Louis. The company bottled a soft drink called the "Joe Louis Punch," but the company floundered and went out of business. Undeterred, Gaston continued his entrepreneurial adventures as America entered the Black civil rights era. He then built and owned a motel, started an investment firm, a savings and loan association, acquired two radio stations and started a construction company. Gaston believed in producing, as well as selling. His favorite line was: "If you build a better mouse trap, people will buy it." A.G. Gaston passed, but his entrepreneurial spirit continues to motivate Blacks to own businesses.[4]

## ❦ QUOTABLE NOTABLES: ❦
### SOUTHERN CONSCIENCE

In the late 1960s, President Lyndon Johnson introduced the term affirmative action and defined it saying: "Don't call it compensatory. Call it affirmative action. It's moving the nation forward. It is going out of the way to bring Blacks into that which they have been long excluded." For President Johnson, affirmative action was corrective action. It was initiated to correct the negative socioeconomic conditions and racial inequalities that existed in all levels of government, business and mainstream White society that had been imposed on Black Americans over the course of 500 years.

## ❦ THE GREATEST SHOWMAN ❦
### OF A BLACK TRAGEDY

For nearly two centuries, America proclaimed Phineas T. Barnum the "Greatest Showman on Earth." Barnum's fame and wealth came from the traveling circus that he operated. His circus was known for popular performers, but also the human oddities and curiosities that he presented to the public. His circus was so popular that it became known as "The Greatest Show on Earth," and later as the Barnum and Bailey Circus. Barnum started upon his lifetime career when he read of an unsuccessful Philadelphia show featuring Joice Heth, an African-American woman who was rumored to have been the nurse of President George Washington. To verify historical association with George Washington, a slave bill of sale, supposedly signed by Augustus Washington, the son of George Washington, was typically posted for public consumption. Barnum paid $1,000 to her owner for the rights to publicly exhibit Joice Heth. Barnum first put Heth on display at Niblo's Garden in New York and billed her as "The Greatest Natural and National Curiosity in the World."

Barnum, promoted Joice Heth as born in Madagascar in 1647, 161 years of age, and weighing only 46 pounds. She was blind, toothless, her skin was shriveled and she was partially paralyzed. Heth told White spectators stories of caring for George Washington as a baby. She recalled events in his youth and songs she had taught him. Heath was an instant success that set Barnum on his way to fame and fortune. On February 19, 1936, Joice Heth died. Barnum exploited Heth even in her death. One commentator wrote: "The funniest part came when the old wench died." In order to gratify public curiosity about Heth's longevity, Barnum arranged to have an autopsy performed in public and charged 50 cents admission. Over a thousand spectators gathered around a surgical table in a makeshift operating theater in New York and watched as David L. Rogers, a surgeon, cut into her body. An autopsy revealed she had only reached the age of 80. Barnum, "the Greatest Showman on Earth," revealed the hoax, while feeding the press stories that ranged from bragging about the deception to being outraged about it. The most that Barnum ever did for Joice Heth was to bury her in his own family's cemetery plot.

Prior to the Civil War, while on a tour through the South, Barnum purchased other slaves and further demonstrated his choice to be a slave master. He publicly whipped a slave and, suspecting him of stealing, sold him at an auction. Barnum was a slave owner who participated fully in the dirty business of buying, selling, whipping and degrading Black people; however, his treatment of Blacks did nothing to injure Barnum's reputation as the world's greatest showman.[5]

## ❦ DID COLUMBUS DISCOVER RUBBER? ❦

There is a story bouncing around that Christopher Columbus was the first European to discover rubber. But, guess where Columbus discovered it? Reportedly when Columbus was in Haiti, he noticed some young boys playing with a ball that bounced. Columbus was curious about the material the ball was made of and where the boys might have gotten the material. They took Columbus into the forest and showed him how they got the rubber from certain trees by cutting the bark of the trees and catching the milky white liquid (latex) that bleeds from the cuts. Once the liquid, or latex, dried, it was spongy and bouncy. Columbus also discovered that the local inhabitants used the strange white liquid to make waterproof shoes and bottles. There is no evidence that Columbus reported his "discovery" of rubber once he arrived back in Europe. His discoveries were land, slaves and tobacco. Consequently, neither Columbus nor Haiti are ever associated with the historical development of commercial rubber.[6]

## ❦ A BLACK MAN WHO LIVED IN A ZOO ❦

Black men, just like Black women, were put on exhibit as freaks. In 1904, the city of New York permitted a public zoo to display a Black human as an animal for commercial profit. Samuel Phillips Verner, a White religious missionary, reportedly purchased a Black male pygmy, Ota Benga, from the African Congo, brought him to America and made a fortune by placing him in the monkey house at the Bronx Zoological Park in New York. To draw large crowds and give the impression that Ota Benga was a primitive cannibal, the missionary filed down sharp points on his teeth, dressed him in a loincloth, scattered bones around the cage, made him dance for the public and fed him a monkey's diet. When several Black ministers raised an outcry against such a degrading exhibition, Ota Benga was set free and sent to a Virginia Seminary in Lynchburg. For a short period, he found some peace and self-respect. But in March 1916, Ota Benga ended his American nightmare by using a gun to kill himself.[7]

## ❦ TELLING IT LIKE IT IS HUMOR ❦

A White ex-slave owner wrote in a letter to his recently emancipated slave: "My dear, faithful, loyal Sambo! That nasty President Lincoln has forced you to accept freedom against my wishes and I am sure against yours. But, being the dear friend and self-sacrificing servant that you are, you don't have to leave this plantation. We all can live like the Civil War never happened. So, stay here with us."

The recently emancipated slave wrote back to his ex-owner: "Thank you, deah, kine, lovin, generous Massa, but I reckon I'll go on and leave. But befo' I go I wants to you to know that I will always remember you the S.O.B that you is and always wuz!"

~ Anonymous

## ❦ CHEW ON THIS! ❦

General Antonio Lopez de Santa Anna, of Texas Alamo fame, was a mulatto Mexican, a mixture of Spanish, Indian and Black. Not too long after the Mexican-American War ended, General Santa Anna traveled to Staten Island, New York, with thoughts of perhaps becoming a permanent United States citizen. In hopes of making his trip as comfortable as possible, he brought some of

Mexico with him. As a small child in Mexico, Santa Anna enjoyed chewing the sap of the Chicola tree. This gummy Chicola resin could be chewed for hours without losing its consistency. Not knowing how long he would stay in the United States and realizing that he would be unable to find the sap in New York, General Santa Anna brought an entire barrel of the limbs and sap with him.

A young American named James Adam, who served as Santa Ana's interpreter, noticed how the old general would constantly cut slices from the tropical plant and place them in his mouth. Adam was unfamiliar the Chicola plant. He asked General Santa Ana about the Chicola plant and was told the chewy substance was called "chicle." When Santa Ana left New York in 1867, James Adam persuaded him to leave the remaining branches of chicle behind. Adam began to experiment with the substance, adding sweetening agents to bolster the flavor. Soon he had taken Santa Ana's chicle and "invented" chewing gum. Adam founded Adam Chewing Gum Company and introduced the product to a ready public which has been chewing ever since. General Santa Ana had unknowingly started a cultural trend and a major multi-billion dollar chewing-gum industry. But until this present day, he is associated only with the Battle of the Alamo. Now, chew on that![8]

## ❦ A REAL LIFE MONOPOLY GAME ❦

Landownership was second only to owning Black people as the primary generator of wealth, social status, political power and voting rights in America. Just like in the board game Monopoly, whoever owned and controlled the most and best land and the businesses on the land could play and win in real-life Monopoly. Black ex-slaves never received the forty acres and a mule they were promised after the Civil War. Moreover, Whites used various legal and extra legal means to deny Blacks the right to acquire and hold public lands. But through sheer determination, Black ex-slaves managed to purchase land. Much of it was poor, low quality, inaccessible and overpriced, but by 1920, Blacks had acquired approximately 20 million acres of land. However, racism grew more intense following World War I, and through violence, intimidation, tax sales, laws of eminent domain and even murder, over 19 million acres of land were taken from Black landowners by the mid-1950s. Numerous government agencies participated in schemes and cooperated with banks and White farmer alliances to take land from Black farmers.

Gaps in crumbling tax records, deed books and the self-righteous mind-set of White authorities hide the true nature of the misdeeds. According to an Associated Press investigation, nearly a third of the courthouses in Southern and border states have been burned down at least once since the Civil War. Records of Black landowners and farmers have gone up in smoke. Immediately after the Civil War, 55–65 percent of all the farmers in the South were Black. Today, they make up less than 1 percent. Black farmers lack access to investment and bank capital, product distribution systems and urban markets. Black farming is nearly extinct. The loss of Black farmlands is high on the Black reparation list. Whatever Black Americans are going to do in the real-life Monopoly game, they will have to do it quickly. In the early 1980s, conservative Whites began using strategies such as gentrification, regionalization, municipal sharing, privatizing, eminent domain and "cool cities" to take back ownership and control of lands in Black urban cities. A new national movement has established White-controlled land banks in every major urban area in the United States and along with natural and man-made disasters, they will eventually make Blacks landless, like the Palestinians in the Middle East. In the game of real-life Monopoly, losing players either go bankrupt or go to jail. In America, there are no get-out-of-jail-free cards for Black losers.[9]

# ❧ TOYS FROM BLACK EGYPTIANS ❧

Black people can take credit for inventing some of the oldest children's games in the world. One of the oldest is shooting marbles. Egyptian children played marbles over 4,500 years ago. Archaeologists have unearthed marbles from among the ruins of temples, and marbles were found in children's tombs. The oldest game of marbles in Egypt appears to have been a set of rounded stones. Later, around 1435, on the Greek island of Crete, children played with polished jasper and agate. The Greek term for polished white agate, "marmaros," evolved into the word "marble." Rules of how the marble game was played were never discovered. The spinning top is another children's toy that goes back thousands of years, to 3,000 B.C. Although adults could have played with the spinning top, it is classified as a children's toy because it was discovered in the gravesites of several children, alongside sets of marbles. The spinning top can be traced from North Africa to the Orient, where it was mass-produced for commercial markets.

Even though it did not become very popular in the United States until the late 1950s, the hula hoop is probably just as old as marbles and the spinning top. In ancient times, Egyptians made hoops from dried and stripped grapevines. Just like in modern days, the Egyptians rolled them, tossed them in the air and spun them around their waists. During the 14th century, a hooping craze swept England. The word hula became associated with the hoop in the early 1800s, when British sailors visited the Hawaiian islands and associated hooping with hula dancing. In the 1950s, the Wham-O Company began manufacturing brightly colored plastic tube rings that were about three feet in diameter and cost about $2.00 each. For over a decade, the Hula Hoop created one of the greatest fads the country has ever seen. The Hula Hoop made the owners of the Wham-O Company very rich, but they could not get a patent on an ancient toy from Egypt and North Africa.10

## 🍃 Blacks in Textiles 🍃

The WestPoint Stevens Company, situated near Dothan, Alabama, is noted for its fine quality linen and dry goods products. This was not always the case. WestPoint Stevens once produced the rough cloth used to make clothing for slaves on Southern plantations. WestPoint Stevens can trace its roots to slavery in the early 1800s. Nathaniel Stevens started a textile company at the outset of the War of 1812 with Great Britain. Samuel Batchelder started the Pepperell Manufacturing Company in 1831. These two major textile manufacturing companies were consolidated into the WestPoint Stevens Company in 1965. Both companies were built on the labor of Black slaves. Southern planters supplied the companies with raw cotton that was milled into both fine fabrics and rough-milled fabric called "Nigger Cloth." The Pepperell's Rock River fabric brand was described in the book, *Men and Times of Pepperell* (a book published by the company in 1940), as "a sturdy cloth heavily bought by Southern plantation owners as clothing for their Black slaves." In the pre-Civil War era, most Northern textile mills concentrated on making cheap fabrics for slaves to avoid competing with British textile mills making finer grade cotton products for White society. In Rhode Island alone, 84 mills made the coarse clothing for Black slaves. The importance of "Nigger Cloth" went beyond its utility. It was used to remind slaves of their place in society.

In 1822, a South Carolina White jury, responding to a legal complaint, emphasized the importance of slaves wearing ordinary clothes to keep them in their place. The jury said: "Negroes should be permitted to dress only in coarse stuffs. Every distinction should be created between Whites and Negroes, calculated to make Whites feel [their] superiority to Negroes." Today, West-Point Stevens Company is America's largest and most successful producer of bed and bath textiles. The company's Lady Pepperell brand remains one of its strongest labels.[11]

## ❦ THE ICE MAN DID COMETH ❦

Frederick McKinley Jones, a Black man, gave this country and the world the first refrigerated truck. Frederick McKinley Jones was born an orphan in 1893 and was only able to attend school through the sixth grade. His invention of the refrigerated truck gave shippers of perishable foods and products long-distance capability. Prior to refrigeration, shippers were limited to using unreliable, heavy blocks of ice. Once the ice melted, it lost its cooling capacity and products would spoil. After Jones' invention changed the transportation of products on land, he also invented a refrigerator unit for train boxcars. Some of his other inventions included, but are not limited to, the defroster, two-cycle gasoline engine, the starter generator and the internal combustion engine, which allowed fuel to be burned inside an engine rather than an external furnace. Frederick Jones registered most of his inventions around 1950.

Jones died in 1961, but his inventions with patents numbers 2,696,086; 2,475,841 and 2,526,874 continue to be used around the world. Thanks to Frederick Jones, refrigerated trucks and railroad cars now supply the daily food needs of large urban and smaller rural populations alike.[12]

## ❦ AN INVENTOR OF SAFETY DEVICES ❦

Richard B. Spike, a Black man, invented a device that made it possible for the typical motorist to drive automobiles with improved safety. Spike created a fail-safe brake that utilized hydraulics and electricity for vehicles with automatic transmissions. Some of Spike's other inventions included the flashing warning signal lights at railroad crossings and the turn signals on cars. Mr. Spike's Fail-Safe Brake is registered under patent number 3,015,522. Even though few Blacks owned automobiles in the early 1930s, Richard B. Spike's automobile safety devices made it possible for the next generation of Blacks to "drive and lean behind the wheel" 50 years later.[13]

## ❧ BLACK WALL STREETS? ❧

At the turn of the 20th century, Black Americans had thriving business communities across America. Two of the largest and most successful Black business districts, called Black Wall Streets, were located in Durham, North Carolina, and Tulsa, Oklahoma. Following the Civil War, Blacks' sense of unity, independence and segregation forced them to build communities, support Black-owned businesses and create their own employment opportunities. Durham had the first Black Wall Street, which was the role model for Tulsa's. The city had over 150 thriving businesses, including a number of Black banks and national insurance companies which boasted more than $200 million in combined assets and employed a large number of Black citizens. The Great Depression of the 1930s caused White business failures all across America. Yet, the Black-owned Mechanics and Farmers Bank in Durham boasted that it did not loose one Black business during the Great Depression. If the Great Depression could not destroy Black businesses in Durham, what did? Durham was killed off by social integration.

The second largest Black Wall Street died a different and more violent death. In the early 1900s, Durham's Wall Street inspired Black entrepreneurs in Tulsa to build a similar business district. By 1920, they had constructed numerous factories, hotels, transportation companies, theaters, restaurants, grocery and clothing stores and retail outlets. Fine residential housing and professional offices for Black doctors, dentists, lawyers and accountants lined the streets within the Black community. Blacks in Tulsa, Oklahoma, were actively practicing group economics, just like Whites and ethnic immigrants. However, Tulsa's White citizens, who had subordinated, exploited and segregated Tulsa's Black citizens, were envious of the prosperity Blacks enjoyed from practicing group economics, doing business with their own people and making their money bounce 8–12 times within their own communities. White envy was subdued racial hate. An incident in which a 19-year-old male accidentally stumbled on a jerky elevator and brushed against a White woman proved to be an incendiary event that gave Whites an excuse to riot and destroy Black lives, property and businesses.

*Faded postcard of Tulsa burning. (Library of Congress)*

For nearly a week, White mobs and thugs robbed and ransacked more than 1,400 Black homes, schools, churches and businesses. Local White police watched the rampaging White mobs attack defenseless Blacks. White pilots from a nearby air force base dropped turpentine bombs on Black homes, businesses and churches. At the riot's end, Whites had lynched and shot nearly 600 Blacks. Tulsa's Black Wall Street had been totally destroyed. During the following year, the surviving Blacks lived in tents donated by the American Red Cross, while Whites bought the burned out or abandoned properties at bargain prices. Whether by the hands of White rioters in Tulsa, Oklahoma, or integrationists in Durham, North Carolina, Black America has yet to recover from the economic losses of slavery, Jim Crow segregation and its two Black Wall Streets.[14]

## ❧ A BLACK OIL PRODUCER ❧

As automobiles increased in popularity, Black entrepreneurs knew they would need gas and oil to operate, so they began to develop supportive businesses with the emerging industries. In 1930, Odessa S. Strickland and a number of other Blacks in Shreveport, Louisiana, pooled their financial resources and organized the Universal Oil, Gas and Mining Company, the first and only Black-owned oil company in the United States. The Universal Oil Company was granted a charter on March 2, 1931. With only $20 in the treasury, Universal, with its Black personnel, began operating and drilling its own oil and gas wells. Within a decade, the company had over 51 employees and nine operating wells in Louisiana, Texas and Kentucky that produced nearly 380 barrels a day. The company's oil was pumped and sold to major White companies.

Realizing that Black landowners with oil deposits were not getting fair payment for their oil leases, royalties and sale of their resources, Strickland invented an "eletronometer," which could locate, trace and measure underground quantities of oil and gas. Experts in the petroleum field felt his machine was the best and most accurate for locating oil deposits. By the late 1930s, Blacks organized the Tiger Oil and Gas Company, another Louisiana oil company. The Tiger Company leased land and drilled for oil in both Louisiana and Texas. Both Universal and Tiger survived bank collapses and the Great Depression of the 1930s. But as the nation approached social integration of the late 1940s, Black Americans increasingly believed it was more important to have access to White businesses rather than for Blacks to have their own businesses. Within a generation, Black-owned oil companies had gone out of business.[15]

## ❧ YOUNG BOYS INCORPORATED ❧

For several years, Young Boys Incorporated was the most powerful and profitable Black business enterprise in America. The federal government estimates that the world trade in illegal drugs is about $400 billion per year. Americans are the largest consumers. America's consumption of illegal drugs made this the land of opportunity for at least one Black family in Detroit, Michigan, called the Chambers. Without Harvard business degrees, the Chambers brothers built the Young Boys Incorporated into an astoundingly successful and profitable business empire. The Chambers brothers' enterprises generated approximately $3 million a day in revenue. Their business employed nearly 500 people and set chilling new standards and concepts in marketing drugs. The brothers specialized in recruiting and employing young boys under 14 years of age from the South to carry and sell drugs. The young boys were well trained marketers and collection enforcers.

The most imaginative aspect of the family business was the age of the drug sellers. Because they were only 14 years or younger, they were beyond prosecution by the law. With a central office in Detroit, Michigan, the Young Boys serviced nearly all of the Mid-Western states. Their annual sales of more than one billion dollars in cocaine and marijuana made it the biggest and most profitable Black business in America. The authorities eventually busted the Chambers brothers. They had made a video of themselves swimming in a pool literally filled with money, and the tape fell into the hands of law enforcement. Like most Blacks who engage in illicit activities for profit, the Chambers brothers did not have an economic structure in their community through which to launder their ill-gotten gains. What did they do? They engaged in conspicuous consumption and painted a target on their own backs.[16]

## ❦ BLACKS INVENTED LOTTERY ❦

Today's state lotteries are a legalized outgrowth of a policy game that Samuel R. Young, a Black man, invented in 1885 in Chicago, Illinois. This game, popularly known as Playing the Numbers, thrived illegally in Black communities across America until the late 1950s. Policy became the biggest Black-owned business in the world, with combined annual sales in the 1930s reaching as high as $100 million dollars and employing tens of thousands of Black people nationwide. Blacks of all class levels, ages and education played the numbers. Groups of Black people owned and operated the policy business in every city. The groups had names such as "Digit Barons," "Numbers Bankers" and "Sportsmen," but the most common name was "Policy Kings." When Blacks controlled policy in Black communities, the Policy Kings were not necessarily viewed as gangsters. To many, they were good guys. They were guardian angels in Black communities. They built businesses, provided jobs, held politicians accountable and capitalized aspiring Black entrepreneurs. Policy dollars bankrolled Black banks, insurance companies, hospitals, businesses and politics. In the decades following the Great Depression of the 1930s, these Black Guardian Angels, or Robin Hoods, were pushed out of the policy game by White gangsters, social integration and state governments.

Samuel R. Young conceived of the policy game while watching gamblers on a Mississippi River boat. After migrating to Chicago, Illinois, Young began selling daily policy in Bronzeville, the city's Black community. To play policy, the number writer would write the bet and give the player a carbon slip as a receipt. Bets could be placed for as little as five cents and such a bet would pay five dollars. The player picked any three numbers between 1 and 78. The illegal daily policy spread to Harlem, in New York, where it was initially operated by Stephanie St. Clair (aka Madame Queen) and Ellsworth Bumpy Johnson.

By the mid-1930s, Al Capone had moved in on Black policy operators in Bronzeville, Illinois. Dutch Shultz, Lucky Luciano and other New York Mafia figures seized the game in Harlem. The newly arrived Italian and German immigrant mobsters saw Black policy as a money-making winner. Believing that Whites had a God-given right to own and control any and everything in Black communities, Whites used their unity, economic and political muscle to take over the illegally operated numbers houses in Black communities. In the decade following the Black Civil Rights Movement, state governments discovered how much money Black Americans were investing in daily policy and decided to take it from organized crime and make it a state operated daily lottery. Fifty years after the Mafia and state governments took over the policy game, Black Americans buy daily lottery tickets that drain rather than aid Black communities.[17]

## ❧ SLAVERY WAS INSURED ❧

Slaves were valuable property, so slave traders and slave-holders purchased life insurance policies to protect themselves from the loss of any slave by accident or natural disasters. By 1810, Lloyds of London held a monopoly on marine insurance and paid off on claims of "natural death" and "perils of the sea." However, slaves had to be examined by one of their representatives for soundness before any policies were issued. Policies valued slaves at two-thirds their market value, with rates set for one to five years. The annual premium for a policy on a Black male valued at $700 cost $11.85 per year. Claims were usually paid 60 to 90 days after proof of death.

Slave traders and plantation owners alike knew their policies could be rendered null and void if slaves escaped, were beyond the borders of the state or died as a result of suicide, dueling, war, neglect, abuse, mistreatment by the owner, riots, insurrections, revolts or law enforcement brutality. Some insurance companies were willing to accept greater risks. Companies like Lynchburg Hose and Fire Company, Albermarle Insurance Company and American Life Insurance and Trust Company advertised in local newspapers and assured their policyholders that neither war nor abolitionists could dislodge their responsibilities to their policy-holders. Most of these insurance companies went out of business after the Civil War.[18]

# BLOOD LINES AND BLOOD PHOBIAS

*"The soul of the flesh is in the blood." ~ The Holy Scriptures*

## Mini Facts

◆ *In the late 1600s, Sir William Phipps, a mulatto man, became the governor of the Massachusetts colony.*

◆ *In the 1860 U.S. Census, most Black mulattoes lived in the nation's urban areas and did not want to be too closely identified with non-mixed Blacks.*

◆ *In 1924, a study by the Carnegie Institute of Virginia concluded that Indians were mostly Negroes and mulattoes.*

◆ *In 1958, R.P. Stuckert, in the Ohio Journal of Science, reported that 57 percent of all White Americans had Black blood and 65 percent of all Black Americans had White blood.*

### 🖤 BLACK BY POPULAR DEMAND 🖤

On May 5, 2005, a *Washington Post* article answered one of Argentina's most enduring mysteries when it explained what happened to the descendants of the hundreds of thousands of African slaves that were shipped into Argentina centuries ago. As late as 1810, Black residents still accounted for approximately 30 percent of the population of Buenos Aires. By 1887, their numbers had dropped to 1.8 percent, and today, Argentina presents itself as an all-White country with a zero Black population. So where did all these hundreds of thousands of African Blacks and people in the Black blood line go?

Until recently, two popular hypotheses have been offered. One claim is that a yellow fever epidemic in 1871 devastated both urban and rural Blacks. Another claim is that in a brutal war with Paraguay in the 1860s, Blacks were put on the front lines where they were all killed. In truth, both hypotheses are little more than popular myths that are being challenged by a number of Argentinian scholars, who openly acknowledge their Blackness and want the Argentinian government to uncover and officially recognize what happened to the country's Black population. Recent door-to-door studies suggest that Black Argentinians neither died off nor were killed off. They just faded into the mixed-race category and became lost in the country's demographics. According to preliminary research, as much as 10 percent of the Buenos Aires residents are partly descended from Black slaves, but they have no idea of their history. Since the Argentinian government has not reflected African racial ancestry in its census for well over a century, most Argentinian citizens accept the notion that there are no Black people in the country. Anti-Black attitudes are so strong that when census or polltakers ask if anyone in the house has any Black ancestors, residents refuse to cooperate or answer, even though some clearly have traces of Black blood.

Miriam Gomes, a professor of literature at the University of Buenos Aires, is part Black and considers herself an Afro-Argentinian. Some of her associates claim they are being harmed by the country's desire to be an extension of European civilization. They want to examine DNA markers in the population and look at the impact of Black culture on the country and get a clearer picture of the percentage of Blacks in Argentina. Francisco R. Carnese, a geneticist at the University of Buenos Aires, said in a *Washington Post* article that: "When you walk around Buenos Aires, you don't see signs of African ancestry. But, you see it in the genes." The census takers intend to include African ancestry in the 2011 census. "If we're not counted," said Gomes, "there's no way to really convince people that we actually exist." Blackness in Argentina is expected to soon return by popular demand.[1]

## ❦ A President with Black Blood ❦

In the 1920s, Warren G. Harding, the 28th president of the United States, publicly admitted the possibility that he could be part Negro. Tongues wagged about Warren Harding's ancestry throughout his term in office. When Harding announced his engagement to Florence Kling in his hometown of Marion, Ohio, her father hit the ceiling, calling Warren G. Harding: "a God-damned nigger." The father threatened to personally blow Harding's head off if he ever trespassed onto Kling property. Kling's expression about Harding's racial heritage was not unusual. Residents in Harding's hometown of Cincinnati referred to him as a nigger, which he never denied. On one occasion, James Faulkner, a friend who was a writer for the *Cincinnati Inquirer*, put a direct question to Harding about his rumored "Black blood." Warren Harding responded: "How do I know, Jim? One of my ancestors may have jumped the fence."

Also, in the 1920s, William Eastbrook Chancellor, a college professor in Worchester, Ohio, claimed he had nothing personal against President Harding, but admitted he was strongly convinced that: "Warren Harding's election to the presidency was a plot by Black people to take over the United States." Professor

Chancellor's concern about a Black plot to overpower a ruling White majority belongs in the same category as a Tooth Fairy fantasy. President Harding may have had Black blood, but he was a card-carrying KKK member who never used his office to help Black Americans. Harding died in office in 1923. Within a year of his death, Congress enacted immigration laws that defined "Black" as a person with "one drop of Black blood."[2]

## ❦ IT TAKES ONE TO KNOW ONE ❦

In July 1969, *Life* magazine published photos of mothers of past presidents of the United States in the midst of the Black Power Movement and made what many perceived was an innocent, but major blunder. From the photo that *Life* ran of Ida Stover Eisenhower, it appeared to many Black Americans and others that she was a Black mulatto. The Life photo was taken on September 23, 1885, the day she married a young German immigrant named David Jacob Eisenhower. Ida Stover Eisenhower was a devoted Jehovah's Witness. She gave birth to six sons, one of whom was Dwight David Eisenhower, who later became the 34th president of the United States. Anthony T. Browder, in his book, *Nile Valley Contribution to Civilizations*, also had a photo of Ida Stover Eisenhower and makes references to her Negro features. Throughout his years of military service and tenure as president, public records do not indicate any references to Eisenhower having African ancestors. If our society were truly color-blind and race-neutral, why is it that nobody wants to be Black? Did Eisenhower do what many mixed-race individuals do — pass for White?[3]

*Ida Stover Eisenhower, Black Blood?*
*(Reprint permission granted from the Eisenhower Presidential Library.)*

## ❦ BLACK BLOOD IN THE OLDEST SENATOR ❦

According to Douglas Hall, a writer for the *Baltimore Afro-American* newspaper, Strom Thurmond, the powerful senator from South Carolina, had several Black relatives, including an uncle and two cousins who were living in Edgefield County, South Carolina, in the same year that Strom Thurmond was presidential nominee for the segregationist Dixiecrat Party. The Black Thurmonds, Robert Thurmond and Eva Thurmond Smith, told the Black press that they were members of the Strom Thurmond clan. Douglas Hall reported further: "It seems like everybody up there in Edgefield, South Carolina, are Thurmonds. They are all colors ... It is an old story and everybody in these parts knows it." Although it was common knowledge that White men had Black mistresses and spread their genes through the Black race, there are still many who continue to believe in the purity of White blood and White skin. The literal rape of the Black race which has occurred throughout American history and accounts for the rainbow colors within the Black race is still not openly discussed in polite circles or among many Whites.[4]

# ❦ FIRST JEWS WERE NOT WHITE ❦

In 2004, the most popular, controversial and financially successful movie was Mel Gibson's *The Passion of the Christ*. As the movie's producer, Mel Gibson went to great lengths to create the realism of last twelve hours of Jesus' life on earth and proclaimed that his movie was true to the New Testament. In the film, Jesus was portrayed as a White man, which contradicts common sense and the Bible. Contrary to the racists who proclaim Jesus was White and the sentimentalists who believe his color is unimportant so long as he is portrayed as White, Jesus was a dark man with African Black features. For Jesus to have materialized on earth as a human, he had to have physical human features that blended in with people living in North Africa at that time.

There is a reason that Bible scriptures repeatedly indicate that Jesus did not have a universal physical appearance. Had Jesus had White, Asian or Hispanics features, he would have stood out like a sore thumb in North Africa. Consequently, Biblical scriptures were very specific in their description of Jesus. His African genealogy is found in Matthew 1:1–16 and Luke 3:23–38. Revelations1:14–15 describe his skin color and hair texture as those of a Black or non-White man. The genealogies of his parents, Joseph and Mary, were both Hamitic and Semitic, closely associated with an African ancestry. In many locations in Europe, Asia and Africa, Jesus Christ and the Madonna, Mother of Christ, are depicted as Black.

Biblical genealogy from Adam to Jesus indicates Jesus and the Jews were Black or non-White. John the Baptist was Jesus' cousin and he had Afro-Asiatic features. When Joseph and Mary sought to escape Herod, they hid in and blended in the population in deepest Egypt, a Black nation. If Joseph and Mary had been White, they could not have been inconspicuous among people with Black, or very dark skin. In Exodus 4:6, Jehovah demonstrates his powers to Moses on the Mountain of Horeb. This demonstration revealed Moses' skin color. Jehovah said unto him: "Put thine hand into thy bosom." And he put his hand out, behold, his hand was white like snow. Jehovah again said, "Put thine hand into thy bosom." And behold, when he pulled it out behold, it was restored like the rest of his flesh. If Moses' hand was already white, it would not be a miracle for God to turn his hand white. However, since he did turn it white, then back to its original skin color, clearly Moses' skin was not white. If Black people were the original people, the first Jews, and all Jews from Adam to Jesus were required to only marry other Jews, Jesus would have to have been non-White. It is biologically impossible for a White Adam and Eve to produce white, yellow, brown and black-skinned offspring.

There are numerous other indicators of the race of Jesus. Justinian the Great, a Roman emperor, minted a gold coin that carried a depiction of Jesus as a wooly-headed Black man. Early statues and paintings depicted Jesus and Mary as Black. A Black Madonna statue is presently stored in the Vatican in Rome and she is venerated in many countries in the world. Worship of the Black Madonna and Isis, the Egyptian goddess, was well established in Europe by 1450 A.D. When Christianity moved from Africa to Europe, the physical features of Jesus and Jews changed. In 1508, Michelangelo was paid to paint the last supper on the ceiling of the Sistine Chapel in Rome. He used his White relatives as models for the paintings. It is ironic that when boxed-in, religious conservatives will insist that the race of Jesus is unimportant. Yet, as demonstrated in the *Passion* film, they do not care, just so long as the color of Jesus and the Jews is White.[5]

## SKIN COLOR TELLS INTEREST

The black-skin gal craves a house and lot,
The brown-skin gal wants a car;
The yaller-skin gal wants all a man's got —
and there you are![6]

## MYTH OF INDIAN AND BLACK ALLIANCES

Here's a myth buster! Alliances are normally created between people or groups who have common interests, needs or predicaments. Since alliances do not normally occur between competing groups, what was the common interest between American Indians and Blacks? If Indian and Black alliances had existed centuries ago, then there would be some historical remnants today. With the exception of some Seminoles, American Indians have never identified with nor championed the cause of Black Americans. White colonists told Indians they were preferred over Blacks and had acceptable blood that could easily mix with Whites. Indians were offered treaty incentives that encouraged them to participate in and profit from Black enslavement. The most noteworthy alliance between Blacks and an Indian tribe was between runaway Blacks and the Florida Seminoles. With the exception of some Florida Seminoles, all of the so-called Five Civilized Indian Tribes, (Choctaw, Chickasaw, Cherokee, Creek and Seminole) treated African Blacks as badly, if not worse, than European Whites. All major Indian tribes were slaveholders, catchers and traders and fought with the Southern Confederacy in support of Black enslavement. In 1865, after the Civil War, the United States government negotiated peace treaties with various tribes that required them to free their Black slaves.

Several famous Indian chiefs were particularly contemptuous in their dealings with Blacks. John Ross, a Cherokee Indian chief who personally owned fifty Black slaves, announced why he held such hate for Black people. Chief Ross said he and his brother understood the importance of Black slaves in developing new lands and routinely sent boats down the Mississippi River to buy and bring back as many as 500 Black slaves to be sold to Whites who were migrating West. In October 1860, in a speech to his tribesmen, Chief Ross attacked White abolitionists, saying: "Slavery has existed among the Cherokee for many years and is recognized by them as legal and they have no wish or purpose to disturb it or agitate it ... It is not an open question among us, but a settled one ... Our locality and institutions ally us to the South." Ross not only felt the South would win the Civil War, but like all of the Five Civilized Indian tribes, he supported the Southern Confederacy because Indians believed in Black enslavement, sovereignty of Indian tribes and land rights.

*Confederate General, Chief Stand Watie*

Another popular Indian leader, Chief Stand Watie, supported Black enslavement, despised Black people and was the last Southern Confederate general to surrender when the Civil War ended. Chief Stand Watie and his tribes carried out the Confederate's "Black Flag Policy" of not allowing Black Union soldiers or their White officers to surrender. In one Civil War battle, Chief Stand Watie ordered his troops to shoot every captured Black soldier wherever they could find them. American Indians understood that Black freedom in America was a social position that could only be granted by, and at the pleasure of, European Whites or American Indians. This social phenomenon alone encouraged American Indians to subordinate and avoid identifying with any form of Blackness.[7]

## 🐛 A BLACK MAN LIBERATED MEXICO 🐛

Vicente Guerrero was a Black mulatto and ex-slave who became the President of Mexico in April 1825. Vicente Guerrero freed Mexico from Spain and emancipated Blacks from 300 years of Mexican slavery. Until the 1800s, White Spaniards oppressed the poorer classes in Mexico, namely Blacks, mulattoes and Indians. When Guerrero and local insurgents defeated Spain's best army, the Mexican masses expressed their gratitude by installing Guerrero as "El Presidente." As the President of Mexico, Guerrero improved the country's social and economic conditions. He built schools and libraries, proclaimed religious liberty, established a coinage system and suspended the death penalty. However, his most profound achievement was to abolish slavery. Even though he used the United States Constitution as a model, Guerrero removed the practice of slavery when he established the Mexican constitution. He immediately ordered the release of every slave in Mexico. Reportedly 10,595 Black slaves and 1,050 Black-mixed mulattoes were still enslaved at that time. In the Mexican constitution, one of its clauses reads: "All inhabitants, whether White, African, or Indian, are free and qualified to hold office and property." Guerrero's emancipation proclamation was put into effect without resistance, except in the territory called Texas.

White Spaniards were the wealth holders. They owned the land and Black/mulatto slaves. They opposed Mexico's governance by a Black man, especially one who lacked a formal education. They conspired and eventually succeeded in driving Guerrero from public office and hanging him. He was buried in Mexico City. His widow and family received a state pension and were honored by having a state in Mexico named in his memory.[8]

## ❧ TOUSSAINT L'OUVERTURE BLINKED ❧

Toussaint L'Ouverture, the slave who freed Haiti, also helped indirectly to free nearly half of what is now the continental United States from French colonial rule. He rose to power during the age of revolution in the latter part of the 1700s and successfully led one of the greatest slave revolts in history. The Black Haitian revolt was so strong that they not only defeated General Napoleon Bonaparte and his army, but also forced France to drain its treasury and have to sell the Louisiana Territory to the United States at a price of five cents an acre. The aftermath of this revolt rendered more certain the final prohibition of the slave trade in the United States.

Shortly after liberating Haiti, Toussaint became magnanimous towards the French and paid a heavy price. The French had no intentions of simply being good losers. A French general invited Toussaint to his home for a conference, assuring him a safe return. Toussaint naively believed the general. When Toussaint arrived, the general declared Toussaint a prisoner, bound and shipped him to France. Upon arriving in France, Napoleon Bonaparte ordered Toussaint imprisoned at Fort Joux, high in the Alps and denied

him any outside communications. During nine months of imprisonment, Bonaparte's soldiers tortured Toussaint to make him
reveal where he had hidden his personal wealth. On April 27,
1803, Toussaint succumbed. He died of neurological complica-
tions and pneumonia. He was buried at St. Pierre, at the foot of the
fort. Had Toussaint lived, he was planning to extend his anti-
slavery fight into Africa. He had saved six million gold francs to
finance his war. However, he made the mistake of entrusting it to
a White American ship captain named Stephen Girard, who
refused to turn the money over to Toussaint's family. Laying claim
to Toussaint's wealth, Stephen Girard became one of the richest
Americans of his day. He founded and financed Girard College in
Philadelphia, Pennsylvania, for Whites only, with Toussaint's
money. Both Toussaint and Haiti paid a heavy price for defeating
General Bonaparte and being the first and possibly the only Black
country to overthrow European colonialism.[9]

## ❦ RACISM ❦

Racism, the offspring of slavery, is a group-based wealth and
power concept. It is a competitive relationship between groups of
people for the ownership and control of wealth, power and
resources. It is used by the wealthy and resource-holding group to
enslave, marginalize, segregate, subordinate, dominate or exclude
a weaker group. Racism is not synonymous with prejudice, bias,
bigotry and discrimination and has, therefore, become one of the
most misused words in the English language.

In earlier times, humans practiced tribalism, which is
different from racism. Racism never existed until the 1500s, when
nine European nations initiated a literal race to colonize the
resources of the newly discovered Western world using slave
labor and the material resources of Africa. Racism was built on
economic development and remained an economic concept

through the 16th and 17th centuries. When England, the world's biggest slave-trading nation, introduced the King James Version of the Bible and encouraged the use of Biblical scriptures to justify slavery, racism acquired a religious foundation. During the early 1800s, pseudo-scientists crafted evolutionary theories linking plants, animals, insects and humans in a descending order of development or evolution. Plants, animals and humans were ranked from the highest to the lowest. By 1859, slavery had maldistributed nearly 100 percent of the nation's wealth, power, resources and control of all levels of government into the hands of European Whites. Black slaves owned and controlled nothing. With educated Whites in control and impoverished and uneducated Blacks on the bottom, Charles Darwin, in his *Origin of the Species*, proclaimed Whites to be superior to Blacks.

In 1860, on the eve of the Civil War, the race was over. European Whites had effectively obtained a monopoly of ownership and control. Charles Darwin's *Origin of the Species* promoted the belief that groups of human beings should be ranked by order based on biological characteristics. Racism then became biological. Naturally, Charles Darwin, as a Caucasian, placed those features that best matched his own at the top of the ranking order. Thus, the myth of superior White skin was born. To protect and preserve superior White skin and blood, public policies required racial identification on birth certificates and all public documents. The Black Civil Rights Movement ended race-based Jim Crow segregation and reduced racism to a personal attitude, but it did not redistribute the ownership and control of resources, wealth and power into the hands of Black people. Racism went underground and re-emerged as conservatism, which maintains the status quo between Blacks and Whites.

*Inequality of Jim Crow segregation. (Library of Congress)*

Racism is a derivative of the word race, a contest. Once the race between nations for economic wealth and power was over, the letter "e" was removed from the word race and the suffix "ism" was added. The suffix "ism" means to maintain the status quo, or prevailing conditions. Racism means doing whatever is necessary to maintain the wealth and power inequalities between Blacks and Whites as a result of slavery and Jim Crow segregation. In proportional and comparative terms, Black Americans are just as impoverished and powerless today as they were in 1860 when the race for ownership and control of wealth and power ended. Black Americans cannot be racist and there is not one recorded instance in this nation's history where Black people have used their collective wealth and power to segregate, subordinate, enslave and exclude other groups. In their present powerless and impoverished condition, Black Americans can only react to racism. Since Whites, Asians, Arabs and Hispanics were slave-holders who benefited from slavery, they can legitimately be called racists, if and when they interfere with or oppose affirmative action, reparations or any other initiatives to eradicate the legacies of slavery from the shoulders of Black people.[10]

## ❦ QUOTABLE NOTABLE ❦

President Harry Truman's racial views were aligned with those of the Ku Klux Klan, an organization he joined in his youth in the 1920s. Truman was elected president of the United States in 1948. In a letter to his future wife, Bess, he wrote in 1911: "I think one man is just as good as another so long as he's not a nigger or a Chinaman. Uncle Will says that the Lord made a White man from dust, a nigger from mud, then He threw up what was left and it came down a Chinaman. He hated Chinese and Japs. So do I. It is race prejudice, I guess. But, I am strongly of the opinion Negroes ought to be in Africa, Yellow men in Asia, and White men in Europe and America."[11]

## ❦ DID GRINGOS STEAL MEXICO'S LAND? ❦

A primary goal of numerous organizations within the National Hispanic Movement is to take control of the Southwestern states. These organizations claim the United States took the Southwest territory from Mexico. According to historical facts, that it is not true. The United States actually won rights to own Texas, California, New Mexico and Arizona as victors in the Mexican-American War. Under the rules of war, the United States government had military and legal justification to lay claim, not only to the Southwest territory, but to all of Mexico. Fortunately for Mexico, the United States government did not fully exercise that right. Instead, the United States purchased 500,000 acres of land — in what is now California, New Mexico, Arizona and Texas — from Mexico for $15 million. The United States government even paid Mexico nearly $4 million in reparation damages. The Southwest Territory had such a low value at that time that according to comparable real estate values, the $19 million the U.S. paid was a substantial overpayment. Comparable American land could be purchased for $5 per acre at that time. Yet, for 500,000 acres of western land, the United States government paid Mexico $38 per acre, six times the normal amount.

Businessmen and politicians generally believed the United States had overpaid for the land. After purchasing the Southwest territory, President Zachary Taylor commissioned Captain William Tecumseh Sherman to explore and survey the newly acquired territory and determine its true value. Captain Sherman spent two years traversing and surveying the sandy, mountainous and cactus-ridden country in which even rattlesnakes had a hard time surviving. When Captain Sherman returned to the White House with his report, President Taylor asked if he believed the land was worth the nearly $19 million dollars and the lives of ten thousand men. Sherman looked at President Zachary Taylor and said: "I've been out West and looked the land over, all of the country, and between you and me, I feel that we'll have to go to war again."

"What for?" asked the President.

"Why," answered Sherman, "to make them take the darn land back."

In Captain Sherman's opinion, the land was not worth the $19 million that was paid for it. Moreover, since the United States won its war with Mexico, it did not have to buy the Southwest Territory. In reality, the United States paid $19 million dollars for land that it legitimately owned.[12]

## ❦ BLACK SARCASM ❦

The code of conduct for slaves required Blacks to be respectful of Whites at all times. Blacks learned how to best them by skillfully using sarcastic humor to express their true feelings. In the dialogue below, a Black Pullman car porter expresses his feeling and frustrations to a White female passenger.

"Why are the passengers looking out of the windows?" a little old White lady asked the Black Pullman car porter.

"We ran over a cat, ma'am."

"You mean the cat was on the railroad tracks?" said the little old woman.

The porter rolled his eyes. "No," he finally replied, "the train done left the tracks and chased it down the alley!"

~ Author Unknown

# CHAPTER 9

# THE ENRICHED AND THE ENSLAVED
*Black people have made everybody rich but themselves.*

## Mini Facts

◆ *In the years immediately after the Revolutionary War, Rhode Island merchants controlled between 60–90 percent of the American trade in African slaves.*

◆ *From 1660 to 1860, White society invested nearly $8 billion in Black slaves, which was more than what they invested in all their other businesses and government enterprises.*

◆ *In 1860, on the eve of the Civil War, free Blacks owned ½ of 1 percent of the nation's wealth; in 2004, over a century later, Blacks still owned only ½ of 1 percent of the nation's wealth.*

◆ *On December 31, 1865, slavery was abolished not by the Emancipation Proclamation, but by the 13th Amendment to the Constitution. President Abraham Lincoln was killed 8 months earlier.*

# ❦ Founding Fathers Left No Fingerprints ❦

According to John Quincy Adams, slavery and its practices dominated the discussions of the Founding Fathers during the drafting of the United States Constitution. They eventually reached a "slavery compromise" at the Constitutional Convention, which recommended the use of vague and illusive language on the topic of slavery. The Constitution drafters judiciously avoided using the words "Negro" or "Black." Even the word "slave" was used only twice. Instead, the writers used very indefinite terminology, such as "those who are bonded," or "persons held in service or labor."

Why did the Founding Father resort to such tactics? Luther Martin, a Maryland attorney who opposed ratification of the Constitution, reported that the delegates "anxiously sought to avoid the admission of expressions and labels which might be odious to the ears of Americans. But, they were willing to admit into their system those things which the expressions and labels signified." The writers and drafters of the Constitution knew the slaves were Black people. But like good magicians, the writers felt they had to make both the images of slavery and Black slaves disappear while codifying Black slavery by using indefinite terms, such as "those bound to service," "such persons," "those imported," "persons held to service or labor," "other persons," and "such male inhabitants." These euphemisms allowed a White nation to disengage its conscience while viciously exploiting, killing and crippling millions of Black people. The Founding Fathers knew that if there were no legal fingerprints, history would have a difficult time identifying and holding the perpetrators accountable for the massive damage they had committed on people of African descent. Using indefinite and ambiguous terms in the Constitution allowed every generation of Whites to enjoy the thrill of being White without the discomfort of paying the bill for injustice.

Frances D. Adams and Barry Sanders write in their book, *Alienable Rights*, about why and how the Constitutional Convention deliberations were kept secret for over fifty years. In 1840, the precise details of the closed-door proceedings in Philadelphia became public. James Madison had kept detailed records of the meetings, and although he was pressured to release his notes, he insisted that they not be made public until all the Founding Fathers were dead. In 1836, Madison, the last surviving member of the Convention, died. John Quincy Adams made Madison's notes available to the public. The notes revealed how the Founding Fathers had conspired to keep the public ignorant of the slavery-related issues and concerns that dominated the discussions and drafting of the U.S. Constitution. Since the Constitution was nearly silent on the issue of slavery, who would have guessed slavery had been such an overriding concern of the delegates? When Madison's notes became public in 1840, abolitionists condemned the Founding Fathers for conspiring and crafting a Constitution that marginalized slavery and erased the identity of the slaves.

It is unfortunate that governmental authorities continue to employ the technique of using broad, indefinite and ambiguous terms to discuss solutions for Black peoples' problems. The technique was used to draft the 13th, 14th and 15th Amendments and thirteen civil rights laws. In the post-Black Civil Rights Movement, Black Americans have been buried under terms like minority, diversity, multicultural, poor people and people of color. These broad and ambiguous terms are racist in nature because they imply that Blacks are no different or have not historically been treated differently than any other population group. Therefore, society uses those broad and ambiguous terms as an excuse to do absolutely nothing to lift the legacies of slavery and Jim Crow segregation from the shoulders of Black Americans.[1]

## ❦ THE LITTLE YELLOW BRICK SLAVE HOUSE ❦

In our nation's capital, between 7th and 8th streets, south of the Smithsonian Institute, there once stood a three-story, yellow brick house that was known as the best private jailhouse for Blacks in America. The Yellow Brick House was used to hold Blacks for almost any reason. Many politicians and businessmen confined their slaves to the jail just for safekeeping while the owner conducted business. William H. William owned this private jail-house and made enough money to purchase two ships for hauling slaves to distant markets. Using his private jail as a collection center, William ran public advertisements offering to pay cash for unwanted Negroes who could be sold into Southern slavery. Solomon Northrup, a free Black who wrote an enduring book about his life as a slave, was once confined to William's Yellow Brick House. In 1841, James H. Birch, a notorious slave trader, drugged, kidnapped and stowed Solomon Northrup in this house before shipping him to New Orleans to be sold. The most dastardly use of the Yellow Brick House was to store and fatten up Black children before shipping them "down the river" into slavery. Unlike the famous yellow brick road that led "over the rainbow," William's Yellow Brick House was a gateway to hell![2]

## ❦ SLAVEHOLDER'S HUMOR ❦

When the first group of captive Black slaves arrived in America, they were led down the gangplank in chains and lined up on the dock. The White ship captain noticed a chained slave muttering angrily to two other slaves. Curious about what was being said, the captain walked over to the chained slaves and said:

"What's the matter with you? You are just like most Blacks. You've been in this country less than five minutes and already you're complaining."[3]

## 🍎 THE FATHER OF THE COUNTRY'S SLAVES 🍎

Following a winter ride in December 1799, George Washington fell ill with a throat infection that restricted his breathing. Washington's doctors followed standard medical procedures of the day and attempted to "bleed" the infection out of him. He was subjected to daily bleedings. As he grew weaker, Washington responded: "I die hard, but I am not afraid to go." On December 14, 1799, just two months before his sixty-eighth birthday, Washington died.

In his will, Washington passed his material wealth and slaves to his wife. He wanted her to enjoy the benefits of owning slaves, but suggested she consider freeing them upon her death. In his will he stated: "Upon decease of my wife, it is my will and desire that all the slaves which I hold in my own right shall receive their freedom." Since he did not free his slaves while he lived, George Washington forced his wife, Martha, to live with them in fear. Martha understood that all the slaves knew that her life stood between them and freedom. She became depressed, fearing that some of the slaves were plotting to kill her. Hoping to find relief, she went to the court and drew up a document that gave her the right to free nearly all her 125 Black slaves while she was still living. Martha Washington lived for another year after granting freedom to her husband's slaves and his conscience. George Washington did in death what he would not do in life. He freed his slaves.[4]

## ❦ A SLAVE SONG ❦

The meritorious manumission policy that rewarded slaves for betraying their fellow slaves appeared in songs sung by Blacks. One of the most popular slavery songs was "Run Nigger Run," sometimes called "The Patteroll Song." It was a simple song that the slaves sang to tout the White gangs who roamed the roads looking for Black runaway slaves.

———⟨◆⟩———

Run nig ... Run,
De Patteroll git ye!
Run nig ... Run,
He's almost here!

*Patterollers check papers. (Library of Congress)*

Please Mr. Patteroll,
Don't ketch me!
Jest take dat nig ...
What's behind dat tree.

This song told of the predicament of Blacks and the deference they held for the White man, but more importantly, it told of the willingness of a Black slave to sacrifice another member of his own race to save himself.[5]

## ❦ THE RAINBOW AND JESUS ❦

Humans assign magical qualities to the rainbow. In fantasies, the rainbow symbolizes a road leading to happy places and pots of gold. It was true for Europeans in the 16th century. In 1645, one of the first American slave ships bound for Africa was named the *Rainbow* and it sailed from Boston to the west coast of Africa, which became their rainbow's end. White slave traders found their pot of gold in the captured African Blacks and Africa's mineral riches. African Blacks became known as black gold and the west coast of Africa was popularly known as the Gold Coast.

After the African Blacks had been captured, chained and stripped of their families, humanity and religion, they were shipped to America. The first slave ship that brought Blacks to America as cargo was named ... *Jesus*. For a hundred years, masters and other authorities used the Bible to condition Blacks for a life of slavery. They were taught to be obedient, humble and Christ-like and to look for the pie in the sky after death. Although the *Jesus* brought them into slavery, the slaves looked to Jesus for rescue.[6]

## ❦ NOT WORTH TWO CENTS ❦

It is sometimes said that a Black person is not worth two cents. At least one White person put his valuation of a Black person on paper. On June 23, 1819, *The National Messenger* in Richmond, Virginia, ran the following advertisement. Was the slave owner seriously interested in the return of Zadock Tucker, or was he simply being sarcastic? The advertisement in the paper read:

### One Half Cent Reward

Ran-away from the subscriber, on the 19th inst. Zadock Tucker.He is about 15 years old, 4 feet high: has an impudent look, and pert mannerof answering when spoken to — had on when he absconded, a velvet roundaboutand domestic pantaloons. He took with him some other articles, which are not recollected. All persons are forewarned against harboring the said boy.Whoever may deliver him to me shall receive the above reward, but no thanks.

~ Benj. Mayfield

## ❦ THE CASTRATION COMPLEX ❦

Castration was a technique to physically and psychologically control Black males. In South Carolina, for instance, one of the harshest slave states, a public policy promoted castration of any Black male slave who ran away from his owner four times. Similarly, in North Carolina, between 1755 and 1765, the state sentenced more than 17 Black slaves to castration for running away. These examples illustrate that slave masters had concluded that the prospect of this horrendous punishment was by itself a means of social control.

In husbandry practices, farmers castrated unruly male livestock to quiet their demeanor and disposition. Most slaveholders hoped that what castration achieved in animals would translate into a social control for Black male humans and curtail their high spirits and potentially malicious and vindictive tempers, which caused them to steal and run away. Slaves were chattel and, therefore, no different from field animals. After slavery ended, Whites continued to castrate Black males as punishment for any real or perceived infraction of Southern racial codes. But, more than anything else, castration was a means of eliminating Black men as competitors for wealth, power and women.[7]

## CONFEDERATE CURRENCY

Governments put images on their money of persons and objects that are of cultural importance. In 1862, Salmon Chase, the secretary of the Treasury, added the motto: "In God We Trust" to the first federal paper money, called the greenback. The sentimental values and history of a people are on their currency. The Confederate South was no exception. The South put cotton and slavery on their notes. During the Civil War, the importance of Southern slavery and Black labor was engraved on approximately 21 different forms of currency in different Southern states. However, placing images of slavery on currency had started as early as the 1820s. By the Civil War, slavery images were familiar on $2, $5, $10, $20 and $50 bills. These images most often portrayed Black slaves working together in the fields planting, carrying or harvesting cotton. Some even pictured Black women with babies on their backs working alongside the men.

The depiction of slavery and its symbols on currency indicated its supreme importance and value. As early as the 1500s when the international slave trade first began to exploit Guinea, West Africa, the British originated the British Guinea, a gold coin that became the chief English currency used by slave traders who took gold and slaves from the country of Guinea. During the Revolutionary War of the 1770s, the United States Treasury put a Black man on the back of the $2 bill that commemorated the Continental Congress' signing of the Declaration of Independence in 1776. The Black man, who is clearly a part of the group depicted on the back of the $2 bill, reportedly is John Hanson, the president of the Continental Congress. These $2 bills were taken out of circulation in the closing years of the 20th century. In the 1940s, the facial profiles of George Washington Carver, a noted Black scientist, and Booker T. Washington, a Black educator, showed up on commemorative fifty-cent coins. In 1976, President Jimmy Carter appointed Elsie Morton, a Black woman, to the position of secretary of the Treasury, which allowed her to sign all United States currency.

Ironically, Black people might have been on the money, but they had little access to much of it. Centuries after slavery, during the civil rights movement of the 1960s, Rev. Martin Luther King Jr. was amazed when he discovered adult Black sharecroppers in Alabama who had never possessed real money or U.S. currency in their entire lives. As sharecroppers, they worked on White plantations for script, which they used to purchase merchandise in local White businesses.[8]

## ❦ BLACKS WERE CASH ❦

Over the past five centuries, Black people have been used in every imaginable way. But, how many people knew that Black slaves were so valuable that they were used as a form of currency by the military during the Revolutionary War? In 1781, General Thomas Sumter established the use of slaves as payment to the soldiers under his command. For example, one colonel who had served with Sumter for ten months was paid three grown slaves and a child. A major was paid three adult slaves. A captain received two adult slaves, and so on according to descending rank. Even privates of the lowest rank in the military received one slave each. General Sumter didn't just pull this pay plan out of thin air. He acquired the slaves that he used as currency from some of the most prominent colonists and Founding Fathers in the colonies.

When Thomas Jefferson was governor of Virginia, he signed a bill granting every White male who enlisted for the war: "300 acres and a healthy, sound Black slave, between the ages of 20 and 60, or 60 pounds of gold or silver." When the colonial army recaptured Georgia, slaves were even given to public officials in lieu of a salary. The British loyalists answered the colonial patriots saying: "If the rebels will give one Black slave for one year of service, let us give two." In this instance, Black slaves were not on the currency. They were cash![9]

## 🌿 AMERICA'S BLACK PIRATES 🌿

Fugitive slaves and free Blacks established Maroon colonies all along the routes of the slave ships, the coastal areas of Southern states from Virginia to Texas and the Caribbean Islands. These coastal areas were made up of numerous barrier islands and coves that provided easy cover for runaways, pirates or outcast criminal groups. These communities were just ripe for pirates. Pirate societies were egalitarian relative to the respectable societies upon which they preyed. Pirates did not mind robbing and kidnapping any- and everybody. When they preyed upon slave ships, they were known to enlist the liberated cargo in their adventures. Luis Aury, a famous pirate with a crew of Blacks who were known as Aury's Blacks, operated out of and ruled Amelia Island, near Jacksonville, Florida. Even though most of the pirates themselves were Black, Aury's pirates trafficked profitably in slave trading. The Black pirates of Amelia Island apparently believed in equal opportunity for pirates. Since slavery was enriching everybody else, why not Black pirates?[10]

## ❧ BLACK LEADER OPPOSED ❧ 40 ACRES AND A MULE

Frederick Douglass was a great Black leader, but in at least one instance, his compromising attitude injured Blacks and was an impediment to newly released slaves receiving reparations. Slavery ended and the nation abandoned nearly five million Black people who had no land, jobs, animals, tools, weapons, clothes, education or protection. Powerless and impoverished, the government left them to either sink or swim, knowing they had never been trained to swim and did not have any boats. Radical Republicans in Congress, such as Thaddeus Stevens, Charles Sumner and George Julian, favored massive wealth and land redistribution to ex-slaves. Unfortunately, Frederick Douglass, the most visible Black leader of that day, was naive about how a slavery-crippled Black race could survive and compete with an advantaged, slave-owning White race.

In 1862, Douglass spoke about what should be done for newly freed slaves. Instead of being an advocate for the forty acres and a mule, Douglass said: "Let them [ex-slaves] alone. Our duty is done better by not hindering than by helping our fellow men ... The best way to help them [ex-slaves] is just to let them help themselves." White racists had the same leave-Blacks-alone attitude. A conservative White congressman spoke for White America when he said slaveholders were sick and tired of taking care of slaves, and it was time for Blacks to work and take care of themselves. In his mind, ex-slaves had to "either work or perish." Within forty years, the 1862 immigration policies brought in 26 million European immigrants who were granted free land, welfare benefits and job opportunities that ex-slaves were denied. In 2005, nearly one hundred and forty years later, conservative Whites and a sizable number of Blacks are still opposed to any public programs or policies to specifically benefit and lift the legacies of slavery off of the shoulders of Black Americans.[11]

## ❦ BLACK AMERICANS, AN ❦ UNPROTECTED CLASS

The United States Constitution codified the exclusion of three groups of people — Blacks, American Indians and women — from enjoying the full benefits of living in the Land of Opportunity. The country's Founding Fathers authorized these exclusions for the sole purpose of handicapping these groups. However, over the course of the last two centuries, government has sought to make amends with American Indians and women by placing them in legally protected classes. Government policies stipulate that Indians deserve to be protected by the government because they were weak, poor and defenseless. Therefore, after the Indian wars ended, Indians were put in a protected class and placed under a "doctrine of trust." This made them wards of the government. The federal government provided Indians with land, medical assistance, tuition-free education, housing, social services, publicly funded bureaus and tax-exempt status. Contrarily, at slavery's end, government abandoned Black ex-slaves, leaving them poor, disorganized, homeless, ignorant, jobless, landless, defenseless and without tools or animals. American Indians receive more for having fought Whites than Blacks received for having enriched, labored and cared for Whites.

Women, like American Indians, are in a protected class. In the U.S. Constitution, the Founding Fathers legally limited women because they were considered an extension of the White male, her protector. Through the centuries, the court system, social chauvinism and cultural customs have kept White women, along with their children, in a protected class. White women co-owned, co-controlled, co-influenced and inherited nearly 100 percent of everything White men owned. In some states, White women had the right to vote two hundred and fifty years before Black women. Black women and their children, like Black men, were in an endangered class rather than a protected class.

No group was any worse off than ex-slaves, but the federal government did not place ex-slaves under a protective doctrine of trust. The Freedman's Bureau was an acknowledgment by the government that Blacks deserved to be placed in a protected class. Under authorization of the U.S. War Department, in May 1865, General O.O. Howard began operating the Bureau of Refugees, Freedmen and Abandoned Lands that was popularly called the Freedman's Bureau. Just like modern-day affirmative action programs, the bureau's short-lived program for freedman was broadened to provide benefits for "poor people" and Southern Whites, who received the lion's share of the benefits. By including Whites and other groups, the racial inequalities and hierarchy remained unchanged. Since Black Americans are still burdened by the legacies of slavery and Jim Crow segregation, government still has a legal and moral obligation to place Blacks in a protected class, just like American Indians and women. Contrary to the wishes of Black civil rights leaders, it should not be necessary for Black Americans to compete with an endless list of newly declared minorities who the government qualifies for affirmative action benefits that they have not earned.

## ❦ GEORGIA: A BUFFER ZONE ❦

In 1732, England issued a royal charter to establish the Georgia colony. Georgia was unique because it came into existence as the thirteenth colony as a socio-political experiment to protect the other colonies. In response to the 1705 Slave Codes and Diversity Act that required five White persons be available to supervise and monitor every Black slave, several philanthropic individuals in London decided to establish the Georgia colony as a buffer colony and to inhabit it with Whites from England's debtor prisons, poverty rows and mental institutions. South Carolina plantation owners were concerned about physical attacks from runaway slaves and Indians who lived in Florida and had long petitioned the Continental Congress to establish some kind of a buffer between South Carolina and Spanish-owned Florida. The Indians and runaway slaves were such a problem to the slave owners that they saw no reason to oppose the British government's decision to empty out their institutions and ship all of their criminals and castoffs to Georgia.

However, three decades later, when the state of Georgia was threatened by hostile Indians and Florida Spaniards, the Georgia colony was short of able-bodied outcasts to fight its battles. This time, the colonial government encouraged free Blacks to migrate into Georgia and defend the state. Many Blacks did and in return for their services, the state promised to grant them the same rights as a person born of British parents, which it never did. However, a mulatto class of free Blacks who passed for Whites did live reasonably well in Atlanta, Georgia, during slavery and Jim Crow segregation.[12]

## 🐛 A RHYME IN THE BLACK TOWN OF BOLEY 🐛

———————————⟨◆⟩———————————

Say, have you heard the story
Of a little colored town
Way over in the nation
On such a lovely sloping ground?

With as pretty little houses
As you ever chanced to meet,
With not a thing but Colored folks
A-standing in the streets.
Oh, 'tis a pretty country,
And the Negroes own it, too.
With not a single White man here,
To tell us what to do, in Boley [13]

## 🌿 WHO WERE BLACK MAROONS? 🌿

Fugitive slaves had no interest in returning to White plantations. They wanted to live in separate communities with their own leaders, political systems and resources. They built economically independent and self-sufficient communities in wildernesses or wherever they could find a safe haven in the Americas or the Caribbean Islands. They wanted to make it as difficult as possible for slave chasers to find them. Runaways who survived combined their skills and resources to build homes, raise crops and livestock. Working together, they created their own languages, customs, arts and laws that blended African traditions with European and Indian ideas. In some instances, they created alliances with Indians, pirates and other social outcasts. Successful communities armed themselves and challenged the notion of Black slavery and White European dominance. Runaways called their newly formed independent colonies, Maroon communities. The largest, most successful and durable Maroon communities were in Spanish Florida, before it became a part of the United States. [14]

# CHAPTER 10

# MILITARY AND WARS

*Black Americans were soldiers in war times,
and hated third-class citizens in times of peace.*

## Mini Facts

◆ *In the 1860s, Stand Watie, a Cherokee Chief, was the first Indian appointed to the rank of general in the Southern Confederate Army.*

◆ *In 1864, Champ Ferguson, a guerrilla fighter for the Southern Confederacy, was hanged in front of U.S. Colored Troops for reportedly massacring Black prisoners.*

◆ *On October 1, 1890, Augustus Walley, a Black Buffalo Soldier, was awarded the medal of honor for bravery in rescuing a wounded trooper under fire by Apache Indians.*

◆ *In 1943, Lt. Charles Hall, of the Tuskegee Airman 99th Pursuit Squadron, was the first Black pilot to shoot down a Nazi plane. His squadron did not lose a single American bomber.*

# 🐛 HANNIBAL, MILITARY GENIUS 🐛

With his military concepts and tactics of warfare being taught in military academies around the world, Hannibal is recognized as the greatest warrior and military mind the world has ever known. Hannibal's father introduced him to warfare during an unsuccessful campaign in the First Punic War. Hannibal swore to his father an eternal hatred for Rome. Hannibal assumed control of the Carthaginian army while in his mid-twenties. Driven by a hatred for Romans, he and his troops marched through Spain and France. He challenged the Roman Empire and conquered most of Italy by performing the astounding feat of crossing the Alps with 50,000 men and 40 elephants. His guerilla warfare tactics and strategies are still taught in military courses around the world.

What is not widely known and accepted, according to J.A. Rogers, is the reality that Hannibal was a full-blooded Black man. Hannibal was born about 247 B.C., northeast of modern Tunis in North Africa. The only firsthand information available about Hannibal is in the writings of White Romans, who respected and feared his military genius, but hated him as an enemy. Consequently, they usually depicted Hannibal as a White man. However, J.A. Rogers asserts that coins in the British Museum in England, and the Museo Kercheriano Museum in Rome, Italy, show Hannibal to have been a pure African with rings in his ears. Rogers quoted Colonel Hennebert, a leading authority of Hannibal, who said: "We do not possess any authentic portrait of Hannibal, but these coins were struck by Hannibal when he was in Italy. In the absence of other information, the most logical argument is that they bore his own effigy. Above all, let us remember that he was an African."[1]

# 🍂 REMEMBER FORT NEGRO, A BLACK ALAMO 🍂

Long before Florida became part of the United States, it was a sanctuary to thousands of runaway slaves seeking freedom and a better life. Equally, a countless number of international crimes and horrendous injustices were committed against Black people in Florida. The massacre of nearly 300 Black women and children at Fort Negro on the Apalachicola River was one of those incidents. In the 17$^{th}$ and 18$^{th}$ centuries, England, Spain and the American colonies were locked into a struggle over the development of southeastern North America. The Spanish crown, the owners of the Florida territory, invited Blacks to migrate to and live in Florida. In two separate treaties, in 1795 and 1819, the Spanish crown declared all Blacks living in Florida free citizens and, therefore, entitled to all the rights and privileges of citizenship. The British fought and lost two wars with America. The last one was in 1812. After that loss, the British decided they could get back at America by going into Spain's Florida territory and providing free Blacks money, military resources and fortified communities. The English helped Blacks build, own and control Fort Negro, which was situated on eight acres at Prospect Bluff on the Apalachicola River, in Spanish West Florida. Fortified communities, such as Fort Negro on the Apalachicola River, and Fort Muse near Jacksonville, Florida, gave Blacks a strong military presence in Florida.

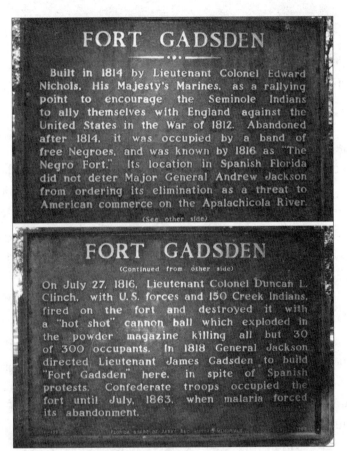

*Front and back of sign at original site of Fort Negro in the Apalachicola National Forest, Florida (Photo by author)*

Fort Negro became a problem for the United States government and Southern businesses that were illegally using the Apalachicola River to transport slave-produced products from Tennessee to the Gulf of Mexico. Nearly 1,000 Black Maroons and Black Seminoles inhabited Fort Negro and monitored the river's boat traffic. White planters and businessmen were angry that their slave-produced products could be controlled by Blacks at Fort Negro and feared that the very existence of a free slave community would serve as a magnet to attract more runaways.

Even though Fort Negro, Florida, was in a foreign country, slave-holders convinced General Andrew Jackson to invade Florida, destroy all Black forts and Black communities and capture any runaway Black slaves.

In 1816, General Jackson launched his first attack on Fort Negro. The fort was a massive structure located atop a 12-foot bluff with walls 18-feet thick and 12-feet high. Undeterred, General Jackson sent 800 American soldiers and 150 Creek Indians down the Apalachicola River to attack the fort. At the time of the attack, most of the men were away from the fort. Only 15 men guarded the fort and the 270 Black women and children who were inside. For more than two weeks, neither General Jackson's soldiers nor his naval fleet could mount the fort's wall or best the Black riflemen. The fort's defenders fought fiercely, that is, until a U.S. naval vessel fired a heated cannon ball that bounced into the fort's armory and set off a massive explosion. The explosion destroyed Fort Negro and killed nearly 300 women and children. Their body parts were buried in mass graves in the rear of the fort. Today, the burial spots are marked by a plaque and noticeable depressions in the earth. The commemorative plaque reads: "This is the burial site of 270 renegade Black slaves." *Webster's Standardized Dictionary* defines renegades as a group who abandons one's group interest and cause to take up the interest and cause of another. Were the runaways renegades? Quite the opposite! They were innocent women and children fighting for their freedom and lives.

The U.S. government subsequently built a much smaller fort called Fort Gadsden within the footprint of the old Fort Negro. Fort Gadsden was burned down two years after it was built. Today, tourist signs and information identify the site as Fort Gadsden instead of Fort Negro. For over a century, the Spanish government had invited Blacks, including these nearly 300 Black freedom fighters and their ancestors, to live in Spanish Florida. Spain guaranteed them freedom and all the rights of citizenship. A generation after General Jackson's invasion and the Three Seminole Wars, the United States marched White Indians, Black Seminoles and recalcitrant runaways to Oklahoma territory, in what is commonly called The Trail of Tears. This trail began running at the mass gravesite behind Fort Negro on the Apalachicola River.[2]

## ❦ SPIES FOR THE UNION ❦

One of America's little known secrets is the key role that Blacks played in the Civil War. Contrary to popular history, the nearly five million free and enslaved Blacks were not passive observers. From the outset, the Union military had a great advantage it termed Black Dispatches, which referred to intelligence slaves collected about the Confederate forces. The Northern Union Army found the prolific information it received from free and enslaved Blacks the single most productive category of intelligence obtained by and acted upon by Union forces throughout the Civil War. Union military leaders counted on their Black spies. The Southern Confederacy was very aware of the damage that Black soldiers and spies were inflicting.

In May 1863, General Lee admitted that: "The chief source of information to the enemy is through our Negroes." General Lee was not the only White Southerner making such public statements. Patrick Cleburne, a prominent Arkansas lawyer, argued that the primary reason the South was losing the war was because while Black slaves were the South's strength at the beginning of the war, they soon became the South's weakness. Clebourne felt that free and bonded Blacks were an: "Omnipresent spy system, pointing out our valuable men to the enemy, revealing our positions, and resources, and yet acting so safely and secretly that there is no means to guard against it." Union military leaders counted on their Black spies.

Slaves were more than just spies. Millions of free and bonded Blacks worked as soldiers, cooks, personal attendants, medical aides, construction workers, common laborers, guides, advisors and rescuers. The more adventuresome free and bonded Blacks spied and reported on Confederate troop movements and fortifications. Blacks aided the escape of many Union soldiers from prison camps, providing them with clothing, food, and hiding them within slave cabins. When the time was right, Blacks guided escaping Union soldiers back to their own military lines, using a covert network. Blacks gave the North an advantage over the South because the Southern Confederacy was surrounded by and dependent on its free and bonded Blacks, who were more than willing to cooperate with the North. The South's detachment from reality became its weakness. Until the final days of the war, ranking officials in the Confederacy as well as slave owners continued to believe they had good relationships with their Blacks, who they thought were happy as slaves.[3]

## 🐛 INTELLIGENT QUOTE 🐛

"In order to get beyond racism, we must first take account of race. There is no other way ... In order to treat persons equally, we must treat them differently." Statement by Supreme Court Justice Harry Blackmun, in the Regents of the University of California v. Bakke case in 1978.

## 🐛 THE FIRST BLACK NAVAL AVIATOR 🐛

At the age of 24, Jesse Leroy Brown became the first Black Navy pilot and was also the first Black Navy pilot to die in combat in the line of duty. On December 4, 1950, Brown's plane was shot down in Korea while he was providing close air support for United States Marines fighting and trapped at the infamous

Chosin Reservoir that bordered Communist China. As a member of the Navy's Fighting Squadron 32, Lieutenant Brown was posthumously awarded the Distinguished Flying Cross, the Air Medal and the Purple Heart. In March 1972, the U.S. Navy honored Lieutenant Brown again when it launched an escort ship, the USS *Jesse L. Brown*, at the Avondale Shipyards in Louisiana. The honors continued in November 2002, when Brown was again honored with a $2.6 million county tax service building in Hattiesburg, Mississippi, which was dedicated in his memory. Lieutenant Jesse Leroy Brown was a pathfinder for Blacks in military aviation.[4]

## ❦ WHO WON THE CIVIL WAR? ❦

Students of history would answer that the North won the Civil War. But an assessment of what the South acquired after the Civil War argues that the Confederate South won the war in nearly every respect. Yes, the North succeeded in transferring some of the wealth and industries from the South to the North and on paper outlawed formal slavery. However, the South suffered fewer military deaths and casualties, received monetary compensation, land reparations, increased their congressional representation and political clout, established formidable Southern culture and code of ethics and recaptured Blacks into semi-slavery under Jim Crow segregation. Even with three amendments to the United States Constitution and more than five civil rights laws, the South was able to re-enslave Black people for another hundred years under the Black Codes. The South effectively dominated national public policy, military budgets, racial policies and Black people's labor through the Black Civil Rights Movement of the 1960s. In a war, the winner takes the spoils. Since the South got all the spoils, then the South won the Civil War.

# AMERICAN INDIANS OWE BLACK AMERICANS

American Indians are indebted to Black Americans for reparations, not withstanding the popular image of American Indians as an oppressed people. In 1790, George Washington encouraged Indians to become "civilized" by modeling their culture after White European colonialists. Indians heeded Washington's admonition and became slaveholders and slave traders like civilized Whites. Colonial treaties rewarded Indians by paying them bounties to capture runaways, pushing Indians deeper into the enslavement system and giving Indians firsthand experience with the strong racial hated that Whites felt for Blacks. Indians did not want to be treated like Blacks and did not willingly identify with Blacks, especially since Indians, too, could enjoy the fruits of Black slavery. American Indians used their Black slaves as a source of revenue and wealth, but also as common laborers, interpreters, teachers and fellow warriors.

When the Civil War ended in 1865, the United States government signed treaties with the five civilized tribes — the Cherokee, Chickasaw, Creek, Choctaw and Seminole — but also the Apache, Fox, Blackfoot, Cheyenne, Comanche, Arapahos, Kiowa, Winnebago and all the remaining slaveholding Indian tribes. In these treaties, the U.S. government gave Indians certain benefits, rights and financial remuneration. In exchange, the tribes agreed to provide their Black slaves with freedom, land, money and full citizenship in their respective tribes. However, within a few years after the close of the war, all of the Indian tribes reneged on every point, with the exception of the Seminoles. Granting full citizenship to Black slaves was particularly important because the treaties granted common landownership to all the tribes and any member of the tribe had full access and rights to everything on the land. When the Indian governing bodies divided the land among individual members of the tribe, Blacks were supposed to have received their fair share. Instead, during the 20th century, all of the tribes violated the treaties and established tribal policies to exclude Blacks from Indian membership and benefits. Some Blacks with American Indian heritage are fighting the tribes and the United States Department of Interior because both have honored these treaties for the last 150 years, but have totally excluded benefits from Blacks. It is amazing that Blacks have marched and demonstrated and filed suits against White corporations, but have totally ignored the egregious behavior of American Indians who refuse to pay what they owe to American Blacks.[5]

## ❦ THE RED BALL EXPRESS ❦

Popularly known as the Red Ball Express, Black soldiers performed a peerless supply service to the United States military during World War II. The Red Ball Express was a military code name for a truck convoy system that would stretch from Normandy Beach to Paris, France, then on to Berlin, Germany. Following the Japanese bombing of Pearl Harbor in 1941, President Franklin D. Roosevelt declared the nation to be in a state of war with Japan. All eligible American males were drafted for combat, with the exception of Black men. Since Black Americans were living under Jim Crow segregation policies and laws, Black males entering the military were assigned to noncombat duty. For the first few years of the war, most Black servicemen were relegated to safe services as cooks, waiters, body servants, drivers and supply personnel.

General George S. Patton's Third Army tank columns needed round-the-clock fuel, food and ammunition, or otherwise, they would grind to a stop. Nearly 75 percent of all Red Ball Express drivers were Black Americans. The Red Ball Express drivers kept an average of 900 fully-loaded trucks constantly rolling, covering as much as 400 miles one way through hostile German territory.

According to one source, when the Red Ball Express came to a halt in mid-November 1944, they had established an outstanding record of achievement and earned a much deserved place in military history. They had delivered 412,193 tons of gas, oil, lubricants, ammunition, food and other war essentials under combat conditions to the front lines. On their return trips, they often used their trucks as hearses to haul the bodies of dead American soldiers to mortuaries behind the battle lines. Like the Tuskegee Airmen, the Red Ball Express did Black Americans proud and established a high level of military performance. Black soldiers in the Red Ball Express helped America and its European Allies defeat the German war machinery in spite of their own country's racism.[6]

## 🍎 A BLACK SPY ON THE RUN 🍎

George Scott, a runaway Black slave, provided the intelligence that ignited one of the Civil War's largest battles. General Benjamin F. Butler, of the Union Army, had been assigned the command at Fort Monroe, which sits on a peninsula at the mouth of the James River in Virginia. When Butler first took command at the beginning of the Civil War, he instructed his troops to be on the lookout for runaway slaves coming through the Confederate lines, and to bring any slaves they discovered immediately to the headquarters tent. George Scott had escaped from a Yorktown, Virginia, plantation. To escape detection, Scott had stayed off the main roads. In so doing, he discovered Southern Confederate forces building new military fortifications between Yorktown and Fort Monroe. Scott arrived at Butler's encampment and described the Confederate fortifications and their locations.

General Butler was surprised and pleased to get Scott's intelligence report, but wanted military confirmation of the reported information. Even though he had just escaped slavery and the South, Scott agreed to lead Union troops back behind Confederate lines to verify his report. Confederate troops discovered Scott and his Union troops behind their lines and fired on them. Scott missed being wounded or even killed when a bullet from a Confederate soldier passed through his coat. Based upon information verified by Union troops, General Butler agreed that Confederate soldiers were planning a major attack on the Union lines. Butler ordered a preemptive attack, but it was poorly planned and executed. The Union lost the battle, even though they had the advantage of the Black slave's spy report. Having done the best that he could do, Scott continued on his journey North to the land of freedom.

## ❧ HO CHI MINH TRAIL IN AMERICA ❧

Ho Chi Minh, who was born in 1890 with the given name of Nguyen Tat Thanh, was Vietnam's greatest political leader. Minh traveled to and was educated in France, China and Russia. In satisfying his intellectual and cultural curiosity, Ho Chi Minh took a tour of America in the early 1920s, as race riots were spreading across the country. White mobs burned down Black Wall Street in Tulsa, Oklahoma, and lynched one Black man a day. He was shocked by what he saw and read. There were daily reports of racial abuse of a powerless Black minority. Racial hatred and Black lynchings were such a normal part of American life that incidences rarely found their way into the local newspapers or radio. When newspapers did report an incident, it often appeared in the comic section of the local newspapers.

Ho Chi Minh was appalled at the treatment of Black Americans, but as an Asian, he never felt personally threatened. Minh collected newspaper clippings about racism and lynchings. He wrote an article about lynching for a French magazine in 1924. When he returned to Vietnam in 1944, the impact of Jim Crow segregation and Whites' inhumanity to Blacks burned in his mind.

Minh initiated a declaration of independence movement to free his people from French domination. In the Vietnam War of 1960s and 70s, some of the most vicious fighting occurred on the Ho Chi Minh Trail.[7]

## 🐦 UNSUNG HEROES OF THE WEST 🐦

Even though they were unwanted, disrespected and unappreciated, more than a quarter of a million Black Union soldiers fought in the American Civil War. When the war ended, the federal government chose to keep nearly 25,000 Blacks in the army to maintain the nation's military readiness and combat effectiveness. However, having Blacks in the military had left a bad taste in the mouths of the Whites in the East, as well as the North and South. In hopes of lowering the visibility of Black soldiers between 1866 and 1917, the government assigned nearly all of them to duty in the West. The army command had other reasons for assigning Black troops to the West. The officers felt that conditions in the West were too harsh for Whites; they had bought into the racial myths that Black troops were more adaptable to disease and Indian warfare than Whites.

The new U.S. Army formed four all-Black regiments — two infantry and two cavalry and assigned them to the Western frontier. Upon seeing these Black Soldiers for the first time, American Indians gave these Black army outfits the name of "Buffalo Soldiers." To them, the hair of the Black soldiers was like the fur of the buffalo. The name Buffalo Soldiers stuck. The Black soldiers quickly established a reputation for courage, fighting and tracking skills and an intense combative spirit. Black Buffalo soldiers hunted and fought Apache, Comanche, Cheyenne and Sioux warriors, while defending other Native Americans from White vigilantes and settlers who sought to take unassigned Indian lands and resources. The Buffalo Soldiers acted as a peace-making force, pursuing Mexican revolutionaries, cattle rustlers and outlaws. They also fought forest fires, protected silver mines and railroad trains from striking workers.

The greatest challenge to the Buffalo Soldiers came not in battle, but from the White people they were supposed to protect. Whites in the West hated Black soldiers as much as Whites did elsewhere in the country. White settlers that Buffalo Soldiers saved from Indian raiders and crooks often expressed little appreciation for them, openly called them niggers and demanded that the federal government replace them with White soldiers. The personal satisfaction Black soldiers found in being Buffalo Soldiers remains an unarticulated mystery.[8]

## ❦ UNRECOGNIZED BLACK WAR HERO ❦

Throughout military history, there have been Black soldiers who deserved to be appreciated and recognized as heroes. However, few can match the war experiences recounted by 84-year-old retired Lieutenant Colonel Emmett Simmons of Los Angles, California. Without a doubt, Mr. Emmett Simmons deserves to be included in the military annals. When he recounts his experiences in the D-Day landings, his first-person stories are more intriguing and spellbinding than the war movies, *Saving Private Ryan, Patton, The Battle of the Budge or The Longest Day*. Black soldiers like Lt. Col. Emmett Simons played critical roles in numerous World War II battles, but their stories, somehow, are conspicuously left out of such films.

Lt. Col. Emmett Simmons provides a thrilling account of the role played by his command and other Black soldiers during World War II. It is noteworthy that Emmett Simmons achieved the military rank of lieutenant colonel in the 1940s while the troops were still segregated. Emmett Simmons demonstrated exemplary leadership, battlefront bravery and personal race consciousness.

On the famous D-Day invasion, he was in command of the all-Black 758th, 763rd and 791st tank battalions which played key roles in defeating both Nazi Germany and Hitler's belief in a superior Aryan race. Simmons' heroics began with the landing on Omaha Beach in 1944, along with hundreds of thousands of Allied troops. He struggled to shore among human body parts floating in a sea of red blood. Within a matter of hours, more than 200 Black soldiers were cut down by crossfire from a German machine gun nest that Simmons helped destroy. He and his Black tank battalions clashed often with the notorious and feared German Panzer Tiger Shark tanks. One of the lead German tanks knocked out one of Simmons' tanks and when five Black soldiers exited under a white flag, they were shot down by German tank soldiers. Simmons ordered his tanks to isolate and capture the crew in the German tank that had killed his men after they had surrendered.

After a short battle, Colonel Simmons and his men subdued the lead German tank, which contained approximately six or seven Germans. Through an interpreter, Colonel Simmons asked a German officer in the captured tank why his crew had killed the surrendering Black soldiers. The German officer responded: "Because they were niggers! Niggers should not drive tanks." Infuriated, Simmons ordered his men to treat the German colonel and his tank crew the same way they treated his Black tank men. And they did.

*Mr. Emmett Simmons holds John Horse Award*
*(Reprint permission from The Harvest Institute)*

One Negro tanker did not like Colonel Simmons' order and reported to military headquarters that Colonel Simmons had failed to respect the rights of German prisoners. Military headquarters immediately suspended Colonel Simmons from the front battle lines and initiated court marshal proceedings against him. General George Patton heard about the court marshal proceedings and intervened on behalf of Colonel Simmons. General Patton demanded that all charges be dismissed against Simmons and that he be immediately returned to his tank command on the front line. General George Patton further said: "The Colonel did what in the hell he was supposed to do. We need more damn officers like him."

Colonel Simmons resumed the head of his tank battalions and continued to spearhead the army's advance towards Berlin, Germany. The unstoppable Black tank units were the first to reach the infamous Dachau Concentration Camp. Colonel Simmons tells how his unit personally drove their tanks through the concentration camp's barbed wire fences and thick walls. Once inside,

Colonel Simmons discovered one of the world's best kept secrets. Of the approximately 9,000 prisoners in the extermination camp, nearly 6,000 were mulatto Blacks. Only 3,000 were Jews. Simmons said the bodies coming out of the gas chambers were stacked up like cords of wood and some of the bodies on the bottom were still moving.

Colonel Simmons is a living eyewitness to the fact that Black prisoners were the majority population within the walls of Dachau Concentration Camp in the final days of World War II. Over half of a century later, neither military or civilian authorities make the point that Black people were also victims of the German Holocaust. Where is the Black Holocaust museum? Where are the reparations for the Black Holocaust victims and recognition for the Black soldiers who rescued them? In 2004, The Harvest Institute, Black America's only national public policy institute, recognized Emmett Simmons' heroism during World War II. Emmett Simmons was given the institute's John Horse Award for standing up for Black people when they truly needed him. (9)

## 🌶 PORT CHICAGO MUTINY 🌶

One of the most shameful examples of military racism in the United States occurred in the Navy yard at Port Chicago, California. On July 17, 1944, an explosion at an ammunition depot shook Port Chicago, killing at least 320 military personnel, including 202 Black enlisted men. The dead Black sailors, who the navy had relegated to common laborers, had been assigned to load live ammunition onto a pair of cargo carriers. Without warning, an explosion occurred that instantly destroyed numerous naval ships and vaporized thousands of tons of explosives, supplies, ammunition and men. Beyond the dead, another 390, mostly Black men, were injured and maimed for life. The explosion was so horrific that it could be seen 35 miles away in the city of San Francisco. Although the explosion was most likely set off by some of the experimental explosive materials called Torpex, a United States naval inquiry claimed the explosion was due to incompetence on the part of the Black laborers who were the handlers and stevedores. All the White officers who were in charge of the ammunition operations were absolved of any responsibility.

The navy then rounded up 400 more Black sailors and assigned them to a similar ammunition-loading facility at nearby Mare Island. Many of the 400 Black sailors were still in shock from the first explosion. Again, the navy assigned White officers to supervise the Black sailors, who were performing the same work with the same explosive materials. The Black sailors understood that the navy was placing their lives at risk. Knowing the danger, all the Black sailors flatly refused to do the loading until the navy instituted safety measures to prevent accidental explosions. Since the Black sailors refused to work during war time, the navy ordered all of them rounded up and charged with mutiny, which carried a penalty of death by firing squad.

Once charged, all but fifty gave in and returned to loading ammunition. The fifty who refused were tried and found guilty of mutiny. After the NAACP failed in its legal appeals, the navy finally decided to free the Black sailors, but assigned them to one year of probation on a remote Pacific Island. As a meager gesture, Congress approved an award of $5,000 for the families of each Black sailor killed in the ammunition explosion. But, adding insult to injury, Congressman John Rankin from Mississippi, reduced the amount to only $3,000 per dead Black sailor. As this saga of Port Chicago unfolded, recruitment posters encouraged young Black men to "Support your country. Join the navy and see the world."[10]

# ❦ BLACK SOLDIERS ON THE FRONT LINES ❦

In times of war, Black soldiers have been overrepresented on the front lines and under-recognized back home. Blacks are generally overrepresented in the military by a ratio of three to four times their percentage of the nation's population. This was especially true in World War II, the Korean War, Vietnam War and the Gulf Wars. Beginning in World War II, racism in the military forced Black soldiers to endure more battle time than their White compatriots, especially the tanker units. In normal combat rotation, White soldiers received a rest after 15 straight days in combat. When General Patton needed tankers on the front line, he called up the Black tankers.

General Patton chose to overuse Black tankers saying: "Send the niggers back up to the front lines." In the famous battle of the Bulge, General Patton forced Black soldiers to fight for 115 days without rest or relief. Black tankers got their rest breaks and a chance to sleep when General Patton and other high-ranking officers were busy giving out military commendations, citations or simply leading public parades down Main Street, U.S.A.[11]

# ❦ BLACK SYMBOLIZED FIGHTING ❦

With the Civil War being fought over Black skin, Blackness, psychologically and symbolically, transmuted into a metaphor for fighting and death. In the early years of the war, the Confederacy established a Southern Black Flag policy that stipulated that all captured Black Union soldiers and their White officers would be shot on the spot at the moment of capture. A few Confederate soldiers even displayed black objects as their fighting trademark. Joseph O. Shelby, of Lexington, Kentucky, declined a captain's commission in the Northern Union Army because he favored state's rights and Black slavery. So, he joined the Southern

Confederacy, fought in every major Confederate campaign in Missouri and Arkansas, and chose to wear a conspicuous black plume in his hat to show his hatred of Black people.

Ben McCulloch, a Tennessean, was another Southern military leader who established a reputation for using the color black in Civil War battles. He wore black to show both his support of slavery and the South's Black Flag policy. McCulloch paid a tailor in Texas to make him a special "fighting suit" — not a uniform — made of black velvet. McCulloch's special velvet fighting suit told all with whom he made contact with that he loved the color black, but he hated Black people.[12]

## ❦ BLACK GERMANS IN THE ❦ REVOLUTIONARY WAR

Stories about the American Revolutionary War typically called forth images of American colonists fighting the British troops for their independence. Most people do not know that the British government hired over 17,000 professional Hessian, or German, soldiers to help them fight the American colonists during the war. The Hessian soldiers had an international reputation as fierce fighters and plunderers. Just the thought of Hessians joining in the Revolutionary War on the side of the British sent shock waves across the colonies. But here is a dirty little secret. General Dunmore of the British Army not only encouraged slave revolts, but had the Hessian military leaders add some additional soul and color to the fighting. The Germans hired a number of free Black mercenaries from Europe to fight for the British government. These hired Black mercenaries, or Black Hessian soldiers, added to the "feldmusik" unit that played the fighting music and kept the "rhythm" during the military marches. Black music had the ability to excite and motivate the soldiers to fight.

During the Revolutionary period, nearly all military units included a drummer, fifer and flag bearer. Although most Blacks were recruited mainly for music and common labor, a few Blacks also served as soldiers and weapons carriers. In a 1784 painting by J.H. Carl, a Black drummer is a part of the Hessian Third Guard Regiment. When the Revolutionary War ended, many of the White Hessian troops stayed in the United States and settled around Lancaster and Reading, Pennsylvania, as well as Frederick, Maryland. The great mystery and possibly a dirty little secret is, what happened to the Blacks who served with the Hessian Army? Did they return to Europe as free men, or did they stay in America as slaves?[13]

## ❧ PIGS IN BLACK HISTORY ❧

The pig has always played a special role in Black people's lives, especially in their dietary consumption. When Black slaves were reduced to the level of field animals, they learned not only how to survive, they also perfected culinary skills and became experts in preparing barbequed ribs, chitlins, pork chops, pork skin and other parts of the pig. However, the pig played another central role in one of the nation's biggest and best planned slave revolts. Contrary to conservative history revisionists, slaves were poorly fed and were kept at a near starvation level. Free Blacks were only slightly better off, but just like slaves, they, too, had to occasionally steal food to survive. In 1799, a Black ex-slave named Gabriel Prosser was caught stealing a pig from his former owner in Richmond, Virginia. The former overseer learned of the theft of the pig and confronted Prosser. However, Prosser was in no mood to be chastised for stealing food to survive, so he attacked the White overseer and bit off his ear. For violating a racial taboo by attacking a White man, Prosser was branded with a hot iron in open court and sentenced to 30 days in jail.

The pig episode was the beginning and not the end of Gabriel Prosser. Several years later, the slave revolt of Tousaint L'Ouverture in Haiti inspired Prosser and convinced him that another major slave revolt was due in America. Prosser then spent a year planning the largest and most far-reaching slave revolt ever conceived in the United States of America. But fate intervened just days before Prosser's plan could be executed. Two slaves seeking their meritorious freedom and the approval of White society betrayed Prosser to White authorities. Gabriel Prosser, along with 26 other slaves, were captured and summarily executed. The state of Virginia reimbursed the White slave-owners for the 26 Black slaves who were executed and probably tossed a pork chop bone to the two slave informers.[14]

## ❧ Blacks Are Unique Patriots ❧

Black Americans, without a doubt, have been this nation's most patriotic and loyal citizens, whether they were enslaved or free. However, for centuries they have had to fight for the right to fight. During every war, Black Americans join the military as a way to express their patriotism and display their bravery. Blacks fought to defend democracy and freedom for others, even though they were not free. Worse, as freedom fighters, historical records omit Black people's heroic deeds and deny them recognition for their unique place in the national annals of patriotism.

Of America's many cultures and ethnic populations, only Black Americans can make two unique claims. First, they are the only population that has fought in support of America in every major conflict, even before the country was a nation. And second, Blacks are the only population group that fought in every major American conflict, and whose mother country has never been at war with America. The United States of America has engaged in hot and cold wars with nearly every European, Arab, Hispanic and

Asian nation. America has fought every Indian tribe, but it has never been at war with a Black African nation. What is the message to Black Americans when they are the most patriotic Americans, yet they are the most exploited, excluded, subordinated and disrespected out-group in America?

## 🌿 THE FORT PILLOW MASSACRE 🌿

In April 1864, nearly 600 Black and White Union troops were encamped at Fort Pillow, a Confederate-built fortification on the Mississippi River just north of Memphis, Tennessee. Major General Nathan Bedford Forrest and approximately 1,500 Confederate troops attacked Union forces inside of Fort Pillow. Using sharpshooters, Forrest's soldiers killed a large number of the Union troops in a crossfire and quickly overran the fort.

Over 262 Black soldiers and dozens of White soldiers surrendered to the Southern Confederacy at Fort Pillow, but Confederate rebels shouted: "No quarter! No quarter! Kill the damn niggers. Shoot them down." Most of the Black soldiers were shot down. Those who were not killed outright were later crucified on tent frames and burned alive. Other Black soldiers were thrown in the Mississippi River to drown. It was rumored that General Nathan Bedford Forrest offered to pay one thousand dollars for the head of any White commander of a Black regiment. General Forrest's attitude and actions toward Blacks made him a hero among Southern states in the Confederacy. When Black Union soldiers learned of the massacre, they responded appropriately. They angrily committed themselves to avenge Fort Pillow. Black Union soldiers pledged to give no quarter, take no White prisoners and make it dangerous for a White to take the life of a Black soldier in the future.

For the remainder of the war, the battle cry of the Black Union troops was: "Remember Fort Pillow!" Blacks were determined to make White Confederate soldiers respect Black lives, manhood and conventional codes of military conduct. In September 1864, General Forrest had an opportunity to place his Southern veteran cavalry in a face-to-face battle with angry Black Union troops. When General Forrest learned that the town of Pulaski, Tennessee, had been reinforced with angry Black Union soldiers, he decided to avoid any further clashes with Black troops. He turned east and attacked the town of Murfreesboro instead.

President Abraham Lincoln had an unrealistic altruistic philosophy of war and was a weak commander-in-chief. When word of the Fort Pillow massacre reached President Lincoln, his cabinet considered executing Southern prisoners of war in retaliation. Rather than standing up for the Black Union soldiers, Lincoln opposed the idea saying: "Blood cannot restore blood and government should not act for revenge." But, General William Tecumseh Sherman was different. General Sherman did not believe in turning the other cheek. He threatened to treat Forrest's rebel troops the very same way they had treated his Black soldiers at Fort Pillow. In his march to the sea, General Sherman burned Atlanta to the ground.[15]

## ❦ THE MASSACRE AT POISON SPRING ❦

Black Americans living in the state of Kansas were among the first recruits into the Union Army for Civil War duty. They were recruited as the First Kansas Colored Infantry. They were the first to see battle and die in military combat. They first saw action on October 28, 1862, when 225 members of the Kansas Colored Infantry confronted 500 Confederate soldiers. They were outnumbered two to one, but they beat the Confederate soldiers with only ten Blacks killed and another twelve wounded. After fighting alongside White Union soldiers at Cabin Creek and Honey Springs, Oklahoma, Major General James Blunt was in a position to compare the fighting spirit of White to Black Union soldiers and he remarked: "I never saw such fighting as was done by that Negro regiment. They make better soldiers in every respect than any troops I have ever had under my command." The First Kansas Colored Infantry continued to distinguish itself in battles in Kansas and Missouri.

But on April 18, 1864, the First Kansas Colored Infantry suffered its only major defeat at Poison Springs, Arkansas. In that battle, approximately 117 Blacks were killed and another 65 were wounded. Most were killed under the Confederate "black flag policy." Black soldiers did not take what happened at Poison Spring lightly. They equated it to the Fort Pillow massacre and began chanting: "Remember Poison Springs and Fort Pillow!" as their battle cry.[16]

## 🍎 HAWAIIAN SENATOR AND BLACK BLOOD 🍎

Senator Daniel Inouye of Hawaii, who served in the U.S. military campaigns in Europe during world War II, commented on the special relationship that existed between his all-Asian company and the all-Black 92nd Infantry Company. Senator Inouye related how the two companies were assigned front-line duty and fought a short distance from each other. Inouye and other Asian soldiers felt it was unfair to assign the Black 92nd Infantry to the most exposed and dangerous front-line positions. But during the advance of the Allied forces, an event occurred on the front line that converted Inouye's concerns for Black troops into a special, lifetime relationship. He became indebted to them.

While attacking a German line, Inouye was wounded three times. The first time, he was hit in the stomach. The bullet that passed through him did not strike any vital organs. Shortly afterwards, Inouye's arm was blown completely off. He tied off the arm to stop the bleeding, then continued to attack the German line.

Finally, he was hit in the leg, lost a massive amount of blood, than passed into unconsciousness. He awoke in a military hospital on the operating table, receiving a blood transfusion. It was customary during World War II to indicate the names of the blood donors on the containers. Inouye felt it was important to remember that of the 17 pints of blood he received, eleven were from soldiers in the 92$^{nd}$ Infantry unit. For his gallantry in combat, Senator Inouye not only received the highest military honors, he also received a lot of life-giving "black blood." Inouye was grateful for both.

## 🐾 PIG CAUSES INTERNATIONAL INCIDENT 🐾

In 1859, on the eve of the American Civil War, the British government and the United States were set to go to war for the third time. On San Juan Island, off the coast of the state of Washington, a shot was fired that was heard around the world. An American farmer by the name of Lyman Cutler had grown tired of mysterious invasions of his yard and garden. One June morning, he walked out on his porch, musket in his hand, and fired. The invader fell dead. Even though he felt some sorrow that it had come to violence, he was happy that he had killed the invader and his property was his once again. Unfortunately, this was not the end. Within a very short time, British authorities on the island heard about the shooting and were on their way to arrest Lyman Cutler. They indicated he would be arrested and taken to mainland British Columbia for a proper trial. But the American military had also gotten the word and would not allow Lyman Cutler to be arrested and tried in a British court.

When Captain George Pickett arrived with American troops, he quickly proclaimed that San Juan Island was American territory and that he and his troops were there to protect American citizens. The British took issue and within a week sent 61 Royal Marines to the island to claim it in the name of Britain. This argument and stand-off continued for at least a year, during which time the British amassed warships in the San Juan Harbor with guns pointed and ready to fire. There is a great likelihood that Britain and the United States would have gone to war had the American Civil War not started in 1861. And all of this conflict was because Lyman Cutler had walked out on his porch in June 1859 and shot dead the intruder in his vegetable garden: a big, fat, black British pig.[17]

## ❦ DOUBLEDAY FIRED CANNON BALLS ❦

It's a little known fact that the Union captain who fired the first shot by the North in the Civil War was none other than Abner Doubleday, who is credited with inventing the game of baseball. In 1861, the Southern Confederates started the Civil War by firing their cannons on Fort Sumter, South Carolina. A surprised Union captain gathered his wits and ordered his men to return fire. He aimed and lit the fuse to the first cannon himself. The battle between the attacking Confederate and Union forces in Fort Sumter lasted several hours. The next day, the United States declared war on the Confederacy. What happened to that captain who fired the very first shot for the Union? You would think that history would remember him for returning fire on the Southern rebels. Instead, Abner Doubleday is better remembered for giving the country its favorite springtime pastime, baseball.[18]

## ❦ DIXIE WANTED SLAVES TO PLAY SOLDIERS ❦

Throughout most of the Civil War, Southern public policies prohibited Blacks from formally joining the Confederate Army. However, Southern Whites did take their personal Black slaves with them to war. It has been speculated that the first Union soldier killed in combat was killed by a Black slave with the

Confederacy. Prior to the end of the Civil War, General Robert E. Lee sensed the South was losing and he asked the Confederate Congress to authorize recruitment of up to 3,000 Black slaves into the Confederate Army. General Lee knew the Union Army was using Blacks as combat troops, while the Southern Confederacy had used slaves strictly as supportive labor. General Lee told the Confederate Congress that Black front-line troops were essential to the South winning the Civil War against the Union Army. General Lee argued that any Black slaves who fought for the Southern Confederacy ought to be set free after the war. A Mississippi newspaper responded to General Lee's request and published a supporter's editorial saying: "Let not slavery prove a barrier to our independence. If it is found in the way, if it proves an insurmountable object of the achievement of our liberty and separate nationality, away with it! Let it perish!" Unfortunately, when the South seemed to be willing to end slavery, it was too late. General Lee had surrendered and war was over.

## ❦ FIGHTING SONG FOR BLACK ❦ UNION SOLDIERS

As the Black Union troops moved into the South to confront Confederate soldiers, the former slaves had a popular marching song. Sung to the lyrics of the "Battle Hymn of the Republic," the former slaves changed the lyrics to:

We are colored Yankee soldiers,
Who've enlisted for the war;
We are fighting for the Union,
We are fighting for the Lord.
We can shoot a rebel farther than a White man
Ever saw — as we go marching on.

Look there above the center,
Where the flag is waving bright.
We are going out of slavery.
We are bound for freedom light;
We mean to show Jeff Davis how the African can fight;
As we go marching on.[19]

## ❦ A Fighting Night Fighter ❦

Private Henry Johnson, a Black man from Albany, New York, was assigned to the 369th Infantry and fought what was probably one of the fiercest hand-to-hand combat battles in Europe during World War I. It was a popular belief at that time that Black men could not and would not stand and fight. Private Johnson's late-night, front-line battle with German soldiers proved the myth to be untrue. While on 12 P.M. to 4 A.M. guard duty in enemy territory, German troops attempted to break through the Allies' line at Private Johnson's post. They rushed him, throwing hand grenades while firing their hand weapons. Although bullets were hitting all around and he was outnumbered by at least thirty-to-one, Private Johnson held his ground and began firing back. He did not have a chance to call for reinforcements.

*Poster: Blacks in World War I (Library of Congress)*

Private Johnson said being alone in pitch darkness was made worse by the fact that Germans were coming at him from all sides. Frightened for his life, Johnson found and began throwing hand grenades. When all the hand grenades were gone, Johnson picked up his rifle and began firing as fast as he could pull the trigger. When his rifle jammed and the Germans were crawling all over him, he used it as a club. Upon hearing a German soldier yell: "Get him! Get him!" in German, Johnson dropped his rifle and pulled out a bolo knife and began to swing. He cut and stabbed a number of German soldiers in the dark. It was over an hour before relief arrived to help him. When the sun came up the next morning, other soldiers from Johnson's command estimated that Private Johnson had single-handedly fought as many as 30 German soldiers.

Several European Allied countries recognized Henry Johnson for his valor and surviving what appeared to have been a battle to the death. When Johnson returned home to America, however, there were no heroes' parades through downtown New York. Such military recognitions and honors were reserved for White war heroes. The only welcome home Henry Johnson received was from his friends and family.[2]

## ❦ BRITISH CIVILIANS LOVED BLACK SOLDIERS ❦

In World War II, Black soldiers endured the same racism in Europe from White soldiers as they had been exposed to at home in the United States. However, one of the great ironies that came out of WWII was that European citizens resented the way White soldiers treated Black soldiers. One British farmer said: "I love the American Black soldiers, but I don't like the White soldiers that they brought with them." The highest levels of the American military condoned White soldiers venting their fury on Black soldiers, vilified British women who associated with Black soldiers and encouraged hotels and bars not to admit Black soldiers. Many British people expressed amazement after meeting Black American soldiers and finding them likable humans that they were not at all like what they had been portrayed to be by White soldiers. Some Brits living in rural villages expressed surprise when they discovered that Black soldiers did not have tails.[21]

## ❦ THE FOUNDING FATHER OF THE KKK ❦

The main character in the Academy Award-winning movie *Forrest Gump* shared a name with an infamous Confederate general, Nathan Bedford Forrest. Forrest Gump, the movie character, was mentally challenged and highly principled, while his namesake, Nathan Bedford Forrest, was an uneducated, unprincipled disciplinarian. Nathan Bedford Forrest established a national reputation as a Confederate general in the Civil War and the 1864 massacre of 262 captured Black Union soldiers at Fort Pillow, Tennessee. Even before he slaughtered the defenseless Black soldiers, Nathan Bedford Forrest had been a slaveholder and international slave trader. As a racist, Forrest was predisposed to any policy or activity that allowed him to hurt or kill Black people with impunity.

*Roots of the Ku Klux Klan. (Library of Congress)*

In the spring of 1867, the first national gathering of the United Ku Klux Klan of America was held in the Maxwell House in Nashville, Tennessee. Based upon his military and racist reputation, Nathan Bedford Forrest was given the title of Imperial Grand Wizard and chosen to head the newly-formed organization.

As a brilliant military tactician, Forrest brought his talents to bear in organizing the Klan. No one knew better how, through elusive tactics, boldness and secrecy, to intimidate and instill fear in an enemy. While Forrest's foremost goal was to protect and elevate White women, he also wanted to use the Klan organization to establish the Black Codes and a peonage system that would force ex-slaves to return to his cotton plantation as cheap labor, share-croppers or convict labor.[22]

## 🐞 PRISONERS TREATED BETTER THAN BLACKS 🐞

For more than four centuries, Black people living in America have fought to secure rights and privileges for other people that they themselves do not have in America. While this fact might be generally known, it is surprising to some to learn that during World War II, German and Italian prisoners of war (POW) were scattered across America and White Americans treated them better than they treated native Black American citizens and soldiers. Starting in 1943, the United States government secretly distrib-uted nearly 500,000 prisoners in camps throughout the South. To the American government, German prisoners were Whites and, therefore, entitled to all the advantages, privileges and value that White skin symbolized and conferred. In the camps, they were provided good food, books, unsupervised work opportunities and regular recreational activities. Unlike Blacks in the surrounding communities and throughout the South, the German and Italian prisoners could sit in the front of the buses, in the best seats on trains, at lunch counters, in restaurants and could attend White-only theaters.

The United States treated German and Italian POWs better than Black soldiers. On United States military bases, Black soldiers ate in segregated mess halls, while German and Italian POWs ate with White soldiers. Moreover, POWs ate better quality meals than Black soldiers. Off the military bases, Black servicemen were often beaten and killed simply for violating this country's segregation laws. There is no known record of a German or Italian POW beaten or killed while attempting to attend a movie or enter a White restaurant. Whether the nation was at war or peace, Whites maintained tight control over Black Americans and kept them segregated and subordinated. A White man speaking to a crowd of Blacks in New Orleans, Louisiana, underscored this point with devastating brutality when he said: "You niggers are wondering how you are going to be treated after the war. Well, I'll tell you, you are going to be treated exactly like you were treated before the war; this is a White man's country and we expect to rule." After WWII ended, a large number of the German and Italian POWs remained in America and were anointed with first-class citizenship. These POWs, along with their anti-Black ideologies, integrated into mainstream White society.[23]

## 🍂 DID JAPANESE INTERMENT SAVE AMERICA? 🍂

When Japan attacked Pearl Harbor and drew the United States into World War II, the federal government took some protective measures for internal security. It required Japanese-Americans to move into relocation camps. For more than 60 years, the justice and fairness of government action towards Japanese-Americans has been questioned, debated and eventually became the basis for reparations. Black slavery and Jim Crow segregation has yet to receive serious political considerations, apologies or reparations. The temporary relocation of the Japanese-Americans during World War II is often referred to as the most shameful episode in American history. This statement is inaccurate, naive and insulting to Black Americans.

While it is true that Japanese-Americans and those of Japanese origin were forced to temporarily live in relocation camps, they were not beaten and murdered, castrated and lynched nor denied an education, religion, community, culture, language, income, family units or the fruit of their labor. The questions that have yet to be asked and answered are first, whether the relocation of Japanese-Americans for a temporary period actually saved America during World War II. And, second, whether the United States should have taken similar measures to insure its internal security following the September 11, 2001, terrorist attacks by Arab Muslims on the New York World Trade Center Towers.

Why similar internal security measures have not been enacted since September 11, 2001, may, in part, be due to a lack of understanding as to why isolation measures were instituted after the terrorist attack on Hawaii. In the fall of 1941, President Franklin Roosevelt was concerned about the vulnerability posed to the nation by persons of Japanese origin living in the United States as hostilities between Japan and the United States escalated. President Roosevelt knew that a country is weakest from the inside. Therefore, it would be very difficult, if not impossible, to stop terrorist attacks once terrorists were inside an open society. President Roosevelt, therefore, ordered Curtis B. Munson, in the Department of State, to conduct a secret investigation to assess the potential of persons of Japanese origin living in America to conduct terrorist activities against the United States. In his report, Munson indicated the vast majority of the 127,000 Japanese living in the U.S. in 1941 would probably remain loyal to the United States. However, on the down side, Munson estimated there were an estimated 600 potential terrorists and a core group of older Japanese Americans, born in Japan, who represented a potential danger. Apparently, this population of older Japanese would identify more with Japan, their country of origin, their religion, and their emperor more than they would identify with the United States of America. Consequently, President Roosevelt signed Executive Order 9066, authorizing all persons of Japanese origin to be relocated to internment camps while the nation was engaged in a war with Japan. The intent of the order was to reduce any possibility of sabotage and espionage within the continental United States. The United States Supreme Court supported Roosevelt's executive order.

The United States did not suffer any major incidents of sabotage or espionage on its soil during WWII. The question that cannot be answered is whether the reason the country did not suffer major acts of terrorism and sabotage was because potential terrorists were not allowed to roam free. Or was it because Japanese Americans would never have done anything to help Japan or harm the United States? With 2 to 3 million Arabs living in the United States, what lessons are to be learned from the Japanese interment of WWII?[24]

## 🐛 A BLACK HARPERS FERRY HERO'S QUOTE 🐛

Before being hanged for his involvement with John Brown to secure weapons from the Harpers Ferry armory to arm escaping slaves, John Copeland Jr., a Black man, said: "I am dying for freedom. I could not die for a better cause."[25]

## 🐛 A BLACK SOLDIER'S PRAYER 🐛

Black Americans have always taken pride in fighting America's foreign enemies outside of the country while they fought their own battles against racist White Americans inside the country. In January 1943, the following *Draftee's Prayer of a Black American Soldier* appeared in a local Black newspaper.

Dear Lord,
Today, I go to war;
To fight, to die.
Tell me, what for?
Dear Lord, I'll fight,
I do not fear,
Germans or Japs;
My fears are here, in America.[26]

# CHAPTER 11

# SPORTS AND SPORTING LIFE

*Those who fail to seize the moment, lose their chance!*

## Mini Facts

◆ *Charles Follis, born in 1879, grew up to become the first Black professional football player in the United States. He played for a team known as the Shelby Blues.*

◆ *In 1915, D.W. Griffith's film, Birth of a Nation, portrayed Blacks in such a negative and offensive manner that it generated race riots and a rebirth of the Ku Klux Klan.*

◆ *In 1927, Abe Saperstein organized a performing Black basketball team called the Harlem Globetrotters. The team was made up of some of the best Black players in the nation.*

◆ *On July 25, 1935, Leonard Tyner, a 13-year-old African American from Chicago, Illinois, became the world's marble shooting champion.*

## ❧ A FIGHTING LITTLE MAN ❧

Nearly a generation before Jack Johnson became the first Black heavyweight boxing champion of the world, George Dixon, a small man who barely weighed 100 pounds, was recognized as the first Black man to win a world boxing championship title. On June 27, 1890, George Dixon defeated Nunc Wallace in the 18th round to win the bantamweight fight. Dixon was considered one of the best bantamweight fighters in the history of the sport. In twenty years of professional boxing, from 1886 to 1906, Dixon fought and won nearly 160 fights. George Dixon was a little piece of leather, but he was well put together. He died on January 6, 1909, and was elected into the International Boxing Hall of Fame in 1990. It took over eighty years to recognize boxing champion George Dixon because Black boxers dominate the sport, but they do not control who will be recognized.

## ❧ DOGS BEST FRIENDS ❧

A number of Southern Black expressions related to dogs such as "putting on the dog" and "turning the dogs loose" have their roots in Black slave culture. Even "hush puppies," a Southern food item, came from Black slaves baking small rolls of corn meal in hog grease and sharing some with the dogs who barked for morsels after smelling the aroma. The expressions "putting on the dog" and "turning the dogs loose" are social expressions used in both White and Black communities to imply going all out to have a good time socially. In general, however, there was a tenuous relationship between Blacks and dogs that goes back hundreds of years. Whites routinely used dogs to catch runaway slaves, escaping prisoners or Blacks who were the guest of honor on a Saturday night coon hunt. Plantation dogs were trained to attack and hunt Blacks. In some instances, dogs were trained to kill running Black persons, especially those Blacks who habitually ran away from plantations or were viewed as a social problem.

The dogs most commonly used to track, attack and kill Blacks were hound dogs. In the South, hunting coon on a moonlit Saturday night was a favorite sport. To keep Black runaways from injuring the chasing dogs and strangling them, the slave owners often equipped the dogs with spiked neck collars. In response to the 1960s Civil Rights marches and demonstrations, Southern police often used what they called "Negro dogs," specially trained to attack Black marchers and demonstrators. A general fear of dogs has been passed down to each new generation of Blacks. Maybe one day, the experiences of dogs and Blacks will improve to the point that they can be best friends.

## ❦ BLACK GENES HAVE IT ❦

Liberals and conservatives alike avoid publicly addressing an issue that constantly haunts every sports enthusiast — the darkening of American sports. Many are curious and wonder if Black people have a special gene that makes them better athletes, or are they better simply because of environment alone? White racists have long claimed that Blacks are more physically endowed than Whites because Blacks are lower in the evolutionary chain. Liberals and civil righters, on the other hand, reject the gene theory and argue that Blacks have succeeded in sports and entertainment primarily because of social conditioning and the specific avenues of opportunities that are open in these areas.

Who is right, the conservative racists or the civil rights liberals? In his book *White Over Black*, Winthrop D. Jordan stated that White slave traders originally chose Black people for slavery because Blacks had stronger bodies and greater physical endurance than Whites, Indians or Asians. He indicated White laborers died quickly from hard labor and field heat. Similarly,

John Perry, in his book, *Myths and Realities of American Slavery*, cited a 1511 report to the Spanish royal government that stated that the work of one Black slave was equal to that of four native Indians. The fact that Black people survived the harshness of slavery when other populations could not seems to lead one to conclude that Blacks have some kind of extraordinary physical abilities. If not, then there must be some socio-psychological explanation for why they dominate nearly every physical sport that they enter.

How do you explain the fact that slaves, who didn't own horses, entered horse racing and became the nation's best horse racing jockeys until racism closed them out in the early 1900s? If they had the natural skills before racism shut them out, would they not still be the best jockeys if racism were to disappear? Blacks entered boxing, football, baseball, basketball and field and track and have dominated these sports for over a century. By the mid-20th century, Black athletes entered tennis, gymnastics, golf, bobsledding and soccer and immediately began to dominate. Rejecting the gene theory makes it difficult to explain how a Black minority population dominates so many sports. There are 800 million Blacks in the world, which works out to one-eighth of the world's population, but they hold all the major world records in running, from the 100-meter dash to marathons. Blacks make up 12.4 percent of the total population in the United States, but constitute 85 percent of professional basketball players, 63 percent of the professional football players and 75 percent of the boxers. It isn't just an American thing either — in England, Blacks are less than 2 percent of the population, but they are 20 percent of the professional soccer players.

In Latin America, the Caribbean and European countries, African Blacks dominate and set performance records, especially in long- and middle-distance running. Gary Kamiya, in his book, *The Black Edge*, argues that Black athletes are advantaged in sports by their distinctive skeletal systems, musculature and metabolic structures. The physical achievements of Blacks is evidence that not all people are equally endowed. Black people have been blessed with some good genes and physical abilities. Liberals and civil rights leaders need to accept it for what it is and move on.[1]

## ❦ Black Musical Geniuses ❦

Thomas "Blind Tom" Bethune (1848–1908) was one of the greatest handicapped, untaught musicians in the history of music. Born into slavery in Georgia, he became the leading musical wonder of his time. Almost blind, unable to read or write and with no training whatever, he had a mastery of music and the piano. He could repeat correctly any selection, however complicated, after hearing it only once. He could play by heart over 5,000 selections from music composers such as Beethoven, Bach, Mozart and other masters. Blind Tom lived and died in poverty, but during his early years, he earned a fortune for his various slave masters. Tom was followed by Sugar Child Robinson, Ray Charles and Stevie Wonder. All were blind Black men with no formal musical training, but recognized as geniuses.[2]

## ❦ The Tiger Roars ❦

Golf sensation Tiger Woods, a Black man, is recognized as the greatest professional golfer that the world has ever seen. After winning three consecutive U.S. amateur championships, Tiger Woods decided to go professional. At 21 years of age, he became the youngest player and the first Black to ever play in and win the Master's Golf Tournament. Since winning it, Tiger Woods has broken nearly every golf record, both domestically and internationally. In the spring of 2005, he won his fourth Master's title and again established himself as the number one golfer in the world.

In responding to his fourth Master's win, Tiger Woods said: "It's pretty neat to have won four before the age of 30 and do something no one else has done." In 2001, when he won the Masters, he also became the first golfer to ever hold all four pro Grand Slam titles simultaneously.

Before Woods, the game of golf was a low-profile and primarily White sport. With the exception of a few Black golfers, Black people viewed golfing only with a hope to caddy or work around the clubhouse. Woods' emotional control, energy and playing skills have popularized the sport. When Woods plays in a golf tournament, he draws staggering numbers of television viewers and on-site, sell-out crowds. Even without his massive earnings in product endorsements, Woods holds the title for the highest grossing professional golfer. He is the model that many players emulate and dream of beating.[3]

## ❦ QUOTABLE NOTABLE ❦

Sam Philips, the founder of Sun Records and the man who discovered Elvis Presley, reportedly said in the early 1950s: "If I could find me a White boy who could sing like a nigger, we could make him a millionaire." Once Elvis Presley became a millionaire and was crowned the King of White Rock and Roll, he allegedly said: "All that a nigger can do for me is to shine my shoes and buy my records."

## ❦ THE BIRTH OF MINSTRELS ❦

Minstrel shows became popular throughout the United States in the 1840s with White men writing the music and using blackface makeup. Thomas Rice and Dan Emmett were two popular blackface minstrel performers, but the most popular musical composer of plantation songs was Stephen Foster. He wrote deep emotional songs to accompany a musical version of *Uncle Tom's Cabin* and other minstrel shows. Through his minstrel songs, Foster gained wealth and fame by making fun of uneducated Black people's speech and their native skin color. Harriet Beecher Stowe's *Uncle Tom's Cabin* inspired Foster to write one of his most enduring hits entitled, "My Old Kentucky Home, Good Night," which became Kentucky's state song. After writing for *Uncle Tom's Cabin*, Foster began to distance himself from the negative images of Blacks portrayed in every aspect of society. Following the Civil War, Blacks formed their own troupes, wrote their own songs and performed on the minstrel stages. Sadly, Black minstrel entertainers imitated White minstrels by blacking up their faces to appear more ridiculous and Sambo-like.

In the 20th century, Al Jolson, a White Jewish singer, and George Gershwin, a White composer, continued performing blackface minstrels and musicals. Al Jolson became a national icon kneeling in blackface and singing, "Mammy" and "Suwannee River." George Gershwin wrote the musical *Porgy and Bess* that promoted demeaning images of impoverished urban Blacks and featured an all-Black cast. In the musical, the lead character, Porgy, sang a song that glorified the status quo of Black people at the time and glorified Black people accepting poverty and laziness as a way of life. Porgy immortalized Blacks' love of poverty when he sang the words: "I got plenty of nothing, and nothing is plenty enough for me." Gershwin's Porgy character was physically hand-icapped, but the song made him appear intellectually handicapped, as well. Poor Porgy.

## ❦ OUR STATE SONGS ❦

All the states have official songs. The state songs of Kentucky, Maryland, Virginia, Florida, Georgia and Texas offer some interesting views about Black people set to music. For example, the state song for Kentucky is "My Old Kentucky

Home." It was officially established as the state song in 1853. With the original title, "Poor Uncle Tom, Goodnight," it became one of Stephen Foster's best-loved minstrel songs. The original lyrics spoke of how the "Darkies are gay [happy]" and "the time has come when Darkies have to part." Lyrics of this song are still played and sung at the start of the Kentucky Derby horse races every May. Other state songs were written by Stephen Foster. In the post-Civil Rights era, Florida's legislators tried to revoke their state song titled "Old Folk at Home" because of the lyrical reference to "Darkies."

*Carry Me Back to Ole Virginny (Library of Congress)*

In at least one state, a Black man wrote the lyrics of a state song. The state song of Virginia, "Carry Me Back to Old Virginny," was written by James Bland, a Black man who died in obscurity and poverty. In recent years, Virginia revoked the song and now has no official state song. The state song of Maryland was written within days after the Civil War began. The original lyrics in the song, "Maryland, My Maryland," vilified President Abraham Lincoln, called Northerners scum and called Southern Confederates to arms. Without a doubt, Texas' state song wins the prize. Texas' state song, "The Yellow Rose of Texas," is a popular song about a mulatto or Black woman who could have been a prostitute. While sung as a folk song, its lyrics glorify the beauty of a mulatto woman's sexual attributes, hinting that not all Texas White males preferred blue-eyed blonds.[4]

## ❦ A TASTE OF BLACK HUMOR ❦

How Black labor was used to enrich European Whites is reflected in the following popular joke:

A White man wanted to cross a river that was deep and swift. He took out his gun and whip, jumped on a Black man's back and said: "Swim." The Black man started to swim, but the river was so swift with a strong undertow, the Black man said: "I don't think I can make it, sir!" The White man said: "Of course, you can," as he began beating the Black man to make him swim harder. When they reached the other side, the Black man expected some words of appreciation or a reward for all of his hard work and suffering. The White man shook his head and said: "No way! Without my help, you never would have made it to America. If I had not kidnapped and beaten you, you would not be standing here on this side of the river."

Isn't it funny that those who oppose reparations for Black Americans use this very same logic? They claim that since Blacks in America are so much better off than Blacks in Africa, that Whites do not owe Blacks reparations. Instead, Blacks owe Whites for having brought them out of Africa. This twisted logic is espoused by right-wing conservatives and, unlike the joke, is not a laughing matter. [5]

# ❦ DID HITLER SNUB JESSE OWENS? ❦

Who snubbed Jesse Owens, reputedly the fastest man alive in the 1930s? When Black athletes from the United States defeated German athletes in the 1936 Olympics, the United States hailed its victory as a humiliation for Germany and a setback for the so-called superior Aryan race. In those 1936 Olympic games, Jesse Owens beat Germany's best track-and-field athletes. Owens bagged four gold medals for America, winning the 100-meter dash, the 200-meter dash, the broad jump and the 400-meter relay. The popular story goes that Hitler became incensed and stormed out of the stadium to avoid congratulating Owens. Such an open display of arrogance fit Hitler's image, but according to William J. Baker, it never happened. William J. Baker, who wrote Jesse Owens' biography, says newspapers made up the whole story. In the days following the Olympic games, Owens insisted he was never snubbed by Hitler. It was only after Owens returned home and America made him a national hero and role model for their image of a Black man, that Owens began saying he had been snubbed by Hitler.

When the American spin doctors went to work, they turned half truths into whole truths. Hitler did not congratulate Owens, but neither did Hitler congratulate any of the other competing Black athletes. He had gotten into public relations trouble earlier when he congratulated some winners, but not all of them. Therefore, the International Olympic Committee advised him to avoid any congratulations. The great irony of the 1936 Olympic games is that Hitler did not snub Jesse Owens or the other Black athletes, but the president of the United States did. President Franklin D. Roosevelt refused a face-to-face meeting with and would not congratulate Jesse Owens even via telephone or letter. An even more sinister irony was that while Jesse Owens was in Germany, he was able to go into any restaurant, any movie theater or sit in the front of any German bus. In America, he could not go into White restaurants or white theaters and the White bus lines made him sit in the rear. Which snubbing do you think hurt Jessie Owens and the Black athletes the most?[6]

## ❦ A DYNAMITE TENNIS DUO ❦

Serena and Venus Williams, two Black sisters, entered the 21st century as the undisputed world champions in professional tennis. For over a century, women's professional tennis was perceived as the sacred turf of delicate White women, just as professional golf was the sacred turf of White gentlemen. The Williams sisters present two problems to the world's professional tennis circuit. They do not fit the classical, stereotypical, tennis player image, being neither White nor classically feminine. Instead, the Williams sisters are tall, strong, talented and Black. Their status as queens of the tennis world has drawn disparaging comments from across America and around the world. However, neither the negative comments nor most White tennis opponents have succeeded in defeating the Williams sisters on or off the tennis courts. The Williams sisters succeeded like Althea Gibson and Arthur Ashe, the first Black woman and Black man to break the color barrier in professional tennis. Although the Williams sisters are constantly reminded by hecklers, referees and sports spectators that they are two Black sisters playing against Whites in a White sport, they are persistent winners.

Serena and Venus Williams not only dominate the world of professional tennis, they set a precedent by being the first siblings, male or female, to ever occupy the top two spots in tennis world rankings. They were the first sisters in tennis history to win a Grand Slam singles title; the first sisters to meet in a Women's Tennis Association Tour final; the first sisters to win the Olympic Gold Medal in Doubles; and the only sisters in the 20th century to win a Grand Slam doubles title together. In 2002, the Williams sisters were recognized as the world's best female athletes and the best female tennis players. Besides being mentally tough, these two women are each nearly six feet tall and weigh approximately 160 pounds. Their hard and fast serves can take the rackets out of the hands of competitors and drive them off the court and into the showers. These young, healthy sisters will continue to challenge and probably dominate women's professional tennis for some time to come.[7]

## ❦ DUTCH SLAVE TRADERS' POEM ❦

Glass beads and brandy and scissors and knives,
And other cheap trash for them giving
The profit at least eight hundred percent,
If I keep the half of them living.
For fetch I three hundred Blacks alive
To the port of Rio Janeiro,
'Tis a hundred ducats a piece for me,
From the house of Gonzales Perreiro.[8]

## ❦ FAST TRACKED BLACK ATHLETES ❦

Following the Great Depression of the 1930s, mainstream American society crowned both Jesse Owens and Joe Louis national heroes. Jesse Owens was called the fastest man alive and Joe Louis was crowned the Brown Bomber, the heavyweight champion of the world. Americans loved, respected and were proud of these two Black athletes. Meanwhile, at least one Black man was being lynched every day in America. The apparent explanation to this hypocrisy was that Owens and Louis were different from other Blacks. Whites saw Owens and Louis as exceptional Blacks in race matters. Both athletes had defeated German opponents and weakened Germany's sense of racial superiority over White Americans. Therefore, Owens and Louis were American heroes because they had embarrassed Hitler and his propaganda machine about Nazis being the "superior race." In the 1936 Olympic games in Berlin, on Hitler's home turf, Jessie Owens won the 100- and 200-meter dashes and the long jump, as well as ran the victorious leg of America's 400-meter relay, while German athletes pulled up the rear.

Hitler's master race suffered its second setback in 1938, when Joe Louis, the son of a nearly destitute Black sharecropper, knocked out Max Schmeling, Germany's premiere boxer and heavyweight champion of the world. Americans equated Joe Louis' victory to the defeat of Nazi Germany. The United States rewarded Louis and Owens by granting them celebrity status and an opportunity to promote American democracy around the world. There is little doubt that Joe Louis and Jessie Owens personally enjoyed the fruits of their celebrity status. However, little of the positive trickled down to the rest of Black America and the glow of their newfound status was short-lived.

When the Black Civil Rights Movement started in the late 1950s, White society called on Joe Louis and Jessie Owens to use their celebrity status to degrade the emerging Black Civil Rights Movement and its aggressive Black leaders. The willingness of these famous athletes to go against their own people cast them into Sambo roles. Both athletes lost their public relations value to White society when they were castigated by Black Americans as "Uncle Tom" sellouts. Shortly thereafter, the Internal Revenue Service (IRS) pounced on Owens and Louis for unpaid back taxes. Having outlived their political usefulness as passive Black role models, they were stripped of all their money, properties and pride. Both died poor with low public respect. Joe Louis, the

Brown Bomber, worked his last days as a doorman for a Las Vegas casino. Jessie Owens was a salesman, smoked a pack of cigarettes a day for 35 years and died of cancer at the age of 66.[9]

## ❦ NOTABLE FACT ❦

Even though Black-produced music was the origin of popular music around the world, like Rodney King, it never got any respect from non-Blacks. For instance, Duke Ellington, one of this nation's greatest musicians, was routinely introduced to White audiences by the club's White master of ceremonies as "the greatest living master of jungle music." White, big band leaders like Benny Goodman and Tommy Dorsey became rich and famous imitating Blacks and playing jungle music that they called "swing." Another form of unique Black music was Jazz. Jazz is a shortened name for what Whites called "jack-ass" music. Up until the late 1950s, many Whites, especially ministers, called Black Rhythm and Blues (R&B) music the "Devil's music." Now when you sit back and relax to some oldies, but goodies, you will know what you are listening to.[10]

## ❦ SPORTS, GLADIATORS AND BLACKS ❦

The majority of celebrity Blacks in America are in sports. Thus a disproportionate number of young Blacks pursue sports as a way to alter their socio-economic conditions. Black athletes are simply employees who have no ownership or control of the sports industry. In reality, they are conditioned bodies, under contract as well-paid gladiators. History teaches that hired gladiators are made up of society's safe, controllable and most expendable people. In the days of the Roman empire, for example, Emperor Commodus collected midgets, the handicapped, criminals, slaves and social outsiders in the city of Rome, brought them into the coliseum and ordered them to entertain the public by fighting each other to the death with meat cleavers. The spectators always cheered and the winning gladiators were presented with lavish meals and female companionship, but rarely, if ever, did they receive their freedom. When a gladiator became too old, injured or failed to perform, the ruling class had little difficulty voting "thumbs down" and condemning the gladiator to death. Considering that most Black athletes wind up either broke and/or permanently injured, Black athletes or Black gladiators of today should not miss the lesson.[11]

## ❦ Great Black Swordsmen ❦

Black is the traditional color for a master swordsman in fencing. Jean-Louis, a Black man, was one of France's greatest swordsmen. He was born in Haiti and died in France at the age of 80. His name and career are still highly regarded in literature on the art of fencing. Since the 1950s, several young Blacks have established themselves as national and Olympic fencing champions. The world ought not be surprised to see Black athletes one day dominate fencing as they do other sports.[12]

## ❦ The Monkey Rides Again ❦

Have you ever heard the expression that someone has a monkey on their back? The monkey on the back was not always about drugs. In the early 1800s, a Black jockey nicknamed "Monkey Simon" was the terror of the horse racing circuit. He was the nation's first Black jockey celebrity. As a slave, Monkey Simons earned his master $100 per ride in every race that he entered. Unfortunately, like many Black jockeys who followed Monkey Simons into horse racing, Black jockeys earned lots of money for the owners of the horses and racetracks. As a Black jockey and a slave, all Monkey Simons got was a racing reputation that has been buried in iniquity for nearly two hundred years.[13]

# REFERENCES

## SOURCES AND NOTES

### 1: NOTABLE FIRSTS AND LASTS

1. *The Michigan Citizen*, March 13–19, 2005, p. A–6; *The Gazette News*, December, 2004, page 11; Internet: www.washingtonpost.com/ac2.
2. Ayres, Thomas. 2000. *That's Not In My American History Book*. NY: Taylor Trade Publishing; The Discovery Channel Documentary, two-part series entitled, *The Real Eve*. 2002.
3. Internet: www.africana.com.
4. Apidta, Tingba. 1995. *The History of Massachusetts*. Boston: The Reclamation Project; Rose, Peter I. 1970. *Old Memories, New Moods*. NY: Atherton Press Inc.
5. Katz, William. 1999. *The Black Pioneers: The Untold Story*. NY: Simon & Schuster Company.
6. Quarles, Benjamin. 1964. *The Negro in the Making of America*. NY: A Touchstone Book; Johnson, Charles, and Patricia Smith. 1998. *Africans in America: American Journey Through Slavery*. NY: Harcourt Brace & Company.
7. *The History Channel*. 2005. A televised program, August 31, Comcast Cable System.
8. Anderson, Claud. 1994. *Black Labor, White Wealth*. Md: Power-Nomics Corporation of America; ., an Internet document.
9. *New York Times* newspaper, Monday, January 29, 2001, Section A–1. "Who Is a Seminole, and Who Gets to Decide?" by William Glaberson.
10. Davis, Kenneth. 2001. *Don't Know Much About the Civil War*. NY: HarperCollins. 106–10.
11. Larrie, Reginald. 1996. "Forgotten Faces: Black Automaker among Early Trailblazers." Published by *African-Americans on Wheels*, winter; Internet: www.utexas.edu.
12. Davis, Kenneth. 1990. *Don't Know Much About History*. NY: Perennial, p. 312.

13. Shenkman, Richard, and Kurt Reiger. 1982. *One Night Stands with American History*. NY: Quill Company, p. 37.

14. Christian, Charles M. 1995. *Black Saga: The African American Experience*. NY: Houghton Mifflin Company; Foner, Eric. 1989. *Reconstruction: America's Unfinished Revolution*. NY: Harper & Row.

15. *The Washington Post*. 1996. "Genetics: DNA Points to African Origins." *Science Notebook*. Monday, March 11, p. 2; *The Washington Post*. 2000. "New Gene Study Supports Out of Africa Theory." Science section. Monday, December 11, A–15.

16. Rodgers, J.A. 1947. *World's Great Men of Color*. NY: A Touchstone Book, p. 555.

17. Adam, Janus. 1998. *Freedom Days: Inspired Moments in Civil Rights History*. NY: John Wiley & Sons Inc.

18. Boyd, Herb. 1995. *Down the Glory Road*. NY: Avon Books, p. 76; Internet www.fdrontwheel,com.

19. McPherson, James M. 1965. *The Negro's Civil War*. NY: Pantheon Books, p. 153.

20. Internet: www. pbs.org/wgbh/aia/part4.

21. Internet: www.africana.com.

22. *Newsweek* magazine. 2005. May 30.

23. Bogle, Donald. 1989. *Toms, Coons, Mulattoes, Mammies, and Bucks*. NY: A Frederick Ungar Book; Potter, Joan. 2002. *African American Firsts*. NY: Kensington Publishing Corporation, p. 75.

24. Wright, Kai. 2001. *The African-American Archive: The History of the Black Experience through Documents*. NY: Black Dog & Leventhal Publishers Inc., p. 32.

25. "The Report." 2001. The Harvest Institute, fall, p. 14.

26. Christian, op. cit., p. 5; Ayres, op. cit., p. 35.

27. Kennedy, Walter D. 2003. *Myths of American Slavery*. Louisiana: Pelican Publish Co. p. 195; Robertson, James Oliver. 1980. *American Myth, American Reality*. NY: Hill & Wang, p. 97.

28. Katz, William. 1986. *Black Indians*. NY: Atheneum, p.60–4.

29. Internet article: www.freedommtrail.org/blackfacts.

30. Taylor, Guintard. 2001. "They Went West." February 28; Fellows, Jarrette Jr. 2001. *American Legacy: The Magazine of African-American History and Culture*. Fall; *Wave*, community newspaper; an article by the executive editor. Englewood, California, p. 2.

31. Wright, op. cit., p. 32.

32. Stewart, Jeffery C. 1996. *1001 Things Everyone Should Know about African American History.* NY: Doubleday Publishers.

33. Johnson, David, and Johnny R. Johnson. 1983. *A Funny Thing Happened on the Way to the White House.* NY: Taylor Trade Publishing; Truman, Margaret. 2003. *The President's House: 1800 to the Present.* NY: Ballantine Books.

34. Davis. Op. cit., p. 143; Jackson, Kennell. 1996. *America Is Me.* NY: Harper/Collins, p. 149; Potter, Joan. 2002. *African American First.* NY: Kensington Publishing Corporation, p. 186.

35. McPherson, James. Op. cit.

36. Potter, Joan. 2002. *African American First.* NY: Kensington Publishing, p. 184.

37. Potter, Joan. Ibid, p. 378.

38. *The American Legacy.* 2002. "Little Known Black History Facts." Spring 8(1):57.

39. McPherson, James. Op. cit., p. 95; Stewart. Op. cit., p. 349.

40. *The American Legacy.* 2002. "Fleeting Fame." Spring 8(1):11–12.

41. Internet document: www.chron.com/content; Potter. Op. cit. p. 393.

42. Potter. Ibid, p. 130; Christian. Op. cit., p. 223 & 235.

43. Apidta, Tinga. 1995. *The Hidden History of Massachusetts.* Boston: The Reclamation Project, p. 40; Edgerton, Robert B. *Hidden Heroism: Black Soldiers in America's Wars. 2001.* NY: Westview, p. 16.

44. Dunnigan, James E., and Albert A. Nofi. 1994. *Dirty Little Secrets of World War II.* NY: Quill William Morrow, p. 125–6.

45. Edgerton. Op. cit., p. 30; Potter. Op. cit.

46. Loewen, James W. 1995. *Lies My Teacher Told Me: Everything Your History Got Wrong.* NY: A Touchstone Book, p. 139.

47. Stewart. Op. cit., p. 37.

48. Stewart. Ibid., p. 64.

49. 10/5/2002.

50. Potter. Op. cit., p. 295.

51. Davis. Op. cit., p. 53 & 98.

52. Clinton, Catherine. 2004. *Harriet Tubman: The Road to Freedom.* NY: Little, Brown and Company, p. 61; *The Palm Beach Post.* 2001. "Searching for Peliklakaha, land of the Forgotten Seminoles," Monday, August 20, by Scott McCabe.

53. Christian. Op. cit., p. 107.

54. Potter. Op. cit., p. 2.

55. A document produced and distributed by *Smithsonian Publication*, in January 2005, p. 26.

56. McPherson, James. Op. cit., p. 230–1.

57. An Internet document: www.triviaweb.

58. Potter, Joan. Op. cit., p. 99.

59. *Uncle John's Bathroom Reader*. 2001. San Diego: The Bathroom Readers' Hysterical Institute, p. 132–3; Christian. Op. cit., p. 4; Anderson. Op. cit.

60. *Jet* magazine. 2005. National Report. Johnson Publishing Company; *Chicago Tribune* newspaper. February 7, Section 3, Business section. 1/21/05; Internet: www.foxnews.com/story.

**2: HEROES AND HEROINES**

1. Johnson, Charles, and Patricia Smith. *Africans in America*, Part 2, PBS.

2. Smith, Jessie Carney. 1994. *Black Firsts: 2,000 Years of Extraordinary Achievement*. Michigan: Visible Ink Press, p. 268.

3. Stewart, Jeffery. Op. cit., p. 4; Ayres. Op. cit., p. 73–6.

4. Schenkman, Richard. 1991. *I Love Paul Revere Whether He Rode or Not*. NY: HarperPerennial, p. 194; Forstchen, William R., and Bill Fawcett. 2000. *It Seemed Like a Good Idea*. NY: Quill Publishers, p. 108–9; Browder, Anthony. 1992. *Nile Valley Contribution to Civilization*. Wash., D.C.: The Institute of Karmic Guidance, p. 260.

5. Kelly, C. Brian. 2000. *Best Little Ironies, Oddities, & Mysteries of the Civil War*. Nashville: Cumberland House, p. 17.

6. The Book Society of Canada Limited.

7. Rogers, J.A. Op. cit., p. 422.

8. Charles Johnson, and Patricia Smith. Op. cit.

9. An Internet document: www.freedommtrail.org/blackflacts.htm.

10. Boyd, Herb. Op. cit., p. 90.

11. *Uncle John's Bathroom*. Op. cit., p. 370; Nofi. Op. cit., p. 32; Clinton. Op. cit., p. 173.

12. "Little Known Black History Facts." 2002. *The American Legacy*, spring, 8(1):55.

13. Katz, William Loren. 1999. *Black Pioneers: The Untold Story*. NY: Simon & Schuster, 114–5.

14. Davis, Kenneth. Op. cit., p. 217–8; Loewen. Op. cit., p. 299.

15. Edgerton, Robert B. Op. cit., p. 130; *Jet* magazine. 2005. "This Week in Black History." Chicago: Johnson Publishing Co. May 30, p. 19; An Internet Document: .

16. This quote was taken from an Internet site: 2/28/03.

17. Loewen, James W. Op. cit., p. 230–4.

18. Ewing, Samuel David. *The Greek Heracles: His Black Ancestry and Legacy to the African Diaspora.* Black Athena, Vol. # 1, pages 476–7 and Vol. # 2, page 270.

19. An Internet document: 10/5/02.

20. *Book of Life, a Narrative by Sojourner Truth.* 1875. Boston, p. 138; Reiss, Benjamin. 2001. *The Showman and the Slave, London, England:* Harvard University Press, p. 85–6.

21. Stewart, Jeffery. Op. cit., p. 333; Christian. Op. cit., p.309.

22. Browder, Anthony. Op. cit., p. 194.

23. *North and South* magazine. 2002. 5(3).

**3: NAMES AND GAMES**

1. Perry, John C. 2002. *Myths & Realities of American Slavery.* PA: Burd Street Press, p. 16–7.

2. Schwartz, Barry N., and Robert Disch. 1970. *White Racism: Its History, Pathology, and Practice.* NY: Dell Publishing Co., p. 11.

3. Shenkman, Richard, and Kurt Reiger. Op. cit., p. 41.

4. "The Report." 2003. The Harvest Institute, spring, p. 13.

5. Fears, Darryl. 2005. "Mexican Stamps Racist, Civil Rights Leaders Say." *The Washington Post*, June 30, page A–10.

6. Aptidta, Tingba. 1998. *The Hidden History of New York.* Boston: The Reclamation Project, p. 121.

7. Steinhorn, Leonard, and Barbara Diggs-Brown. 1999. *By the Color of Our Skin.* NY: A Plum Book, p. 114–5.

8. Barry N. Schwartz, and Robert Disch. Op. cit., p. 20.

9. Bryson, Bill. 1994. *Made in America.* NY: William Morrow and Company, p. 85.

10. Reed, John Shelton, and Dale Volberg Reed. 1996. *1001 Things Everyone Should Know About the South.* NY: Doubleday, p. 40.

11. http://emergingminds.org/diduknow/2004jun04

12. Kennedy, Stetson. 1959. *Jim Crow Guide: The Way It Was.* Boca Raton, Fla.: Florida Atlantic University Press, p. 213.

13. Author's discussion and editorializing on a rare racial incident that occurred in North Carolina.

14. An Internet document: www.americasdebate.com.

15. Malcomson, Scott L. 2000. *One Drop of Blood.* NY: Farrar Straus Giroux, p. 98–109.

16. Information for this factoid can be found in 2001 public records and newspaper reports on the governor's office in California and President George W. Bush appointees to federal positions.

17. Richard Shenkman, and Kurt Reiger. Op. cit., p. 39.

18. Author's editorializing on a popular rumor within Black America.

19. Shenkman, Richard. Op. cit., p. 27.

20. Christian, Charles. Op. cit., p. 116, 154.

21. Shenkman, Richard, and Kurt Reiger. Op. cit., p. 32; Shenkman, Richard. *Legends, Lies, and Cherished Myths of American History*, p. 137–9.

22. Bryson, Bill. Op. cit., p. 118.

23. *The Daytona Beach News-Journal.* 2004. "Neighbor to Neighbor." Wednesday, November 17, p. 9–C.; Sontag, Debbie. 1989. "Names to Stand Out With." *The Washington Post.* Monday, June 12, C–5; Young, Yolanda. 2005. *USA TODAY.* "A Name doesn't have to be a Burden." June 3, p. 15–A.

24. Scott, John Anthony. 1974. *Hard Trials on My Way.* NY: Alfred A. Knopf, p. 232; Kelly, Brian C. Op. cit., p. 38.

25. Wright, Mike. 1999. *What They Didn't Teach You About the American Revolution.* Calif.: Presidio Press, Inc., p. 50–1; Internet document: www.liunet.edu/cwis.

26. Mullane, Deirdre. 1993. *Crossing the Danger Water.* NY: Doubleday Books, p. 184.

27. Davis, Kenneth. Op. cit., p. 75.

28. Original author unknown.

29. Doug, Hill, and Jeff Weingrad. 1996. *Saturday Night: A Backstage History of Saturday Night Live.* NY: William Morrow, p. 117–8.

30. Shenkman, Richard, and Kurt Reiger. Op. cit., p. 194; Apidta, Tingba. 1995. *The Hidden History of Massachusetts*, Boston: The Reclamation Project, p. 30.

31. "What is the secret of African quilts?" An Internet document: Amazing Africana, Black History Facts,  10/11/2003.

## 4: SEX AND SEXUAL TABOOS

1. Bower, Claude G. 1929. *The Tragic Era.* NY: Houghton Mifflin Company, p. 80–5.

2. Boyd, Herb. Op. cit., p. 211.

3. Wright, Mike. Op. cit., p. 297.

4. Jordan, Ervin L. 1995. *Black Confederates and Afro-Yankees in Civil War Virginia.* Charlottesville: University Press of Virginia, p. 127.

5. Thompson, Marilyn W. 2003. "Woman Claims Thurmond as Father." *The Washington Post*, p. 1–A, Sunday, December 14.

6. Perry, John C. Op. cit., p. 228.

7. Ayres, Thomas. Op. cit, p. 115.

8. Shi, David E., and Holly A. Mayer. 1999. *For the Record: A Documentary History of America,* Vol. 2. NY: W.W. Norton & Company, p. 43.

9. Christian, Charles. Op. cit., p. 81; Clinton, Catherine, and Michelle Gillespie. 1997. *The Devil's Lane: Sex and Race in the Early South.* NY: Oxford University Press, p. 125.

10. Smith, Jessie C. Op. cit., p. 346.

11. *Jet* magazine. 2000. "This Week in Black History." Johnson Publishing Co., June 5, p. 19.

12. Edgerton, Robert B. Op. cit., p. 196.

13. Roger, J.A. 1970. *Sex and Race. Volume II.* St. Petersburg, Fla: Helga M. Rogers, p. 190; Clinton, Catherine. 2004. *Harriet Tubman: The Road to Freedom.* NY: Little, Brown and Company, p. 68–9.

14. Perry, John C. Op. cit., p. 12; Segal, Ronald. 2001. *Islam's Black Slaves: The Other Diaspora.* NY: Farrar Straus and Giroux; an Internet document: www.faithfreedom.org.

15. "A Dream of Wings," by Jeff Hardy, Mobile, Alabama *Register*, Washington Bureau; an Internet document:

16. Shenkman, Richard. Op. cit., p. 90.

17. Schafer, Daniel L. *Anna Madgigine Jai Kinfsley African Princess, Florida Slave, Plantation Slave Owner.* Florida: University Press of Florida; Hyman, Ann. 2003. "The Amazing Life of Anna Kingsley," Book review section, The Times-Union, Jacksonville, Sunday, May 18, p. G–4.

18. Davis, Burke. 1960. *The Civil War: Strange & Fascinating Facts.* NY: Wings Books, p. 148–9.

19. "African Aspects of the Puerto Rican Personality," an article by Dr. Robert A. Martinez, Baruch College, City University of New York, NY.

20. *Uncle John's Bathroom Reader.* Op. cit., p. 317.

21. "Racist for Feminism! The Odd History of the Civil Rights Bill." 1994. By Jamie Malanowski, *The Washington Post,* Feb. 6, p. C–5.

22. *Jet* magazine. 2003. Johnson Publishing Company. December 22, p. 38; an Internet document: Africana Amazing Black Facts, www.african.com.

23. The author editorializes about the role that Black Women played in the development of the frontier. Facts contained in the factoid are based upon the author's personal knowledge.

24. Farquhar, Michael. A Treasury of Great American Scandals. 2003. NY: Penguin Books, p. 3–6.

25. Shenkman, Richard, and Kurt Reiger. Op. cit., p. 136; Rodney, Walter. 1982. *How Europe Underdeveloped Africa*, Wash., D.C.:Howard University Press, p. 79.

26. Shenkman, Richard, and Kurt Reiger. Ibid. p. 52.

27. Shenkman, Richard, and Kurt Reiger. Ibid. p. 93.

28. Reed, John S., and Dale V. Reed. Op. cit., p. 75.

29. Shenkman, Richard. Op. cit., p. 134–6; Shenkman, Richard. Op. cit., p. 27.

30. *Jet* magazine. 2005. Chicago: Johnson Publishing Company, April 11 p. 4.

31. "African Native's Homecoming." by Ann M. Simmons. 2002. *The Los Angeles Times,* World Section, Saturday, May 4, A–3.

32. Clinton, Catherine, and Michelle Gillespie. Op. cit., p. 109–10.

33. *Uncle John's Bathroom Reader.* Op. cit., p. 124–5.

34. Shenkman, Richard. Op. cit., p. 68.

35. Edgerton, Robert B. Op. cit., p. 219.

36. Shenkman, Richard. Op. cit., p. 71.

37. Rogers, J.A. 1944. *Sex and Race*, St. Petersburg, Fl.: Helga M. Rogers. Volume III, p. 309–15; an Internet document: www.lucky-mojo.com.

38. Webb Garrison. Op. cit., p. 63.

39. *Uncle Johns Bathroom Reader*. Op. cit., p. 324.

40. Loewen, James W. *Lies Across America*. Op. cit., p. 273.

41. Black Folk Humor: Originator unknown.

## 5: PRESIDENTS & THEIR SCANDALS

1. Reportedly are comments of Dick Gregory, a Black social commentator. The comments of Fidel Castro, the president of Cuba, were aired in a special Comcast cable TV broadcast.

2. Apidta, Tingba. 1995. *The Hidden History of Washington,* D.C. Boston: The Reclamation Project, p. 35.

3. Shenkman, Richard, and Kurt Reiger. Op. cit., p. 12.

4. "The Report." 2001. The Harvest Institute. Spring, p. 10.

5. An Internet document: www.rightwingnews.com.

6. *Uncle John's Bathroom Reader*. op. cit., p. 155.

7. Apidta, Tingba. *The Hidden History of Massachusetts.* Op. cit., p. 58; Kennedy, Stetson. Op. cit., p. 30.
8. Johnson, David E., and Johnny R. Johnson. Op. cit., p. 15–6.
9. Farquhar, Michael. Op. cit., p. 17–9; Jones, James H. 1981. *Bad Blood: The Tuskegee Syphilis Experiment — a Tragedy of Race and Medicine.* NY: The Free Press.
10. Rodney, Walter. Op. cit., p. 83; Sobel, Robert. 2000. *The Pursuit of Wealth.* NY: McGraw-Hill Company, p. 61–2.
11. O'Brien, Cormac. 2004. *Secret Lives of the U.S. Presidents.* Philadelphia: Quirk Books; Whitney, David C. 1967. *The American Presidents.* NY: Doubleday Company.
12. Ayres, Thomas. Op. cit., p. 113; O'Brien, Cormac. 2004. *Secret Lives of the U.S. Presidents.* Philadelphia: Quirk Books; Whitney, David C. 1967. *The American Presidents.* NY: Doubleday Company.
13. O'Brien, Cormac. Op. cit., p. 228.
14. Tamarkin, Bob. 1993. *Rumor Has It.* NY: Prentice Hall General Reference, p. 33–4.
15. Key, V.O. 1949. *Southern Politics.* NY: A Vintage Book.
16. Shenkman, Richard, and Kurt Reiger. Op. cit., p. 53.
17. Allen, Chaz. Op. cit., p. 163–4.
18. Tindall, George Brown, and David E. Shi. 1999. *America: A Narrative History.* Fifth Edition, Volume 2. NY: W.W. Norton & Company, p. 817.
19. Shenkman, Richard, and Kurt Reiger. Op. cit., p.193.
20. Edgerton, Robert B. Op. cit., p. 52.
21. David C. Whitney. 1967. *The American Presidents: Biographies of the Chief Executives from Washington Through Nixon.* NY: Doubleday and Co., p. 135; Edgerton, Robert B. Op. cit., p. 26.
22. Shenkman, Richard. 1993. *Legend, Lies and Cherished Myths of World History.* NY: HarperPerennial, p.120; Berlin, Ira. 1974. *Slaves Without Masters,* NY: Pantheon Books, p. 16.
23. Apidta, Tingba. 1993. cit., p. 59–60; Kolchin, Peter. *American Slavery.* NY: Hill and Wang, p.184.
24. Tamarkin, Bob. Op. cit., p. 34–6.
25. Gahlinger, Paul. 2004. *Illegal Drugs.* London, England: Plume Books; Wright, Mike. Op. cit., p. 1; Shenkman, Richard. Op. cit., p.127; Siegel, Ronald K. 1989. *Intoxication: Life In Pursuit of Artificial Paradise.* NY: Pocket Books, p. 260–2.

26. Anderson, Claud. 1997. *Dirty Little Secrets About Black History, Its Heroes and Other Troublemakers.* Maryland: PowerNomics Corporation of America.
27. Wilson, Amos. 1998. *Blueprint for Black Power.* NY: Afrikan World InfoSystems, p. 681; *Family History Resource File, Freedman's Bank Records.* The Church of Jesus Christ of Latter-Day Saints, # 3.
28. Raphael, Ray. 2002. *A People's History of the American Revolution.* NY: Perennial Books, p.10–2.
29. "The Report." Harvest Institute Newsletter. Washington, D.C.
30. Cruse, Harold. 1987. *Plural but Equal.* NY: William Morrow Company, p. 82; Meir, August, and Elliott Rudwick. 1966. *From Plantation to Ghetto.* NY: Hill and Wang, p. 192–3.

**6: CONSERVATIVES AND SAMBOS**

1. Jackson, Kennell. Op. cit., p. 27; Malcomson, Scott. Op. cit., p. 145.
2. Perry, John C. Perry. 1996. Op. cit., p. 26; Banks, William M. *The Black Intellectual.* NY: W.W. Norton & Company, p. 150.
3. The author's personal sentiments which were contained in a number of speeches and media interviews. The facts congealed from a variety of historical documents.
4. *Egotrip's Big Book of Racism.* 2002. NY: Regan Books, p. 32.
5. An Internet document: www.rightwingnews.com.
6. Davis, Kenneth. Op. cit., p 242; Information on Dr. Walter Williams' book, entitled Black Confederate Soldiers, on the Internet: 2/28/2003.
7.Potter, Joan. Op. cit., p. 297; an Internet document: www.free-dommtrail.org/blackflacts.
8. Spalding, Henry D. 1978. *Encyclopedia of Black Folklore and Humor.* NY: Jonathan David Publishers, p. 378.
9. *The American Directory of Certified Uncle Toms, 1st Millennial Edition.* 2002. CBIA & DFS Publishing.
10. An Internet document: .
11. Loewen, Kenneth W. *Lies Across America.* Op. cit., p. 47–8.
12. Bellant, Russ. 1988. *Old Nazis, the New Right, and the Republican Party.* Boston: South E. Press.

**7: BUSINESS AND BUFFOONERY**

1. McPherson, James. Op. cit., p. 368–9.

2. Axelrod, Alan, and Charles Phillips. 1992. *What Every American Should Know About American History*. Mass.: Adams Media Corporation, p. 26; What's Black Rice? Black History Facts at 10/5/2002.
3. Potter, Joan. Op. cit., p. 293; an Internet document at: www.cs.georgetwwn.edu.
4. Higham, John. 1997. *Civil Rights & Social Wrongs*. PA: Pennsylvania State University Press, p. 61–5.
5. Reiss, Benjamin. 2001. *The Showman and the Slave*, England: Harvard University Press, p. 1–3, 26–7; Who Made P.T. Barnum Famous? An Internet document at .
6. *Uncle John's Bathroom Reader*. Op. cit., p. 163–4.
7. Jackson, Kennell. Op. cit., p. 224.
8. Shenkman, Richard, and Kurt Reiger. Op. cit., p. 125.
9. "African-American Village, Land Taken from Blacks Through Trickery, Violence, and Murder," by The Associated Press. Information at www.imdivedrsity.com 10/6/2002.
10. Panati, Charles. 1987. *Panati's Extraordinary Origins of Everyday Things*. NY: Perennial Library, p. 368–71.
11. "WestPoint Stevens: Textile firm linked to rough Negro cloth slaves had to wear." 2002. By reporter James Cox, *USA TODAY*, Thurs. January 21, p. 9–A.
12. Mapp, Ray, and Shannon H. Mapp. 2002. *The Miracles of Black Inventors and Scientists*. Black Miracles Chart Publishing Company.
13. Black Miracles Chart. Ibid.
14. Wilson, Amos. Op. cit., p. 423.
15. Burton, Willie. *The Blacker the Berry: A Black History of Shreveport*. Shreveport: *The Times*, p. 33–4.
16. Charles Laurence, reporter for the *London Daily Telegraph*, London, England.
17. Thompson, Nathan. Kings: *The True Story of Chicago Policy and Numbers Racketeers*. Chicago: The Bonneville Press, p. 11–6.
18. McPherson, James M. 1965. *The Negro's Civil War*. NY: Pantheon Books, p. 96; Williams, Eric. 1944. *Capitalism and Slavery*. NC: The University of North Carolina, p. 105–9.

## 8: BLOOD LINES AND BLOOD PHOBIAS

1. Reel, Monte. 2005. "In Buenos Aires, Researchers Exhume Long Unclaimed African Roots." *The Washington Post*, Thursday, May 5.

2. Shenkman, Richard, and Kurt Reiger. Op. cit., p. 216.

3. Browder, Anthony. Op. cit., p. 143.

4. Black Press USA.Com/News/Article, 12/28/2003.

5. Montagu, Ashley. 1965. *Man's Most Dangerous Myth: The Fallacy of Race.* NY: World Publishing Co., p. 317; Browder, Anthony T. 2000. From the Browder File, Wash., D.C. The Institute of Karmic Guidance, p. 70–2. New World Translation of the Holy Scriptures; Mosley, William. 1987. *What Color Was Jesus?* Chicago: African American Images.

6. Spalding, Henry D. Op. cit., p. 315.

7. Malcomson, Scott L. op. cit., p. 92.

8. Rogers, J.A. *World's Great Men of Color*. Op cit., p. 183–5.

9. Rogers, J.A. Ibid., p. 219, 235–6. Rogers, J.A. *100 Amazing Facts about the Negro*, p. 12.

10. Browder, Anthony T. Op. cit., p. 18–9.

11. An Internet document at: rightwingnews.com.

12. Shenkman, Richard, and Kurt Reiger. Op. cit., p. 86; Davis, Kenneth. Op. cit., p. 143.

**9: THE ENRICHED AND THE ENSLAVED**

1. Perry, John C. Op. cit., p. 53; Adams, Francis D., and Barry Sanders. 2003. *Alienable Rights: The Exclusion of African Americans in a White Man's Land*, 1619–2000. NY: HarperCollins Publishers, p. 51.

2. Apidta, Tingba. *The Hidden History of Washington*, D.C. Op. cit., p. 18.

3. Spalding, Henry D. Op. cit., 1972.

4. Davis, Kenneth. Op. cit., p. 141; Johnson, Charles, and Patricia Smith. Op. cit., p. 204.

5. Malcomson, Scott. Op. cit., p. 226.

6. Christian, Charles. Op. cit., p. 12.

7. Clinton, Catherine, and Michelle Gillespie. Op. cit., p. 79–82; Bradley, Patricia. 1998. *Propaganda and the American Revolution*. Mississippi: University Press of Mississippi, p. 18.

8. The source of this data is Dahleen Glanton, *Tribune* national correspondent, in an article on May 27, 2003, that talked about "Confederate Money Talks." John W. Jones exhibit of Confederate Currency, *The Color of Money,* was on display at the Martin L. King National Historic site, in Atlanta, Georgia.

9. Raphael, Ray. Op. cit., p. 339.

10. Rymer, Russ. 2000. *American Beach: How Progress Robbed a Black Town and Nation of History, Wealth, and Power*. NY: Harper-Perennial, p. 11.

11. Kolchin, Peter. Op. cit., p. 211.

12. Berlin, Ira. 1974. *Slaves Without Masters: The Free Negro in the Antebellum South*. NY: Pantheon Books, p. 9.

13. Malcomson, Scott L. Op. cit., p. 127.

14. Berlin, Ira. Op. cit., p. 158; "The Report." 2003. The Harvest Institute Newsletter, winter, p. 7.

## 10: MILITARY AND WARS

1. Rogers, J.A. *100 Amazing Facts about the Negro with Complete Proof,* written in 1940's and published in 1957.

2. An Internet document at: www.tfn.net/SeminoleWar; "The Report." 2003. The Harvest Institute, winter, p. 2.

3. Perry, John C. Op. cit., p. 220.

4. *Jet* magazine. 2005. Chicago: Johnson Publishing Co., March 21, p. 22.

5. Garrison, Webb. 1992. *Civil War Trivia and Fact Book*. Nashville: Rutledge Hill Press, p. 247; Malcomson, Scott. Op. cit., p. 92.

6. "Little Known Black History Facts." 2002. *The American Legacy*. Spring, 8(1):56.

7. Edgerton, Robert B. Op. cit., p. 108.

8. Taylor, Guintard. 2001. "They Went West." American Legacy: *The Magazine of African-American History and Culture*. Fall, 7(3):52.

9. "The Report." 2003. The Harvest Institute Newsletter. Winter, p. 4.

10. Packard, Jerrold M. 2002. *American Nightmare: The History of Jim Crow*. NY: St. Martins Griffin, 197–8.

11. A Comcast cable on Washington, D.C., Channel 32, entitled: *Silent Heros*. The program was presented on February, 2003.

12. Garrison, Webb. Op. cit., p. 29.

13. An Internet document at: www.vondonop.org/HessianFAQ.html.

14. Johnson, Charles, and Patricia Smith. Op. cit., PBS series on Comcast Cable Washington, D.C.

15. McPherson, James M. Op. cit., p. 221, 231; Christian, Charles. Op. cit., p. 200–1; Loewen, James W. Op. cit., p. 191; Edgerton, Robert B. Op. cit., p. 32–3.

16. "Before Glory, the First Kansas Colored Infantry was First in Battle: A Moment in Time," a 1998 monthly series from the Kansas State Historical society; Check: www.kshs.org.

17. Allen, Chaz. Op. cit., 115–6.

18. Robertson, Dale. 2002. *Little Known Facts*. NY: Citadel Press, p. 25.
19. *The Baltimore Chronicle and the Sentinel*, published Feb. 6, 1997.
20. Edgerton, Robert B. Op. cit., p. 87.
21. Edgerton, Robert B. Ibid., p. 206.
22. Loewen, James W. *Lies Across America*. Op. cit., p. 16; Bowers, Claude G. Op. cit., p. 310.
23. "War in the Gulf: WWII German Prisoners were based in area POW Camps," by C.J. Christ. Internet site: www.crt.state; Dunnigan, James. Op. cit., p. 125.
24. Bruns, Roger. 2000. *Almost History*. NY: Hyperion Company, 224–6.
25. An Internet document at: www.freedommtrail.org.
26. Zinn, Howard. 1990. *Declaration of Independence*, NY: Harper-Collins, p. 88.

## 11: SPORTS AND SPORTING LIFE

1. Perry, John. Op cit., p. 17; *Egotrip Big Book of Racism*. Op. cit., p. 175; for additional information on the possible genetic and superior physical abilities of Black athletes, visit Gary Kamiya and www.archive.salon.com.
2. Rogers, J.A. *World's Great Men of Color*. Op. cit., p. 559.
3. Klein, Frederick C. 1997. "Tiger Masters Masters." *Wall Street Journal*, April 15, p. A–16; Jet magazine. 2004. Sports section, p. 48, January 4.
4. Anderson, Claud. 1994. *Black Labor, White Wealth*. Maryland: PowerNomics Corporation.
5. This joke was originally told by Whitney Young, Civil Rights leader, to illustrate how Whites benefited from centuries of Black enslavement and yet, felt Blacks ought to feel grateful.
6. Shenkman, Richard. *Legends, Lies, and Cherished Myths of American History*. Op. cit., p. 100; *Uncle John's Bathroom*. Op. cit., p.127.
7. An Internet document at: www.watsonwaterchallenge.com.
8. Apidta, Tingba. *The Hidden History of New York*. Op, cit., p. 29.
9. Edgerton, Robert B. Op. cit., p. 126–7.
10. Edgerton, Robert B. Ibid., p. 124. An Internet document at: www.rapcoalition.org/political.
11. An Internet document at: www.triviaweb.co.
12. Rogers, J.A. *World's Great Men of Color*, p. 7.
13. Jackson, Kennell. Op. cit., p. 213.

# INDEX

## A

## B

Black Hospital, 49
  Provident Hospital and Training
  School, 49
Black National Constitution, 78
Black representative, 41
boycott, 50
  Free Produce Movement, 50
college graduate, 41
  Twilight, Alexander Lucius, 41
female aviator, 55
  Bessie Coleman, 55
first humans, 18
guest in the White House, 39
  Wheatley, Phillis, 39
insurance company, 53
  African-American Insurance
  Company, 53
killed in the Revolutionary War, 44
  Attucks, Crispus, 44-45, 107,
  108, 187
  Snyder, Christopher, 44
legal Black Town, 53
  New Philadelphia, 53-54
Mexicans, 56
Miss Americas, 117
  Charles, Suzette, 117
  Williams, Vanessa, 117
novelist, 38, 144
  Wilson, Harriet E., 38
painter, 40
  Johnston, Joshua, 40
Post-Slavery Black Governor, 17
president, 16
professional Jockeys, 42
  Anderson, George "Spider", 43
  Clayton, Alonzo, 43
  Conley, Jess, 43
  Henderson, Erskine, 43
  Kentucky Derby-winning
  jockeys, 43
  Lewis, George, 43
  Murphy, Isaac, 43
  Perkin, James, 43
  Simms, Willie, 43

  Walker, Billy, 43
  Winkfield, Jimmie, 43
scalping, 27
Slavery Apology, 57
  J.P. Morgan Corporation, 57
sow and reap wheat in the New
World, 1
Supreme Court Activist, 55
  John Jay, 55
U.S. Congress, 43
  Menard, John W., 43
  Revels, Hiram Rhoades, 44
Underground Railroad, 51
  Ferandina Beach, Florida, 51
  Spanish Florida, 52
  St. Mary's River, 52
Underground Railroad Conductor,
52
  Loew's Hotel, 52
  Still, William, 52
Woman Doctor, 41
Follis, Charles, 301
Ford Theater, 175
Forrest Gump, 293
Forrest, Nathan Bedford, 285, 293-
294
Fort Gadsden, 267
Fort Muse, 265
Fort Negro, 265-268
Fort Pillow Massacre, 285-287
Forten, James, 50
Fortune, Robert L., 68
forty acres, a mule, 34, 47, 131, 162,
217, 258
Foster, Stephen, 31, 306, 308
Founding Fathers, 16, 50, 93, 149,
164, 185, 187, 209, 248-249, 257,
259
Franklin, Benjamin, 92-93, 139, 140,
184
Freedman's Bureau, 186-187, 260
Freedom Riders, 20
French Legion of Honor, 126
Fugitive Slave Law, 7, 48, 53, 186

# S

# T

# Y

# Z